POLICY AND RATIONALITY:

THE REGULATION OF CANADIAN TRUCKING

HAROLD KAPLAN

Policy and Rationality: The Regulation of Canadian Trucking

UNIVERSITY OF TORONTO PRESS
Toronto Buffalo London

© University of Toronto Press 1989
Toronto Buffalo London
Printed in Canada

ISBN 0-8020-5725-X

Printed on acid-free paper

Canadian Cataloguing in Publication Data

Kaplan, Harold, 1936–
    Policy and rationality

    Includes index.
    ISBN 0-8020-5725-X

    1. Trucking – Government policy – Canada.
    2. Trucking – Law and legislation – Canada.
    I. Title.

HE5635.A6K3 1989   388.3′24′0971   c88-095096-x

62763

This book has been published with the help of a grant from the Social Science Federa-
tion of Canada, using funds provided by the Social Sciences and Humanities Research
Council of Canada.

Contents

Acknowledgments

I wish to thank the various groups that helped finance my research on this study: the Social Sciences and Humanities Research Council, Transport Canada, the Max Bell Research Programme in Business–Government Relations (Faculty of Administrative Studies, York University), the Joint York University/University of Toronto Programme in Transportation, and the Minor Research Grants Fund (Faculty of Arts, York University). I also want to thank those York University graduate students who served, with great dedication and intelligence, as research assistants: Douglas Allan, Shannon Bell, Stella Catsamaki, Michael Dartnell, and John Finney.

Abbreviations

CCMVTA	Canadian Conference of Motor Vehicle Transport Administrators
CI	cognitive-instrumental
CITL	Canadian Industrial Traffic League
CN	Canadian National (formerly Canadian National Railway or CNR)
CP	Canadian Pacific (formerly Canadian Pacific Railway or CPR)
CTA	Canadian Trucking Association
CTC	Canadian Transport Commission
CVOR	Commercial Vehicle Operators Registration
ECC	Economic Council of Canada
HTA	Highway Traffic Act (Ontario)
LTL	less-than-truckload shipments
MTC	Ministry of Transportation and Communications (Ontario)
NDP	New Democratic Party
OHTB	Ontario Highway Transport Board
OMRB	Ontario Municipal and Railway Board
OO	owner operators
OTA	Ontario Trucking Association
PAO	Public Archives of Ontario
PCV	public commercial vehicles
PCVA	Public Commercial Vehicles Act (Ontario)
PNC	public necessity or convenience
TL	truckload shipments

POLICY AND RATIONALITY

1

Policy Failure: A Systems Approach

In recent years there has been growing scepticism about government's ability to solve public problems. The earlier conviction that government must intervene to correct market failures has been dampened by growing, unmistakable evidence of policy failure or what some economists have called 'non-market failure.' For example, earlier in this century, Canadian and American governments decided to regulate certain industries as a means of correcting alleged market defects. The various transportation industries were among the first to be so regulated. By the 1970s, however, these policy agendas were dominated by claims that regulation had failed and should be dismantled.

'Policy failure' is a useful, shorthand phrase; but the question, more accurately phrased, is why governmental efforts to solve socio-economic problems, even when backed with sincere, good intentions and substantial amounts of money, produce such disappointingly modest results. The problem is not why this or that policy sometimes disappoints, but whether policy performance consistently, inevitably disappoints. And, if it does, what persistent, structural factors explain this inevitable gap between intention and results.

The advocates of deregulation – for example, most North American economists – not only tried to show that regulatory programs had failed but also explained why. Although much of the literature on policy failure provides a useful but unsystematic description of all the things that can go wrong, the deregulators offered a more systematic explanation of regulatory failure that has something to say about the sources of failure in any policy sphere. According to this view, most regulatory programs had been created in order to protect the public from certain, typical industry abuses, but the regulated industry subsequently captured the program, eliminated the watchdog function, converted government officials into sponsors and protectors of the regulated industry, and transformed the program into a legal means of cartelizing the industry. Why this occurred can only be understood within the context of a more general viewpoint, which I call 'political realism.' It is naïve, realists tell us, to think of political leaders as white-coated scientists objectively seeking the right answers and effective solutions in a laboratory-type, seminar-like setting. Rather they are rational, self-interested optimizers playing a very different, political game. Their major goal is to maximize the inflow of support for themselves: votes for politicians, money and power for administrative agencies. They manipulate policy decisions as vehicles of securing that support. Thus, capture was inevitable. Regulation imposed heavy, concentrated burdens on a relatively small group, the regulated industry, while providing small amounts of benefits scattered over a very large population. Under such conditions, it is politically rational for the industry to fight back; it is not rational or feasible for the public to counter-mobilize. And government officials, playing the political game, simply respond to the more intense pressures. This argument rests on some very general assumptions about what motivates policy makers, how they formulate decisions, how we should explain policy outcomes. To assess the argument's usefulness as a theory of policy failure, one must examine these assumptions. At this basic-assumption level, the argument has two central problems. First, it sees the isolated, self-interested individual as the basic unit; it either ignores social systems, treats them as derivatives or consequences of individual decisions, like a market, or treats systems as nothing more than ad hoc strategic instruments, like a coalition or contract. Second, this argument tries, in good micro-economic fashion, to explain behaviour as the outcome of a few simple initial assumptions about what always motivates all behaviour. Such an approach assumes that all action is governed by the same set of premises, that people always pursue one kind of objective, or that only one kind of game – a political one – is invariably played.

Such substantive and theoretical concerns are the focus of this study. Using Canadian transportation and more specifically trucking policy as my focus, I try to assess the achievements of regulatory programs, to identify sources of shortcomings or failures, and to see if these specific-case explanations have anything more general to teach us about the sources of policy failure. How valid is the 'capture and cartel' explanation of regulatory failure, and the more general theory of policy making on which this explanation rests? I begin, in this chapter, by criticizing the individualistic and one-game-only picture of policy making. In its place, I offer an approach derived from social-systems theory and from the Weber/Parsons/Luhmann tradition in sociological theory. By providing an initial account of how a hypothetical, 'healthy' policy system works, one then can ask how these systems typically go wrong. In other words, I approach the problem of policy failure by trying to identify some characteristic system malfunctions or 'pathologies.'

MULTIPLE GAMES, DIFFERENTIATION, RATIONALITY

My approach begins with the assumption that people, including political leaders, play different games or participate in different, specialized action systems. Each game has its own distinctive premises, ground rules, strategies or 'moves,' roles, specialized language, and definition of successful performance. When the players produce clear, distinct definitions of each game and tend to play them serially and separately, when specific kinds of situations are governed by a single, appropriate game, there is structural differentiation among the games. Behaviour is not monotonic; people will invoke one game or another, depending on their initial definition of the situation. A one-game model of a policy system explains some aspects of that system but not others, because sometimes, although not always, that is the game being played. The way in which these games interconnect, for example the extent to which they are differentiated or intrude on each other, becomes an important question.

To provide a minimal, loose definition of a complex concept, I define 'rational behaviour' as the informed, consistent, reasonably effective pursuit of certain well-articulated objectives. Rational actors formulate a relatively clear, precise notion of what they are trying to achieve, work with a reasonably useful, accurate picture of reality, adjust means to ends, and assess the impact of their action on the environment. Less-rational behaviour occurs when one is confused, deceived, inconsistent, or unfocused – either in defining objectives, selecting means, assessing results, or perceiving reality. Rational behaviour is consistent, articulate, directed, informed. Irrational behaviour is aimless, muddled, self-defeating, often self-deceiving.

The existence of structured games enhances the individual's ability to behave rationally. Any game creates a clear framework, sets objectives, suggests various strategies, defines success and failure, helps us interpret other people's moves. To play that game is to behave rationally within the context of that game. In other words, each game generates its own distinctive kind of game-specific rationality. A more elaborate, complex game suggests to us a greater array of more sophisticated options, allowing us to be very clever, subtle players. Thus, as the game develops, it expands the possibilities for game-specific, rational conduct.

The more differentiated the games, the greater the scope for individual rationality. At a macro-level, a game is more likely to undergo development, and thus permit more rational individual conduct, if the game is separated from others and allowed to evolve in its own terms. At a micro, specific-situation level, individual actors are more likely to behave in a clear-headed, consistent, directed fashion if they understand what game is being played. If it is unclear which game is being played, or if several games are being played concurrently, individuals are more likely to be muddled, deceived, or self-deceived about their own objectives, the intentions of others, or the significance of specific events. I am not arguing that complete differentiation, that the pure performance of any game, is possible or desirable; to the contrary, my central argument is that these games always intrude on each other because each performs vital functions for the others. None the less, overlap and intrusion among the various games is one systemic source of irrational conduct.

COGNITIVE-INSTRUMENTAL AND POLICY GAMES

This study will focus on four games. We begin by examining the relationship between cognitive-instrumental problem solving, hereafter referred to as the CI game, and politics.

In the CI game, players are trying to formulate accurate descriptive generalizations and usable, effective programs of action. One type of the CI game is a policy-oriented one, in which we seek effective responses to public problems. To act rationally in this game is to acquire a sophisticated cognitive appreciation of the complex realities surrounding a given problem, to assess the strengths and limits of various solutions, and to monitor the results of one's actions so that corrections can be made. In this game, as in the political one, we often confront a 'decision-making vacuum': we wish to play the game rationally (others demand this of us) but we lack the capacity to do so and we are not sure how to fill this void with appropriate behaviour. There are many inherent obstacles to CI rationality: the problems are often complex and rapidly changing; data are inadequate or difficult to interpret; there often are conflicting, equally plausible answers; we often lack the time or resources to pursue more research or analysis; and it isn't certain whether further analysis will produce results that justify the additional cost. But if players are *trying* to find solutions to policy problems, they are playing a CI game, however much their behaviour falls short of some rational, problem-solving standard.

Elected and administrative officials often portray their own activities as pure CI problem solving. The present policy exists because it is a necessary solution to a serious, obvious problem. Official policy histories say that, for example, problem A emerged and became more and more serious; after some initial uncertainty, we all came to realize that policy Y was the best solution; but based on further experience we could see some limitations in Y and so we adopted the new, improved version, Z, which is present policy. The policy problem sits there, like Gaul, waiting to be conquered; and formulating public policy is largely a matter of veni, vidi, vici.

Political realists set out to demonstrate the naïveté of this account and to show that in fact a different kind of game, a political game, was being played. In the political game, a policy 'problem' exists for you if your interests are being threatened. This problem exists for a policy system if you are able to push your concerns onto that system's agenda. In your view, the substantive problem is that your interests are being threatened; the solution is the removal of this threat. There will be as many definitions of the problem and as many versions of the desired solution as there are affected interests. Solutions get adopted not because they are thought adequate responses to some public problem (dirty water, unsafe products, excessive competition in the trucking industry) but because the people advocating this solution have applied more resources, with greater persistence, than their opponents. Because politicians are trying to maximize interest-group support for themselves and for the proposed policy, the substantive merits of argument are less important than the resources commanded by their sponsors, and the real facts are less important than what the key groups claim is true.

Political rationality, then, is the intelligent pursuit of one's self-interest: a private group's interest in advancing its economic objectives, a politician's interest in getting re-elected, an administrative agency's interest in more power and bigger budgets. The rational political actor canvasses the field of players to ascertain their viewpoints and resources, avoids unnecessary quarrels, seeks allies, avoids wasting resources on lost causes, and recognizes when to compromise. Politicians see themselves less as solvers of policy problems and more as mediators, trying to patch together a majority or find some broadly supported, middle-ground solution.

Although much has been written about the limits to CI rationality, vast amounts of rationality are often attributed to players in the political game. The same people who cannot deal intelligently with policy problems apparently have no trouble identifying their vested interests, linking those interests to policy options, and devising clever strategies for advancing those objectives. In this study, I assume that rational behaviour is equally problematic in both CI and political games, for roughly the same reasons. Furthermore, the systems pathologies described in this study are crucial obstacles to the pursuit of both intelligent policy solutions and rational political conduct. Although political realists often imply, and micro-economists explicitly say, that politics is the only game being played, I assume this game coexists alongside, and doesn't simply supplant, the CI game described above. Because we are to some extent self-interested optimizers, politics intrudes into all other games. A purely CI game may generate interesting ideas, but only politics can link these ideas to the vested interests of certain players and thus create the support needed to sustain these ideas. But as any empirical account of any policy sphere demonstrates, the key players are not purely, solely political optimizers. They care about whether the policies adopted do in fact solve problems, right wrongs, protect people, alleviate suffering; and they often pursue their own convictions about the best solutions, even at the expense of their support-maximizing interests. The key question, then, is exactly how these two games coexist and interrelate.

AFFILIATIVE GAMES

Although political and CI games are different, the perspectives in these games have certain similarities: rationality is defined in terms of achieving visible results, much of our action is a means to some end, and much of our thinking is strategic, oriented to consequences; we assess ideas and actions as specific, cold instruments; we assess people as well in terms of their ability to perform and move us toward certain objectives; our links to others are calculative and temporary. By contrast, in the affiliative game, we create and allocate loyalty or attachment: a diffuse, unconditional, emotionally charged, stable form of support. When people mutually display loyalty to each other and to a common social system, the result is 'solidarity.' In the family, love-based relations, communal or ethnic-group settings, we have a broad, open-ended set of obligations (diffuseness) to certain persons who stand in some special relationship to us (particular-ism). We do not vary the obligation in response to short-run fluctuations in the other person's performance; we do not offer it in exchange; and we do not shop around for a better deal. Affiliation creates strong bonds between some people but in the process also creates boundaries and exclusions, creates antipathies or tension between insiders and outsiders, one system and another. If clear system identities and boundaries emerge, one can play this game rationally.

The affiliative game intrudes on all others because, whatever the game, we prefer clarity, stability, and predictability in our dealings with others. If people regularly interact over a period of time, they will try to draw a boundary around this interaction, structure their interaction through commonly understood roles and ground rules, resist intrusions from outsiders, and try to preserve this structure. Thus, the people concerned with a given policy sphere regularly build policy systems, sometimes referred to as subgovernments, policy communities, issue networks, iron triangles. By allocating our loyalty and antipathy, we identify ourselves and locate ourselves in social-structural terms. We similarly identify and locate others. Because we often find acting as part of a team intrinsically gratifying, collectivities tend to evolve from cold, limited-purpose, convenient instruments into more unified, organic, solidary systems, commanding the member's diffuse support and thus better able to mobilize resources for collective goal attainment.

EXPRESSIVE-APPRECIATIVE GAMES

People also derive intrinsic gratification by acting out their personal convictions or character before an appropriate audience. Commitments, it seems, are a kind of energy that seek out opportunities for release or expression, preferably before an audience that shares such commitments and thus is likely to be impressed, moved, or entranced. For this audience, appreciation also is intrinsically gratifying. When there is maximum communication between audience and performer, i.e., expressive rationality, the gratificational potential of the performance is maximized. Otherwise, the audience is confused and unmoved, the performer frustrated. One achieves this rationality and develops a relatively elaborate, sophisticated expressive game by investing parts of the performance with standardized meaning, in other words, by drawing upon common, expressive symbols.

A symbol is an indicator or label standing for some referent. An expressive symbol usually carries a strong emotional charge, has multiple referents, and thus strong evocative power. Symbols are compacted, multivalent catalysts, capable of triggering elaborate, intense responses.

One can extend the amount of rapport and understanding between performer and audience by basing the performance on such symbols, on familiar, stylized moves with elaborate, commonly understood meanings. Frequently repeated stylized performances, with commonly understood meanings, will be called 'rituals.'

Expressive-appreciative action is omnipresent because it performs vital functions for all other games. Aside from its apparent, surface meaning, every act reveals something about the actor's long-term objectives, motives, or character. Other players inevitably respond not only to the ostensible meaning, which usually corresponds to the primary game being played, but also to the deeper, indicative, symbolic meaning. Underlying messages of the right sort, such as reassurance or indications of respect, become symbolic pay-offs, which these other players seek and find intrinsically gratifying. Moreover, in both political and CI games, the immediate objectives one pursues are often small links in a long means-end chain. The key objectives we seek may or may not be attained. They will be attained far in the future, if at all, and even if attained, may or may not solve problems to the extent we hope. Expressive performance – for example, the ritualistic reaffirmation of one's adherence to these objectives – provides people with some of the short-run gratification needed to sustain their motivation and keep such games going. In affiliative games, ritual is an important vehicle through which system members reveal and renew their loyalties and remind colleagues of mutual affiliative obligations.

POLICY FAILURE AND SYSTEMIC RATIONALITY

Policy success presupposes cognitive-instrumental rationality. Policies are more likely to be successful if the key players work with accurate pictures of reality, formulate some clear images of the problems to be solved, define reasonably precise objectives, accurately perceive their own actions, and gain some insight into what impact their actions have on the environment. Such CI rationality is a necessary but not sufficient cause of policy success; one may proceed in this reasonable, well-informed manner and produce plausible solutions, which none the less fail to solve problems, perhaps because no one at present knows of any good solutions. However, suppose the key players proceed on the basis of misinformation and self-deception, dwell largely within a world of myth and fantasy, engage in inconsistent, self-defeating actions, and cannot clearly define the problems they are addressing or the solutions they pursue. Not only is the resulting policy unlikely to be successful, but one may have found in such CI irrationality a key source of policy failure. Rather than ask how well Canadian policies have solved transportation problems, I will pursue more modest questions: To what extent were these policies based on a clear-headed, unmuddled, reasonably articulate approach to transportation issues? And if the approach was incoherent or misinformed, as we often find it to be, what factors produced this muddle or stood in the way of a more intelligent approach to such issues? In short, we will search for sources of policy failure by trying to identify the major obstacles to cognitive-instrumental rationality.

To some extent rationality is a personal achievement. Individuals play any game with varying amounts of skill. Policy failures in specific cases can sometimes be attributed to strategic blunders or mistakes in reading evidence, that is, to ad hoc, random acts of personal irrationality. As well, the structural context of action facilitates or impedes rational decision-making. Irrational conduct can be 'systemic,' as opposed to ad hoc and personal, in two senses: first, certain distinctive, patterned kinds of irrational conduct consistently reappear; and, second, they reappear because they are the product of recurring system malfunctions, not of individual mistakes. These typical, recurring irrationalities will be called 'systems pathologies.' In the following examination of transportation issues, I not only ask 'what went wrong' but focus on the question of what things repeatedly go wrong.' What typical pathologies inhibit the pursuit of CI rationality; and what are the underlying structural or systemic sources of these pathologies?

POLICY, RATIONALITY, AND DIFFERENTIATION

The answer provided in this study, my overall argument, can be summarized as follows. Complex systems have a horizontal dimension (the extent to which there is differentiation among various games) and a vertical dimension (the extent to which each game is organized as a cybernetic hierarchy). The pathologies described in this study result either from a breakdown in game differentiation or from some vertical malfunction. Here we pursue the first kind of malfunction; below we describe the vertical dimension.

To restate an earlier point, we are more likely to behave rationally if we pursue games one at a time, if we clearly understand what game is being played at any given moment, and if we thus can rigorously pursue the logic of one game. This argument can be illustrated by drawing on political realism, which showed how political intrusions into a CI game inhibit the pursuit of CI rationality. For example, the system may be unable to pursue the most effective policy solutions because they command insufficient support or challenge too many vested interests. Politics unduly restricts the range of policy solutions given serious consideration. Sometimes we pursue ineffective solutions because it is not in the interests of well-placed groups to have the problem solved. Politics also diminishes our ability to think clearly or talk intelligently about policy issues. Each group will produce and claim general validity for what in fact are self-serving, distorted assertions, which only include evidence compatible with the group's interests. When each team retains its own experts and produces its own data, an already fragile, imperfect, data-collecting, data-interpreting process is further discredited and weakened.

Our culture says that leaders should devote themselves to a purely CI game. Because two games are being played simultaneously when only one is legitimate, the leaders must deceive. The leaders must deny they are playing politics and must hide their strategic manoeuvring behind a legitimate, seminar-like, problem-solving façade. For example, if leaders make a concession to group X, they must say it is because they were impressed by the substantive merits of X's arguments not by X's ability to wield rewards and penalties. When deception fails, mass cynicism results.

POLICY AND DRAMA

Expressive intrusions into either the CI or political game produce a pathological process that I call 'ritualization.' A belief or demand is torn from its original supportive evidence or rationale and transformed into a highly charged end in itself, whose value is to be regularly, ritualistically reaffirmed. The idea or belief is no longer an intellectual instrument to be applied in specific situations and judged on the basis of evidence or experience; it is viewed instead as a positively charged, static quality. It becomes the subject of expressive performance, something to be solemnly intoned rather than used. Given ritualization, I may no longer understand what game is being played and I easily deceive myself. I may think I am exerting effective pressure on politicians or endorsing a proposal that will solve specific problems, when in fact I am engaged in an intrinsically gratifying, self-contained, consequence-free performance. In 'ritual combat,' two sides will stage an elaborate fight over some proposal that apparently has important practical significance; but in fact the fight is a self-contained, expressive performance, an end in itself.

POLITICS AND DRAMA

If I know my actions and words will be examined for latent, symbolic messages, I stage my action so that it sends out the covert messages I want. Because people will treat the correct underlying messages as rewards, as symbolic pay-offs, I can often provide such rewards in place of the substantive solutions being demanded by some group, giving them not the solution they demand but instead a sympathetic hearing, a show of serious concern, a formal inquiry, and group representation on the inquiring body. Here politics intrudes on the expressive-appreciative game because the latter is being manipulated by clever performers to win support from a less-knowing audience; and both intrude on the CI game because symbolic reassurance is being offered in place of real solutions to policy problems.

All of this requires deception. My covert messages are effective only when they seem natural rather than studied. My appearing to get on with solutions is a reassuring, symbolic reward only if it is thought to be a genuine effort. For the deceived group, the outcome is a politically irrational one, because the group has been diverted from its major purpose and fobbed off with something much less meaningful.

THE VERTICAL DIMENSION: STRUCTURE AND EVENTS

Earlier we said that the extent of differentiation among games is the horizontal dimension of complex systems; we turn now to the vertical dimension. Complex systems tend to assume a hierarchic form; or, to put it another way, hierarchy permits simple systems to become more complex. Stable, more general, shared ideas and commitments become the higher-level context for action and experience in specific situations. To simplify the discussion, I treat system hierarchies as if they had only two levels: a process level consisting of visible events and a structure level consisting of latent, taken-for-granted beliefs and commitments. Thus, in each game, the structure sets the rules and objectives, creates a repetory of strategic moves, and indicates how one keeps score; the process level contains a history of games played, the moves made by various players, and who won or lost.

The structure level regulates, controls, partially defines lower-level phenomena. Our cognitive-instrumental culture largely shapes how we interpret data or events and what questions we think worth asking; our moral culture shapes what objectives we think worth pursuing; higher-level understandings about correct ground-rules and roles shape individual conduct in specific situations. Policy oriented, CI games tend to form a higher-level policy culture: a standardized, widely accepted view of what the problems are and which solutions work best. A policy culture contains those tacit, taken-for-granted, often unstated premises on which specific CI processes are based. That we often do not clearly see our presuppositions makes them all the more influential and difficult to change, all the less subjected to scrutiny or criticism. One of the mistakes in the micro-economist approach to policy failure, sometimes duplicated in political realism as well, is a tendency to ignore these top-down influences, to treat the players as isolated actors improvising responses to specific situations. Similarly, many studies of policy making focus too much on process, over-emphasize the give and take of conflicting interests involved in short-run, tactical skirmishes, and often miss the longer-term structural regularities that control any policy field.

In cybernetic hierarchies, influence and causality flow in both directions. Action in part is an attempt to implement higher-level beliefs, but implementation means linking a simplified, general idea to a messy, complex, not easily foreseen reality. Ideas are transformed when applied, never simply implemented in some mechanical fashion. One also develops ad hoc, pragmatic responses to unforeseen circumstances, which eventually work their way upward and redefine higher-level commitments.

In any given game, the individual's ability to behave rationally often depends on the content of this higher level and its relationship to specific-level action or evidence. A properly functioning hierarchy, based on a two-way flow of influence, is a systemic source of rational decisions. For example, if one distinquishes between higher-level objectives and specific-level strategies, one can be more intensely committed to the former, but adopt a more tentative, calculative, flexible approach to the latter. One can allow greater diversity, change, and complexity at lower levels partly because these levels must be more finely attuned to varied, changing situations but also because the higher-level commitments provide a stabilizing context. Hierarchic perspectives, by helping us see that there are many, equally plausible, specific-level ways of achieving higher-level objectives, encourage freedom of choice, experimentation, and variety at specific levels. Bottom-up influences are pragmatic and adaptive; top-down influences reassert the system's identity, self-direction, and autonomy.

In the CI game, the existence of a higher-level policy culture is a systemic source of individual, problem-solving rationality. Through a higher-level cultural framework, one can store lessons and engage in cumulative learning; one can solve earlier, simpler problems and then move on; one can pursue long-term objectives by constructing complex means-ends chains, or 'plans.' In the political game, a hierarchic perspective liberates us from the sole pursuit of immediate, tactical victories. One tries not only to win specific games (process-level power) but to alter the rules to one's advantage (structure-level power). Our ability to play the political game rationally is enhanced if we have higher-level credit – e.g., access, trust, good working relations, reputation, alliances, IOUS – that we can draw on. It is rational political strategy to build and preserve such a higher level. Given a hierarchic perspective, we avoid ruining long-term relationships for the sake of secondary, short-term gains.

HIERARCHIC PATHOLOGIES

At the same time, malfunctioning hierarchies systematically produce irrational behaviour. If there is inadequate two-way influence between levels, our political culture may incorrectly summarize past lessons, we may trust people we shouldn't, the reputations we assign to others may be groundless, we may pick the wrong allies or cling to no longer useful alliances. Similarly, a dogmatic, simplistic policy culture will regularly generate ineffective policy solutions; it becomes an obstacle to clear thinking about policy problems, a trap, a systemic source of self-deception and confusion. In the transportation case that follows, much of what went wrong could be attributed to maladaptive, higher-level beliefs. Some of the pathological processes that produced such ideas are themselves the products of malfunctioning hierarchies. I call these vertical-dimension or hierarchic pathologies.

'Vertical disjunction or disconnection' is a breakdown in reciprocal causality and the two-way flow of influence between levels. When higher and lower levels are disconnected, cognitive beliefs are cut off from evidence, proposals from rationales. Commitments are no longer the crucial guides to actions or predictors of what people will do. There is a gap between rhetoric and practice, between what people say and what they do. System members may alter what they do but insist no change has occurred, or they may embrace new ideas but continue the old practices. Because the commitments are not implemented, they are not subjected to the test of experience. Disconnection and ritualization go together. Ideas cut off from specific-level evidence or implementation instead become objects of expressive reaffirmation.

In 'self-closure,' there is too much top-down influence and self-direction, too little bottom-up learning or adaptation. Rather than apply or test our beliefs, we set out to prove them correct, select only the confirming evidence, and, not surprisingly, find what we are looking for. In this way, we more thoroughly lock ourselves into the limited perspectives of a given culture. We shield that culture from the challenges but also from the useful lessons of specific-level experience. 'Fundamentalism' is the attribution of excessive, sweeping validity to what in fact are partial truths or the attribution of vast curative powers to policy proposals of limited significance. In the political game, a 'fundamentalist strategy' is marked by inflexibility, a high moral tone, a refusal to compromise, and, often, a resulting ineffectiveness. Fundamentalism involves an inability to see things in proper hierarchic perspective. One assigns long-term, higher-level importance to something relatively specific and temporary; or in strategic terms one fails to see the distinction between minor skirmishes and the larger war. Fundamentalism is a specific case of 'misattribution,' a failure to identify the correct structural location and significance of events, acts, or ideas, a tendency to assign them either too much or too little importance. Thus, one reads too much into a trivial remark, focuses on the least important part of a document and ignores the more important parts, burns up much of one's resources over secondary issues. Fundamentalism most often involves overattribution, in which we overload some item with far more significance than is justified.

In 'grounding' or 'legitimation,' we attribute certain qualities to an idea or practice mainly because these qualities are widely valued. We anchor some specific item by linking it to higher-level commitments. To justify some practice, we argue (sometimes correctly, sometimes not) that it helps attain important, shared values. If the higher-level values are vague or multivalent, one can ground almost any practice in them, and it is difficult to say whether this involves misattribution or not.

OTHER PATHOLOGIES: TOO MUCH, TOO LITTLE COMMITMENT

'Fixation' is the allocation of rigid, excessive commitment to certain ideas or practices, to the point where one no longer is able to criticize the idea, to recognize its limitations and its proper structural place, or to trade it off against other valued objectives. Fixation and fundamentalism go hand in hand: if one has found such a magic remedy or a sweeping truth, one obviously should cling tenaciously to it, and only to it. Through fixation, fundamentalism, and ritualization, a tentative, limited hypothesis is converted into an unqualified, frozen, not-to-be-questioned truth. Irrational behaviour often results. We may remain unalterably committed to certain goals when our best interests would be served by a change in direction. Or a short-run means to some end is confused with, perhaps pursued at the expense of, our longer-term, more-important objectives. Through these pathological processes, ideas outlive their original rationale or supportive evidence. They become disconnected from, impervious to, new evidence or experience.

Through a process I call 'inertia,' one remains excessively committed to current practice not out of any enthusiasm for it, as in the case of fixation, but because one has an inordinate fear of change and the unfamiliar. One overvalues the familiar, the here and now, the known evil, even though conceding that a change might be for the better.

'Ambivalence' is the opposite of fixation. Rather than assign too much commitment to item X, we cannot clearly define our attitude to it. X becomes true/false, good/bad. Instead of a debate between two different viewpoints, which might help resolve the underlying tensions or inconsistencies, each actor internalizes these inconsistencies in muddy, yes/no, 'on the one hand/on the other hand' statements. Rather than concede that X has both costs and benefits, strong and weak points, and then arrive at some aggregate judgment, we are locked into approach-avoidance cycles, moving toward X but then backing away, arguing in the first chapter of our report that X is good but in the second chapter that X is bad. Ambivalence is a neurotic symptom, a sign of our unwillingness to resolve certain contradictions in our thinking.

PATHOLOGIES: COMMITMENT TO WHAT?

In some cases, our viewpoint is confused or fuzzy because we are unambiguously, perhaps intensely, committed to ideas or objectives that cannot be defined.

Members of a social system can process large amounts of information and often engage in sophisticated communication because they share a distinctive vocabulary, in which specific terms convey rich meanings, in which short terms summarize complex phenomena. But unless there is a frequent renewal of the link between name and substance, the two may become disconnected. As the concept is frequently used, the meaning erodes, information is lost, the idea becomes increasingly simple, and, if the process is carried to some logical conclusion, the idea becomes an empty cliché, a label without substance. One might call this process 'loss of meaning' or 'intellectual entropy.'

Running counter to entropy, but producing similar irrational results, is 'symbolic accretion,' the tendency for an idea or practice to acquire multiple referents, unrelated to its original meaning. Through this process, a sharply defined term is converted into a condensed, multivalent, emotionally charged symbol, capable of evoking strong responses from an audience but less capable of conveying clear meaning or fostering calm, measured discussion. When people talk in empty labels or condensed symbols, they think they are engaged in meaningful communication but usually are not. Similarly, agreement on terms that have unclear or no referents creates an illusion of consensus.

Symbolic accretion and ritualization are linked. A vague symbol, overloaded with multiple, unrelated meanings, cannot be used or assessed; rather, it invites expressive affirmation or rejection.

WHAT TO SAY WHEN YOU HAVE NOTHING TO SAY

It is inherently difficult to play either the political or CI game rationally. Data often are limited and difficult to interpret, the situation complex and changing. As players, we often confront a decision-making vacuum: we want to play the game rationally but we have no promising clues about what to say or do next. Because others expect us to do something, rather than confess our bafflement, we must somehow try to fill this void. Saying something irrelevant or inappropriate rather than remaining silent, advocating something without good reason but merely to fill a silence, is a process I call 'political sublimation,' borrowing Freud's assumption that energy, prevented from moving toward its immediate objective, will seek out alternative, second-best routes.

Some of the pathologies noted in this study are attempts to fill a silence or decision-making void through unjustified leaps of faith, through the groundless adoptions of certain viewpoints. Some ideas capture our imagination and support not because there is evidence or good reason to support them but because they are presented in a dramatic form, which we find intrinsically gratifying. What makes certain ideas interesting or captivating is a question we pursue in this study. In 'wish fulfilment,' we take something to be true because we wish it were – for example, assuming that people behave as we think moral people should behave. In 'projection' or 'transferrence,' we fill a void by assuming that this situation is basically the same as another, so that the experience and thinking of the other can be applied unaltered and uncritically to this situation. For example, we assume that railway ideas can be extended to other transportation modes or that American experience and data can be applied to Canadian cases. When we look eagerly for a magic cure that worked elsewhere and should work here as well, projection is linked to fundamentalism.

When playing a political or CI game and in doubt about how to proceed, but compelled to say something, players often fall back on an expressive reaffirmation of standard, common values. Here we fill a void in one game by turning to another, just as, when in doubt about the validity of an argument, we may base our response on the affiliative credentials of the arguer.

In the following chapters, we examine these and other system pathologies as a way of understanding what went wrong in the specific case we study. In the last chapter we turn to the question of why these pathologies occur.

My purpose is to examine the case of trucking regulation for some clues of more general applicability to problems of policy success and failure. I return to this problem in the last chapter. Chapters 5, 6, and 7 focus on trucking regulation in Ontario; chapters 2, 3, and 4 describe the larger Canadian transportation context. Chapter 2 sets trucking within the context of Canadian transportation policy and develops the notion of a pathological policy culture. Although it is a long and perhaps tedious chapter, it advances the theoretical argument and provides much of the descriptive context for what follows. The gap between culture and reality, the inadequacies of the policy culture, are examined mainly in chapters 2, 3, and 5. In chapter 3, I characterize trucking as an industry and, in chapter 5, I examine the impact of trucking regulation, in both chapters trying to juxtapose hard evidence with the culturally standardized viewpoints. Chapters 4 and 6 examine obstacles to the pursuit of political rationality. Chapter 4 focuses on the Canadian Trucking Association and describes the role of trucking issues in federal-level politics; chapter 6 focuses on the Ontario Trucking Association and thus adds to our account of one province's regulatory system. In chapter 7, which again concentrates on Ontario, I try to describe the overall structure of a stable policy system, emphasizing how structure makes top-down demands on individual players. In the last chapter, I raise some questions about what all this suggests about the more general problem of policy failure.

Because this study is an attempt to summarize and interpret a large body of data, rather than provide a detailed narrative of specific events, it would be tedious and not particularly helpful to readers if I were to cite all the primary sources considered in arriving at each assertion. For example, my characterization of the Canadian Trucking Association's viewpoint on railway acquisitions of trucking companies is based on a careful reading of all the relevant trade journals and all the newsletters CTA regularly sends to its members, among other sources, during the 1950–70 period. I doubt if readers would be better off knowing all the specific dates of these journals and newsletters. Instead I have divided each chapter into titled subsections and provide at the back of the book a description of the sources used in each of these subsections.

A word on nomenclature might be in order. 'The industry' means the Canadian trucking industry. 'Politicians' refer to elected officials, 'administrators' to appointed officials, and 'government officials' to both politicians and administrators. 'The minister' refers to a position, role, or office; when I refer to specific incumbents, I name them. In referring to 'the minister's viewpoint' or 'the ministry's viewpoint,' I mean the relatively stable, official policy viewpoint emanating from that office. The 'policy professionals' are those economists, social scientists, engineers, and assorted experts who make their living by developing transportation ideas, who are paid by universities, governments, interest groups, or others to engage in research, define the facts, write the studies and reports.

2

The Canadian Transportation Culture

An elaborate, stable culture has dominated Canadian thinking on transportation in the twentieth century. This culture consists of widely accepted, taken-for-granted premises about what the transportation problem is and what policies would best deal with that problem. In some important respects, herein summarized, this policy culture was an obstacle to clear thinking about transportation problems, an impediment to the pursuit of cognitive-instrumental rationality.

This culture has been a remarkably stable one. Although its origins reach back to the mid-nineteenth century, reflecting early governmental involvement in transportation concerns, most of the current culture developed between 1890 and 1925. By the mid 1920s, the central ideas were in place, and very little has been added since. Throughout most of the twentieth century, royal commission reports, governmental policy statements, and interest-group submissions have largely reiterated standard themes. There is little in the recent deregulation debates that cannot be found in the 1962 report of the Royal Commission on Transportation, the MacPherson report; and little in MacPherson that cannot be found in the 1917 report of the Royal Commission on Rail Transportation, if not earlier. In fact, the culture is excessively stable. Despite great changes in transportation realities, the prevailing thinking has been frozen, static. The resulting transportation debates have involved a repetitious recycling of stale, overly familiar ideas.

Over a period of decades, the key ideas were not merely reiterated but transformed into a set of condensed, affectively charged symbols. Other central ideas in this culture were clichés or platitudes, hollowed-out, empty phrases, concepts that had a name but not much meaning. There was vast agreement on the importance and validity of these concepts but little ability to define their meaning. Hence, the consensus was illusory. The system assumed that these consensual values could be used to solve specific policy problems; but when it tried implementing these values, their meaning vanished, the concepts crumbled in one's hands. Thus, many of the key ideas in this culture had minimal impact on specific-level policy. Instead, these ideas set the stage for resource-consuming, highly dramatic, but basically fruitless 'great debates.'

One can see a number of system pathologies at work in this case: loss of meaning, symbolic accretion, ritualization, vertical disjunction, fixation. The transformation of cognitive-instrumental concepts into clichés or condensed symbols helped produce a highly static culture. The policy system was excessively committed to ideas that lacked substance. Transportation issues were debated through these vague, charged symbols, which evoked strong positive or negative reactions and thus created an illusion of meaningful communication but which, in fact, conveyed little precise meaning and thus produced muddled discussions. It was difficult to assess or criticize such vague concepts, and difficult to use them or alter them in the light of experience. The ideas became cut off from specific-level behaviour and events. They were less problem-solving, reality-defining instruments, to be used and assessed in performance terms, than static, correct values, whose importance had to be frequently reaffirmed. Rather than tackle new problems, unearth new empirical findings, or formulate new concepts, the players repeatedly fell back on ritualistic restatements of the unquestioned, very familiar themes and symbols. Major policy statements and 'research findings' issued by governments, interests groups, and royal commissions often were little more than a chain of these consensual symbols strung together. The apparent attempt to work with, debate, and implement these ideas, in fact, was largely a stylized, grandly rhetorical, expressive drama.

This policy system, however, did not think of itself as being locked into a cycle of ritualistic reaffirmations. For political reasons, the players had to emphasize how much progress was being made and to de-emphasize the extent to which transportation debates continued to rotate within well-worn grooves. Each report, proposal, or policy statement, then, was hailed as a bold, new departure, a major revision in previous transportation thinking. The fact that these exciting new ideas did not produce appropriate changes in official policy could be explained by the 'planning vs politics' theme, which saw these new ideas being undermined by selfish vested interests and faint-hearted politicians.

An apparent consensus based on positively charged, vague symbols obscured the internal contradictions in this policy culture. Canada's transportation culture was based on an unintegrated set of multiple, inconsistent themes, a list of valued but conflicting objectives. To apply such a culture to specific policy issues, one must clarify the relationship between its conflicting objectives. Ritual restatements of conflicting objectives failed to produce this clarification. A crisp debate between differing viewpoints might have provided some clarification; but the illusion of consensus, the fact that everyone seemed to agree on central values, helped obscure differences and smother conflict. In place of debate, each player internalized the culture's commitment to conflicting objectives and thus produced muddy, ambivalent, yes/no statements, which reflected but did not help resolve the basic conflict. For example, the famed MacPherson report began with a ringing affirmation of free-market principles and a call for less government intervention, proceeded at great length to list justifiable exceptions to this rule, and wound up endorsing almost all existing policies.

Because these conflicting objectives could not be realized simultaneously, and because all these objectives were genuinely valued, the central problem in Canadian transportation policy was to find optimum trade-offs among these objectives in day-to-day decision-making. Influenced by the American tradition, both federal and provincial governments in Canada delegated to independent regulatory boards the authority to make these trade-offs in specific cases – and thereby delegated the core of transportation policy-making. Thus, the disjunction one finds between general-level ideas and specific events or policies was paralleled by, and re-enforced by, a structural gap between the minister responsibile for transportation and the appropriate regulatory board. According to the culture, specific decisions must be made in an 'independent,' judicial manner; and ministerial involvement in these crucial, specific decisions constituted 'political interference.' To a great extent, the key policy decisions were made through many detailed cases, whose importance was often insufficiently appreciated. Instead, the key players assumed that policy would emerge from the system's more dramatic events, from great debates, royal commissions, and ministerial white papers. If the culture contained conflicting objectives, ministers and commissions were urged to resolve these inconsistencies with some once-and-for-all, definitive statement of general principles. The resulting statements, however, largely restated the familiar themes, including all-embracing ambivalent references to conflicting objectives. Thus, the minister engaged in the manipulation of general-level symbols; the great debates, while expressively gratifying, often led the system down blind alleys; and the regulatory boards quietly ground out policy.

Before proceeding, we must add one important qualification to these generalizations, especially the 'static culture' hypothesis. Although no new ideas of consequence appeared after the 1920s, some reallocation of emphasis among the old ideas occurred. From the outset, the culture contained both pro-government, interventionist, and pro-market, non-interventionist objectives. On this issue, however, one can discern a large, arc-like shift in priorities. From roughly 1890 to 1940, the case for interventionism steadily gained support; after the Second World War, emphasis shifted to the non-interventionist themes in this culture. Although the 1940s were the key turning point, the case for less intervention, for example, the notion that the railways should be liberated from the dead hand of regulation, began to gather strength early in the twentieth century. Thus, the recent campaign for deregulation was the culmination of a very gradual, long-term shift in internal cultural priorities.

This chapter describes the major themes that make up the Canadian transportation culture, indicates how this culture was applied to specific transportation problems, like price, examines how the early railway-based culture was extended to trucking questions, and reviews cultural responses to the truck vs rail controversy. We then consider the extent to which the post-war shift toward non-interventionism represented a departure from the previous classic pattern.

NON-INTERVENTIONIST AND INTERVENTIONIST THEMES

Canada's transportation culture contains an unresolved, conflicting commitment to both interventionist and non-interventionist objectives. On the one hand, transportation is simply one kind of service-providing market, to be judged mainly on the basis of how efficiently it delivers this service. The transportation companies should provide a high quality of service at minimal cost; they should strive for maximum efficiency in internal operations and transfer the benefits of low operating costs to users in the form of low rates. Any market creates winners and losers. The more efficient, imaginative, innovative companies gain at the expense of others. Although the losers will want government to intervene on their behalf, government should avoid any action that impedes healthy market adjustments or props up weak, lazy firms.

On the other hand, transportation is not merely another market or industry. It is an essential service, an industry on which all other industries depend. Efficient freight handling, translated into lower rates, means lower prices for all Canadian consumers. Conversely, transportation inadequacies hurt the entire economy. For these reasons, transportation is a public necessity, a public utility, an industry whose effective functioning is essential to the public interest. When market forces fail to generate a network of healthy transportation industries, government must intervene to secure such a network, perhaps through subsidies, perhaps by intervening to prevent business failures. In transportation, market solutions often prove inadequate because most transportation modes have high fixed costs and thus constitute natural monopolies. Firms must construct an elaborate, expensive infrastructure at the outset and thereafter cannot make short-term supply adjustments in response to market fluctuations. In such a setting, competition can be destructive because it creates uncertainty about future demand and discourages firms from undertaking an optimum level of long-term capital investment. Government must intervene to dampen these destructive forces.

Having restrained competition and thus weakened the protection that competition normally provides to users, government must fill this gap with legal protections. Government should sponsor and promote a healthy transportation industry but must also protect shippers, passengers, and the general consumer public from abuses that can result from the carriers' monopolistic power. Public policy rather than the marketplace must strike a fair balance between the needs of transportation providers and users.

THE CANADIAN THEME

Many aspects of the Canadian transportation culture can be found in other nations; but some elements in this culture focused on the distinctive features of Canadian transportation and drew appropriate policy conclusions. By and large, this attempt to define the Canadian condition strengthened interventionist elements in the transportation culture.

Canada is a nation of vast miles and relatively few people. Only in a narrow corridor running from Montreal to the United States border at Detroit and Buffalo does one find a large stetch of continuously urbanized settlement. Outside this corridor, cities are scattered across a thin, east-west ribbon, which rarely extends more than 100 miles from the United States border. Vast distances, cultural diversity, and uneven patterns of regional economic development conspire to make national unity a central Canadian concern. Proximity to the United States, and the tendency for parts of Canada to form north-south links with parts of the United States as opposed to east-west links with other regions of Canada, exacerbate problems of diversity, disparity, and disunity. Free, untrammelled market forces appear to strengthen these north-south links at the expense of national unity. Nation building apparently would require persistent governmental attempts to redirect market forces. Helping to create national unity always has been viewed as one objective of Canadian transportation policy; or, to put it differently, transportation always has been considered an instrument of nation-building policy.

Given the large distances involved and the limitations of Canada's private capital market, one would probably need government funding to establish the transportation infrastructure. But the problem might go far beyond laying the tracks and building the seaways. Perhaps an unassisted, private transportation market would never be viable under Canadian conditions. The distances might always be too vast and the markets too small to produce decent profits for private companies. Compared to the United States, transportation in Canada always has consumed a larger share of the gross national product. Compared to the United States, a much smaller amount of freight travels each year on each mile of Canadian rail or Canadian roads. Permitting free competition among transportation firms might mean that already small markets would be further subdivided, providing a viable return for none of the carriers. Competition in transportation was assumed to be inherently destructive, but perhaps especially destructive in Canada. Furthermore, subsidies or legal restraints might always be needed to ensure that goods moved east and west, rather than north and south, and to ensure that Canadian goods headed for Europe or Asia were shipped to Canadian rather than u.s. ports.

From the outset, the Canadian economy became heavily dependent on the export of unprocessed or semi-processed, resource-type commodities. Over the long run, one might question the wisdom of this dependence and urge measures to diminish it. Over the short run, however, the health of the economy depended on Canada's ability to move these goods quickly and cheaply, and this in turn required an efficient, inexpensive transportation system. Vital national interests were involved. If the market could not ensure cheap, speedy transportation of goods headed for export, the government must.

EARLY RAIL POLICY

These themes dominated Canada's initial thinking and policies on railway transportation. In the latter half of the nineteenth century, adequate, relatively inexpensive transportation was considered essential to the forging of unifying, east-west links. The railways would promote economic development in Atlantic and western Canada by linking these regions to the urban markets of Ontario and Quebec. Railways would also help Canadians settle the northwest before Americans did. But unassisted, private enterprise seemed unequal to this task. The distances to be spanned were great, and indigenous sources of private capital modest. If an undirected free market in transportation prevailed, many parts of Canada might be served only by U.S.-owned railways, linking Vancouver to Seattle or Winnipeg to Minneapolis. Other parts of Canada might not be served at all. An east-west railway network, located entirely north of the border, and built largely with federal government money on federally donated lands, seemed the appropriate response to nation building under distinctively Canadian conditions. In the 1870s, as part of its National Policy, the federal government committed itself to financing the construction of a railway from Ontario to the Pacific, using as its instrument a quasi-public corporation, the Canadian Pacific Railway (CPR). With the tracks built, the federal government helped CPR become a full-fledged private corporation. Later, the prevailing culture viewed this CPR story as a successful reconciliation of interventionist and non-interventionist objectives. The government had intervened to build the infrastructure but then stepped aside to let the railway be operated on a business-like basis. Dissenters, for example, on the left, questioned whether it was appropriate to endow a quasi-public company with massive amounts of federal land and money and then allow it to carry those assets into the private sector.

It was assumed that railway competition, especially in Canada, always produced destructive results: rate wars, falling wages, dangerous economizing on vehicle safety, and a flight of private capital. This assumption was apparently confirmed by the collapse of four private eastern Canadian railways in the early 1900s – although in fact a serious economic recession explained the collapse far better than 'destructive competition.' On non-interventionist grounds, politicians initially resisted the 1917 royal commission's recommendation that government weld these four defunct companies into a single publicly owned railway for eastern Canada. At the same time, one presumably needed government to salvage the wreckage left by these private companies, to guarantee eastern Canadians adequate rail service, and to spare us from a fresh cycle of destructive railway competition. Pulled in both interventionist and non-interventionist directions, the federal government eventually, reluctantly, accepted the royal commmission recommendation and, in 1923, created a publicly owned railway, the Canadian National Railway (CNR).

After 1923, the Canadian railway system became a duopoly, consisting of one privately owned and one publicly owned railway. With characteristic ambivalence on the interventionist/non-interventionist, public/private question, federal officials were not sure whether the CNR was to provide a yardstick for the privately owned company's performance, or the reverse. On one point, however, there was agreement. Because competition in transportation was destructive and unnecessary, the two firms were urged to 'rationalize' their operations, which meant eliminating all those cases in which they competed against each other.

THE REGIONAL-PROTEST THEME

Through overattribution, fundamentalism, and symbolic accretion, 'the railways' became a powerful, emotionally charged, multivalent symbol in Canadian life. From the time of Confederation, rail transport had been seen as a key catalyst for economic development. Because the railways became symbolic expressions of the nation's faith in its economic future, rail lines were built in great bursts of enthusiasm, based on unrealistic optimism about future markets and population densities. Because far too much faith was placed in the vast catalytic power of adequate, inexpensive rail transport, these periods of enthusiastic construction would alternate with periods of economic recession, when the railways, and the Canadian government, would become preoccupied with problems of overcapacity and operating deficits. Overattribution, overconstruction based on rash optimism, was a major source of the railways' chronic financial problems. But, since the railways were symbols of Canada's bright prospects, it was heretical to urge a more restrained pace of construction during the economic upturns.

Transportation generally, and rail specifically, was also viewed as the leveller of regional differences and the great national unifier. Rail would achieve all this by linking less-advanced regions to the urban markets of central Canada. When the promised regional economic development failed to materialize, no one dared suggest that too much importance had been attributed to rail as sole catalyst. Instead, positive overattribution turned into negative overattribution; excessive hope became excessive blame.

According to interest groups and provincial governments in Atlantic and western Canada, Confederation had been based on the promise that federal powers would be used to promote the lesser-developed regions; but in reality the federal government and the railways exploited and suppressed these regions for the benefit of Ontario and Quebec. The National Policy protected industries in central Canada with high tariffs but raised domestic prices and made it more difficult for farmers and resource industries to sell their products abroad. Cheap rail rates had been promised, as a stimulus to regional economic development; but in practice the railways charged lower rates in urbanized Ontario and Quebec, exerted monopoly-type power over farmers and small shipping companies, and thus compelled other regions to cross-subsidize central Canada. In reply, the railways said it was cheaper to move freight in central Canada and therefore sound business practice to charge less in that region. To the regional protestors, however, the railways were not so much businesses as instruments of national policy, in this case, a policy of promoting regional economic development through reduced rail rates. Relying on market forces and business-like principles would simply enshrine the economic dominance of central Canada. At the same time the protestors denied that it was cheaper to ship goods in central Canada and thought that small shippers were being compelled to pay for inefficient rail management. For example, rail costs and rates could be cut if the two companies did more to rationalize, that is, eliminate, the 'needless duplication of service.'

Regional protestors wanted government to correct railway abuses. This protest strengthened interventionist elements in the transportation culture and drew the government into a larger transportation role. At the turn of the century, the federal government created an independent regulatory board to ensure that the general level of rail rates was 'reasonable' rather than excessive and that rates did not discriminate against some shippers (e.g., western farmers) for the benefit of others. Later, when regulated rates failed to produce the desired regional economic expansion, the protestors sought low, subsidized rates. The federal government responded with two major acts, both given definitive form in the 1920s. The Maritime Freight Rate Assistance Act provided cash subsidies to compensate the railways for a major reduction in the railway rates on freight moving from the Atlantic region to other parts of Canada. In the Western Grain Transportation Act, the so-called Crow's Nest Pass legislation or more simply 'the Crow,' the government froze at their 1897 level the rail rates on grain moving to ports for sale aboard. In this case, no subsidy was provided; by carrying grain at these low rates, the CPR would be compensating Canadian taxpayers for earlier federal government generosity. These two acts, along with a federal policy guaranteeing the maintenance of rail service on small-town branch lines, became central tenets of Canadian rail policy. To western and Atlantic Canada they were economic magna cartas, belated attempts to fulfil the promise of Confederation and to redress central Canada's historic exploitation of other regions.

THE INTEGRATED NETWORK THEME

Transportation professionals assumed that each mode had its own distinctive strengths and weaknesses, that a natural division of labour existed in the transportation market. In the nineteenth century, for example, inland shipping was less expensive than rail but slower and not operative throughout the year. Compared to rail, inland shipping was especially suited to moving large amounts of low-valued, bulky goods during non-winter months. Through a process of transference or projection, it was assumed that such differentiated roles would characterize the expanded, post-1920 transportation system. To paraphrase the MacPherson report's comment on the various modes: there is a need for all and a place for each. According to this cultural theme, any transportation mode or company could perform most efficiently if it concentrated on those tasks it best performed. If each company sought out its own differentiated market niche, if each focused on its area of distinctive strength, the resulting transportation market would achieve maximum efficiency.

This theme had both interventionist and non-interventionist implications. By rewarding those firms that most efficiently provided a given type of transportation service, the market would allocate firms to their proper niches. If government subsidies encouraged a firm to try retaining some service that other firms could more efficiently provide, government would be delaying rather than assisting these market-based allocations. At the same time, perhaps these market processes worked too slowly or ineffectively and would need some government help; or perhaps these processes, while ultimately beneficial, created unacceptable short-run disruptions, which government must cushion. The central purpose of transportation policy, then, was to guide each firm to its right niche. One needed 'comprehensive transportation planning,' designed to achieve an efficient, role-differentiated but integrated transportation network. To produce such a plan, government must adopt a multi-modal, system-wide transportation perspective.

On the basis of this model, one could criticize existing practices. In reality, and in sharp contrast to this model, one found narrow, unimodal perspectives, fragmentation of authority, and ad hoc responses to immediate crises. While the federal government controlled most modes, the provinces retained jurisdiction over trucking. In trucking, the Canadian scene was 'balkanized' by ten different provincial regulatory systems. Even for those modes under federal jurisdiction, the most recent federal regulatory body, the Canadian Transport Commission (CTC), allocated each mode to a different subcommittee and provided for little co-ordination or communication among these subcommittees. For most of the twentieth century, federal politicians remained obsessed with one mode – rail – and obsessed with one issue – the financial decline of the railways. Even later, when federal perspectives broadened, the cabinet had separate policies on rail, on maritime shipping, and on airlines, but did not have a transportation policy.

THE PLANNING VS POLITICS THEME

Apart from the survival of unimodal perspectives, why did federal politicians make so little effort to plan comprehensively or to build a rational, integrated transportation network? If everyone believed in planning, comprehensiveness, and integration, why didn't these values filter down to specific levels and correct the fragmented, haphazard practices? The policy professionals explained this disconnection between culture and practice by developing a 'principle vs politics' theme. Doing the right thing often meant stepping on toes. Sound economics, cognitive-instrumental rationality, 'principle,' and efforts at 'reform' always lost out to 'entrenched, vested interests' because politicians were unable to make the 'difficult decisions.'

After 1945, the planning vs politics theme, taken in conjunction with the notion of an integrated network, was often used to support non-interventionist conclusions. According to this view, we would be much less inclined to call for a government-prepared comprehensive plan if we first looked realistically at how transportation policy is made. Government usually responds to the noisiest pressure and thus gets drawn into many ill-conceived interventions. When people protest a proposed increase in railway rates, for example, the government responds with rate freezes and further subsidies. Government should and could facilitate the proper market adjustments, but it usually resists them. Consequently, government could help us achieve an efficient network simply by de-intervening, by undoing the damage caused by its present policies. Shippers in Atlantic Canada would benefit more from healthy rail/truck competition in that region than from a rail-only federal subsidy that stifled the growth of an Atlantic trucking industry. Railways could more easily find their right niche if they became less reliant on government subsidies, if they had the freedom to exit from branch-line markets, and if they could raise rates to a cost-based level. But such sensible de-interventions are unlikely to occur. Interventionist mistakes are very difficult to undo, because each mistake creates beneficiaries with a vested interest in that program's continuance. Thus, prairie towns could kill any move to curtail branch-line service; and no political party would risk losing seats in Atlantic or western Canada by questioning the Maritime rate subsidies or 'the Crow.'

The problem with this interpretation was that it assumed too much consensus on the correct policies and attributed too little cultural legitimacy to the 'vested interests.' The regional protestors were listened to not only because they commanded votes but also because transportation had always been viewed as an instrument for promoting regional economic development. Both the demands of regional protestors and the more market-oriented 'correct principles' favoured by policy professionals derived their legitimacy from the same culture, albeit from different themes in that culture. And neither view was a more faithful, more legitimate expression of that culture. This culture was difficult to implement because it contained internal contradictions – a commitment to transportation as a business but also to transportation as an instrument for promoting regional equity – not because selfish interests blocked the implementation of agreed-on values.

LEFT AND RIGHT

The transportation culture embraced conflicting values, created an illusion of consensus, obscured differences in viewpoint, discouraged the emergence of sharply defined, contending viewpoints. Instead of a debate between interventionists and non-interventionists, this culture produced statements that simultaneously advocated both. As a result, those people who saw politics in left vs right, interventionist vs non-interventionist terms had difficulty fitting transportation issues into this framework and often wound up ignoring these issues. The transportation policy system operated outside this ideological mainstream. The election of a more right-wing or more left-wing federal cabinet would not have produced notable, predictable changes in transportation policy.

The right (for example, the Canadian Manufacturers' Association [CMA]) and the left (for example, the New Democratic Party [NDP]) often debated the question of whether transportation was a business or policy instrument, but this was mainly ritual combat, confined to general-level symbolism and disconnected from more specific policy proposals. Moreover, each camp was ambivalent. The two began with different premises but converged on the same policies. The right opened with ringing pro-market principles but, given problems of regional development, the resource-based, export-based economy, etc., wound up accepting many interventionist exceptions to these principles. The NDP urged government to engage in 'comprehensive planning' and to help create an 'integrated transportation network' that would carry goods in the most efficient manner possible, a position not very different from anyone else's, and a position that conceded the desirability of assessing transportation industries in terms of business-like efficiency.

The concept of 'regulation' had never been defined in left vs right terms. Before 1975, both left and right had sometimes portrayed transportation regulation as a welfare or subsidy program for certain corporations, as a way of providing unjustified protection and profits to certain firms at the expensive of consumers and other firms. In the early 1970s most players had difficulty deciding whether deregulation was a move to the left or right. At first, the NDP showed some sympathy for dismantling regulatory programs that were nothing but hidden subsidies to certain businesses. In the end the party decided to oppose deregulation because it would give more power to newer, non-unionized companies and because it would open the door to U.S. take-overs and a loss of Canadian jobs in deregulated industries. Eventually, the right adopted deregulation, but this outcome had not been an obvious or inevitable one.

Among transportation issues, only the CNR/CPR relationship could produce a clear left/right confrontation, mainly because both sides decided to treat this issue as a surrogate or symbol for the larger debate over private vs public enterprise. The right opposed and the left supported the government's various attempts to 'recapitalize' the CNR, that is, to assume some portion of the corporation's accumulated capital debt. For the right, CNR's inability to reduce that debt on its own demonstrated how inefficient crown corporations were, compared to private firms like CPR. In reply, the left noted that, while the CPR had benefited from incredible federal largesse before presenting itself to the private capital market, the CNR had inherited the unintegrated rail lines and the vast, accumulated debts of four bankrupt companies. The right thought it inappropriate for the federal government to be both regulatory umpire of the rail system and owner of one major firm in that system; but this view incorrectly assumed that the cabinet intervened in specific regulatory decisions and that the cabinet was strongly committed to public ownership and to CNR interests. We now examine how these themes were applied to important, specific issues: the truck vs rail conflict, trucking regulation, and the question of transportation pricing.

ROAD VS RAIL

Whatever financial problems the railways had been experiencing before 1920 were aggravated by the emergence of airlines, pipelines, buses, automobiles, and trucks in the 1920s and 1930s. The rail corporations decided to accept a lesser role in passenger service, to fight for the more lucrative freight market, and to focus their counter-attack on trucking. At first, trucks had confined themselves to short intra-municipal trips, for example, moving goods to and from railway stations and thus performing useful, ancillary services for rail. After 1925, however, trucks began to move goods between cities, to undertake fifty- and seventy-mile trips, in direct competition with rail. In 1928 the two railway corporations, backed by the railway unions and by municipal officials from the many 'railway towns' in Canada, began a major political campaign designed to convince both the federal and provincial governments that they must restrict the spread of trucking. No trucking company should be authorized to operate in a market then served by rail. If provincial governments were unwilling to restrain trucking in this manner, jurisdiction should be shifted to the federal level, where the railway's problems were better understood and where the appropriate restrictions on trucks were more likely to be approved. The resulting road vs rail debate dominated the transportation agenda for at least forty years.

The railway case was grounded in standard cultural themes. Because competition in transportation tended to be pointless and destructive, the federal government must act to curtail road/rail competition and to protect its elaborate investment in the existing rail infrastructure. By moving beyond short, intra-municipal trips, the truckers were exceeding their appropriate market niche. They were able to encroach on the railway niche only because the provincial taxpayers paid for the truckers' right of way, the highways, and thus gave trucking an unfair competitive advantage. The fact that the railways were heavily regulated, while the truckers were not, allegedly gave the latter additional advantages. The trucking industry had a notorious reputation for low wages, long hours, and false economies in vehicle maintenance – matters which, in the railway case, were all governed by strict federal standards. In line with the Common Law obligations of the common carrier, the railways could not refuse service to any customer they were legally authorized to serve, i.e., could not engage in 'service discrimination.' The railways needed board approval of rate changes and often waited years for a decision. By contrast unregulated truckers could pick and choose among clients, could skim off the attractive trips and ignore the others, and could alter rates at will.

The truckers' response also was grounded in standard themes. The truckers attributed their gains to certain 'natural' market advantages, like flexibility in setting routes, minimal loading time, and an ability to accommodate smaller shipments. The truckers had been able to underprice rail partly because steady improvements in truck technology produced larger, safer, faster, and cheaper vehicles – thus falling per-unit operating costs for truckers. In other words, recent gains were legitimate; trucks were finding their true market niche, not poaching on the railway's. Railway operating costs were high and uncompetitive because militant railway unions secured excessive wage and hour concessions and successfully resisted the introduction of labour-saving devices. Because the railways had excessive capacity resulting from earlier, unduly optimistic forecasts about future rail use, the only long-term solution to the railway's financial problems was to discontinue service, to shrink supply until it corresponded to demand. But this allegedly was a principle vs politics problem. Railway managers and federal politicians refused to acknowledge the real sources of railway deficits because such an analysis called for 'difficult decisions,' for example, shrinking rail service and standing up to railway unions. Even if truckers benefited to some small degree from a highway subsidy, the extent of subsidy paled when compared to the vast federal largesse that had been heaped on the CPR in its early years and on the CNR through recent recapitalizations. Moreover, the Maritime and Crow's Nest subsidies encouraged certain shippers to use rail and thus impeded the emergence of a healthy trucking industry in Atlantic and western Canada. The trucking position on federal railway regulation was ambivalent. Sometimes they attributed rail inefficiency in part to the extraordinary delays, red tape, and bureaucratic interference involved in federal regulation; on other occasions truckers said that the railways secured whatever they wanted and that such ineffective, toothless regulation could not impose significant competitive disadvantages on rail.

Both economically and politically, the railways' campaign against trucking was a mistake. The railways, although focusing on the trucking threat, had been hurt just as much by the rise of pipelines, largely resulting from Canada's conversion from coal, carried by train, to oil and natural gas. The railway's financial problems stemmed largely from an imbalance between the thriving east-west trunk line, linking major Canadian cities, and the underutilized, money-losing, north-south branch lines, linking large cities and smaller towns. The only solution to this imbalance problem was to have trucks serve more of these lower-volume north-south routes, which meant further shrinkage in the railway's market share. Moreover, although the railways persisted with their campaign well into the 1950s, it should have been apparent to them, as early as 1926, that neither the provincial nor the federal governments had any intention of restricting the growth of trucking. Government, everyone said, must not try to promote the economic health of one mode by impeding the normal market development of another. As trucking gained more ground, its new-found importance became a fait accompli, which no government would consider undoing. The railway's political campaign against trucking merely delayed, by some twenty-five years, the preparation of a market-based strategy for recapturing lost customers. Not until the 1950s did the railways move to renew ageing terminal and moving equipment, adopt diesel engines, introduce automated communications networks and automated loading and unloading processes, introduce lower rail rates in areas where trucking offered a competing alternative, acquire custom-tailored (e.g., refrigerated) boxcars, and enter the trucking business.

THE SEARCH FOR DISTINCTIVE MARKET NICHES

For more than forty years, the policy professionals attempted to find a definitive, correct solution to this road vs rail controversy. Both in its economic and political manifestations, the conflict seemed destructive, wasteful, and unnecessary. The two sides should have concentrated on developing market strategies rather than wasting their time lobbying. Even in the marketplace a natural harmony existed. Each of the two modes performed different, complementary, non-competing functions; thus, each side should have found and defended its distinctive niches. Instead, road and rail foolishly tried to maximize their market share, to seek any and all gains at the expense of the other mode, to duplicate service better provided by the other. For example, it was wasteful duplication for the railways to cling to their small-parcel 'express' service, when trucks could better perform this service. As each mode came to appreciate its distinctive role, this conflict and duplication presumably would give way to role differentiation and complementarity. To hasten this process, government must remain 'even-handed,' must avoid playing favourites. This was a very appealing, universally endorsed argument. Everyone wanted to believe that a natural harmony of interests among transportation modes existed and that the current controversy was just transitional.

If this concept were to resolve the road/rail controversy or generate a correct policy, the professionals would have to indicate exactly what the correct niches for the two modes were. This they were unable to do. Professionals repeatedly solemnly intoned the niche concept as one of the great transportation truths. But, when it came to specifics, they usually provided little more than illustrations, designed to show that truck and rail had different strengths. For example, rail companies are slower in responding to technological innovations and short-run market shifts because rail requires large capital investments in immovable tracks and in equipment and vehicles with long lives. Trucking is the more flexible, adaptive mode because the truckers' capital costs, largely the purchase of trucks, constitute a much smaller percentage of total costs and because trucks have an average life of only five years. Because the loading and unloading of trucks is simpler, less expensive, and involves less handling of goods, trucking is more appropriate for uncrated, fragile, or small shipments. Trucks are more suited for trips involving irregular, zigzag rather than straight-line movement. Truckers are better able to adjust their timing to the wishes of the shipper, especially when the shipper's order fully loads one truck. Trucking thus is more appropriate for the shipper requiring fast delivery, for example, the shipper of perishable goods.

To go beyond mere illustrations, the professionals urged a careful study of operating costs. If we could determine the operating costs of each mode for a given kind of trip, we could determine which mode was able to provide that service at less cost and therefore which mode should rightfully offer that service. But the data on trucking costs were not available; and the data on railway costs were subject to very different interpretations, depending on how one allocated fixed costs to various trips. All the professionals could provide on the costs issue were plausible, possibly correct hypotheses. Because trucks had lower terminal costs, that is, lower loading and waiting costs, the professionals assumed that trucks would be more efficient for shorter trips, where terminal costs constituted a relatively large percentage of total operating costs and where the trucks' advantage would weigh heavily. Because boxcars were larger than trucks and because it was easier to extend a train by one boxcar than place a second or third truck on the road, rail was probably more efficient in coping with very large shipments. Moreover, the train, once loaded, had lower line-haul costs; that is, it could move goods at less cost per ton-mile than could the truck. The professionals concluded that trucks were best for short trips, 30 miles or less, involving smaller shipments of fragile, uncrated goods, while rail was more efficient in carrying large amounts of wheat, ore, and coal on 700- or 800-mile trips. But this argument, while assigning to each mode one extreme end of the freight market spectrum, left unresolved and still disputed the vast middle ground, i.e., most of the market.

According to the professionals, as the length of the trip increased, the railway's superiority on line-haul costs would become more pronounced. At some crucial threshold, X miles, the truck's advantages in terminal costs would be neutralized, and trucking would cease to be the more efficient carrier. One could apply the same argument to size of shipment and conclude that at Y tons the trucking niche ended and the rail niche began. If we could define X and Y, the crucial turning points in shipment size and trip length, we could identify the boundary that separated the road and rail niches. Rail, trucking, and many other groups accepted this challenge and produced a mountain of conflicting evidence about X and Y that in the end convinced no one. Although they had opened this line of inquiry, the professionals never defined X or Y, primarily because the examination of operating costs proved to be a fruitless, speculative venture. Although all major commissions and studies after 1930 tried to define niches through an analysis of operating costs, each concluded that its data on costs were unreliable and that the next study must collect better evidence on this all-important topic.

The power of these concepts rested largely on blind faith and wish fulfilment. Why must each mode have its own distinctive niche, distinct from the correct niches of other modes? Why was it unthinkable that a mode might have no sphere in which it was more efficient than all the others? Why rule out the possibility that there might be considerable overlap in the niches of various modes? If so, there would be constant competition for those middle grounds, those areas of overlap, in which no one mode had an obvious market superiority. Moreover, as long as the freight market was divided into more- and less-attractive segments (a concept considered below), there would always be intense, inter-modal competition for the more attractive segments. No mode would accept the less-attractive segments as its proper niche. And this search for the truckers' correct niche mistakenly treated trucking as if it were like rail, a homogeneous industry with easily summarized patterns.

The prevailing wisdom also assumed that these differentiated niches were a fixed, inherent, immutable attribute of the transport market, to which trucking and rail companies must adapt. In fact, technological developments kept redefining the 'correct niche' of each mode. With steady improvements in highway construction and truck design, one had to keep revising upward any estimate of the maximum distance or size of shipment that trucks could efficiently deal with. In 1930 people debated whether the truck could efficiently carry goods on 50-mile trips; in 1987 they were debating truck efficiency on 650-mile trips. As well, a niche could be altered through the market strategies pursued by the various modes. Not even technological advances could be treated as a given because some modes, and some companies, were more alert than others in perceiving and exploiting these advances. When truckers introduced specialized vehicles for carrying items like oil, long steel beams, lumber, and manufactured cars, the niches had to be redefined; when the railways countered with custom-tailored boxcars, a further redefinition was necessary. The appearance of piggyback dramatically redefined the truck/rail relationship in the 1950s, and sealed containers redefined things again in the 1960s. What the professionals had to say about niches simply summarized recent market trends rather than predicted the future or served as a guide to future policy making. Because the niches were always in flux, why assume that, some day, the transportation industries would arrive at a competition-free, stable division of labour? It made more sense to assume that the transportation system would always be in a state of transition from one division of labour to another and that, as a result, there would always be economic and political conflict among these modes.

Politicians repeatedly reaffirmed their undying commitment to the 'complementary niche' concept; but it would have been very impolitic to say exactly what kinds of service truck and rail should provide or to try allocating the contested, more-attractive areas of service to one mode or another. There was a great deal of 'ambivalence,' some said 'hypocrisy,' behind the universal call for comprehensive planning. The federal government actually approximated this kind of planning during the Second World War, when it assigned various kinds of traffic to specific modes; but in 1945 everyone agreed that only a wartime emergency had justified such high-handed, authoritarian procedures, and no one favoured extending them into peacetime.

Government, everyone agreed, must be 'even-handed,' but this concept, like complementary niches, proved to be less a usable cognitive-instrumental concept than an empty, remote-from-reality symbol. Everyone thought this concept crucial and repeatedly invoked it, in the most reverential terms, but no one could define or apply it. Almost any action a government might take on transportation matters would have a differential impact on various modes and thus would violate the principle. Interpreting the concept in this manner, politicians invoked 'even-handedness' whenever they had decided to take no action at all and needed a rationale for inactivity. The concept implied that a blank slate or a state of initial fairness existed and that government must not create imbalance. In fact, both truck and rail saw the other as having benefited unduly from past policies. Because the status quo was unfair and imbalanced, each side favoured not an even-handed but a corrective policy. Although the protagonists provided elaborate historical reconstructions, designed to compare federal concessions to railways with the truckers' hidden highway subsidy, the various royal commissions invariably found the data inconclusive and urged further study – another dead end. And no politician was interested in overturning present policies on the basis of ancient history.

To becloud the concept even further, the road and rail groups sometimes argued that any significant change in the status quo could be seen to violate 'even-handedness,' because present market conditions and existing public policy constituted a norm or baseline to which the various modes had become adjusted. Any policy-induced change in that norm would be unfair because it would create a sudden windfall for one mode and a similarly unanticipated, unearned set-back for another. Thus, even if the federal government should have provided a cash subsidy to the railways in exchange for the frozen rates on grain shipments or should have made trucking as well as rail eligible for the Maritime rate subsidies, current attempts to redress those old wrongs would greatly disrupt present market relations between rail and truck.

Concepts like 'differentiated niche' and 'even-handedness' probably encouraged politicians to see transportation as a multi-modal network, as a 'system,' and to recognize that the specific actions they took in response to the problems of one mode usually had serious, ripple-like effects on other modes. For the most part, however, the attempt to resolve road/rail controversies by invoking these concepts produced grandly rhetorical, largely expressive debates, which had little impact on specific policy outcomes.

TRUCKING REGULATION: FEDERAL OR PROVINCIAL?

Although the federal government was given jurisdiction over most forms of transportation, the British North America Act, for obvious reasons, said nothing about motorized vehicles. In the 1900–25 period, provincial and federal officials interpreted the provincial authority over roads and highways to include the regulation of motorized vehicles. In 1932, when a consensus emerged on the need for trucking regulation, trucking was assumed to be part of provincial jurisdiction and the creation of regulatory regimes for trucking a provincial responsibility. The two rail corporations, however, had been pressing for a federal assumption of jurisdiction over interprovincial trucking, for the so-called 'federalization' of trucking. Again the railways invoked standard cultural themes. According to their argument, one would never get comprehensive planning or an integrated network until all the modes were within one government's jurisdiction. The alternative to federal control over trucking was balkanization, ten disparate regulatory systems. By giving preference to local companies and harassing out-of-province truckers, each province would create protectionist barriers to interprovincial free trade. The provinces would adopt a sponsorship approach to trucking, the federal government would be compelled to defend rail, and the result would be rival sponsorship and federal/provincial competition rather than even-handed policies and comprehensive planning.

In 1935, the recently named transport minister, C.D. Howe, repudiated the 1932 accord and announced his intention to proceed with federalization. Confronted by strong opposition from the provinces, Howe at first delayed and then, in 1939, abandoned this move. Aside from provincial opposition, Howe's efforts were undermined by a 1937 federal report which said that because only 3 per cent of trucking freight moved across provincial boundaries, the federal government could assert jurisdiction over only a very small portion of the market. Intraprovincial trucking, most trucking, would remain with the provinces. Rather than solve the balkanization issue, federalization would create a small eleventh regulatory regime to stand alongside the ten provincial ones.

Aside from Howe, the dominant federal approach was to appear interested in federalization but in fact to assign it very low priority. Federal officials had to appear interested because they could not seem to oppose 'comprehensive planning' or favour balkanization. But the provinces were determined to retain jurisdiction; and federal officials never thought the issue sufficiently important to warrant a head-on collision with the provinces. The truckers had become provincial allies. The railways wanted federalization; but this support, standing by itself, made the cabinet look like a puppet of the railways and therefore hurt more than it helped.

During the war, the federal government assumed jurisdiction over trucking; but in 1946 these powers were restored to the provinces, despite railway protests to the contrary. In 1949, the Canadian Supreme Court, subsequently upheld by the British Privy Council, declared that the provinces lacked constitutional authority to regulate interprovincial trucking and that the federal government must assume responsibililty in this sphere. This decision extended federal jurisdiction to the total operations of any trucking firm that engaged to any extent in interprovincial traffic, which gave the federal government control over most of the industry. The provinces and the trucking industry urged on the federal government a solution that, while nominally complying with the terms of the 1949 decision, would in effect leave things as before. According to this plan, the federal government would designate the provinces as agents of federal authority on interprovincial trucking issues; the actions of provincial boards and legislatures on these issues would become federal policy. Although federal officials proceeded from a position of great advantage, trucking remained, as before, too unimportant to fight over. The federal minister accepted the provincial plan and in effect retained the pre-1953 structure. As a result of this court decision, however, provincial jurisdiction over interprovincial trucking rested on federal delegation and therefore could be redefined at any time by a majority in the House of Commons.

THE NEED TO REGULATE TRUCKING

Largely through projection, it was assumed that all the newer, post-1920 transportation modes, like the older ones, should be regulated. Railway-type regulation should be extended to trucking even though two more-different industries could not be imagined. Railway regulation had been essential because the rail was a natural monopoly, an industry with too little competition. Trucking regulation was essential to curtail excessive competition.

According to the standard, widely accepted view, trucking was characterized by low capital requirements, easy entry, and no economies of scale, all of which produced a chronic pattern of oversupply, excessive competition, insufficient profit levels, and high failure rates. Too many small, inexperienced, undercapitalized firms struggled to meet their short-run cash-flow problems by exploiting employees, skimping on vehicle maintenance, and undercutting other truckers' rates, even if this meant carrying goods at less than operating costs. In the long run, most of these firms would fail, but in the short run they would either weaken the 'serious,' established firms or compel the latter to engage in equally disreputable, cost-cutting practices. And while the rate-chiselling marginal firms fell like flies, there would always be new entrants to take their place and maintain the pressure on 'reputable' firms. Given this rapid turnover, shipping firms could not acquire the experience needed to assess carrier reputations and would always be vulnerable to exploitation. Trucking once again proved that competition in transportation tended to have destructive consequences; in this case, underpaid, sleepy drivers operating unsafe vehicles, gypsy firms making promises they could not fulfil, gypsy firms offering low rates but losing or damaging cargo as a result of inexperience, and shippers trying to press claims against bankrupt or vanished trucking companies. Even after 1945, when the culture came to view inter-modal competition as basically healthy, competition within the trucking industry still was considered cutthroat and destructive.

Invoking a railway-type regulatory system would presumably correct these problems. The 1932 federal/provincial trucking accord defined a model regulatory system for trucking, embodying the prevailing wisdom of that day. All truckers would be required to secure an operator's licence; the licence would be issued only if the proposed service constituted a 'public necessity or convenience'; licences would only be issued to 'fit,' financially sound, reputable applicants; each licence would stipulate the kind of service the licensee could provide; within his sphere of authority, no licensee could engage in service discrimination; there would be mandatory, minimum standards on wages and hours, vehicle maintenance, insurance coverage, and claims processing; and trucking rates must be fair, compensatory, and not discriminatory. Disagreement seemed to be confined to one issue: whether the truckers should be required to secure provincial approval for their rates, as in the standard, railway model, or whether truckers should only be required to file their rates with the province.

TRUCKING REGULATION: APPARENT CONSENSUS,
REAL DISSENSUS

In characteristic fashion, everyone had agreed on a vague, positively charged symbol: 'regulation.' But the result was a mock, illusory consensus that obscured important differences in viewpoint and smothered what might have been a useful, clarifying debate. Behind everyone's repeated ritualistic reaffirmations, there were varied and conflicting versions of what trucking regulation was supposed to achieve.

One version, urged mainly by the two rail corporations and their municipal-council allies, might be called punitive or restrictive regulation. The purpose of entry control, in this version, would be to confine trucking to a subordinate, intracity role, to prohibit trucks from entering a market already served by the railways, to preserve long-distance freight for the railways. This version was grounded in the cultural assumption that competition in transportation was at worst destructive and at best inefficient, pointless duplication. Complementary niches must surely mean that trucks and trains should perform different roles. A similar but more widely accepted version viewed regulation as a penalty or burden, a form of policing, a set of restraints. Because the railways were shackled by regulation, even-handedness required that government impose these same restraints on trucking. For example, no one mode should have the advantage of being able to alter rates without securing a board's approval. 'Regulation as policing' also rested on the traditional assumption that carriers, including truckers, tended to abuse their power and that shippers needed legal protection from such abuses. Only regulation would stop truckers from giving inappropriate, discriminatory rate discounts to shippers with superior market leverage, from engaging in service discrimination, refusing to process claims, or making reckless promises to shippers. But much of this argument involved an unthinking projection of railway experiences onto trucking. As the truckers correctly asked, should one assume that shippers required the same legal protection whether dealing with a two-firm rail industry or with a very competitive trucking market made up of many small firms?

A third, 'industry sponsorship' version, best articulated by the truckers but more widely supported, viewed regulation primarily as an attempt to strengthen and 'rationalize' a vital, but inevitably volatile, fragile industry. Entry control would reduce the number of truckers and thus resolve the problem of chronic oversupply. It would screen out those marginal, disreputable firms, whose cutthroat tactics produced the volatility. Even if some of these marginal firms slipped through the licensing net, their ability to undercut reputable firms would be restricted by legally imposed performance standards and by a legal insistence on compensatory rates. The railways supported trucking rationalization because they, like the reputable trucking firms, often felt threatened by the 'cutthroat tactics' of 'gypsy truckers.'

In a fourth version, regulation, more specifically entry control, was viewed as a mechanism for finely tuned, small-scale or 'micro-market' economic planning. The movement of a certain category of goods between two specific places can be defined as a micro-market. In this version of trucking regulation, an application to provide additional service in a given micro-market should be granted if there was an unmet demand for service and if the additional service, as described in the application, would not financially cripple existing carriers. The licensing board should plan or adjust supply and demand in each micro-market. It should protect shippers from too little carrier competition, which would result in over-priced, inadequate service; but it also should protect carriers from excessive entry, undue fragmentation of the market, and inadequate profit levels. Because there were thousands of micro-markets in each province, such detailed economic planning must be implemented through the resolution of many small cases, ideally by an 'impartial, non-political' board.

Thus far, micro-market planning meant assessing the impact of a trucking application on the currently licensed truckers; but the railways and some policy professionals wanted the provincial boards to engage in inter-modal planning, to consider the impact of a trucking application on all transportation companies serving that micro-market. Because the provincial board would have to decide which mode could most efficiently serve a given micro-market, truck licensing decisions would become a mechanism for 'comprehensive transportation planning.' But truckers saw railway-inspired, anti-trucking motives behind such grand phrases. More important, no provincial politician wanted to enmesh provincial licensing boards in the rail vs truck quarrel or to stimulate new federal/provincial disputes by seeming to encroach on railway questions.

THE CULTURE OF RATES

No single transportation issue attracted more attention than price. (The carrier issues a schedule of 'rates' from which the 'price' of a specific trip can be derived.) Here as well, the culture was dominated by vague, positively charged symbols that were easy to reaffirm but difficult to define and hence difficult to apply to specific cases. The consensus was that rates must be fair and reasonable (as opposed to excessive), cost-based, compensatory, not arbitrary, and not discriminatory. Everyone favoured 'rate regulation,' that is, a governmental effort to ensure that rates met these requirements. But there remained serious confusion about what these terms meant, how rates should be judged, and what rate regulation entailed. That various groups disagreed on something so important as rates is not suprising. Rather than try to debate such disagreements, it was assumed that everyone agreed and that all one need do is define correctly the substance of this consensus.

What resulted was another dead-end debate, which did little to resolve or even clarify the major questions. As T.C. Douglas, then federal leader of the NDP, said in 1966, the freight-rate issue was like the peace of the Lord: it passeth all understanding. The carrier's operating costs on a specific trip will reflect the distance travelled, the size of the load, and the kind of goods involved. According to the prevailing culture, the rates charged by a transportation company for any specific kind of service should cover the operating cost for that service, should help retire a portion of fixed costs, and should provide a fair return on investment. Rates derived in this way are considered cost-based, rational, or scientific, as opposed to arbitrary, ad hoc, groundless. It is wrong for carriers to exploit their market leverage, charge unreasonably high rates, and secure excessive returns. At the same time, when a company charges rates below its operating cost for that service, it is guilty of 'non-compensatory pricing,' a practice that occurs (a) when inept managers do not know what their costs are and run at a loss until driven out of business; (b) when a company receives a government subsidy to cover its losses; (c) when a company subsidizes a money-losing service with excess profits earned on other kinds of service, usually called 'cross-subsidization'; or (d) when the company is engaged in 'predatory pricing,' undercutting its competitors in order to drive them out of the market and thereafter instituting much higher, monopoly-level prices. If rates are cost-based, so that operating efficiencies are translated into lower rates, the firm or mode that can provide a given type of service most efficiently will come to dominate this niche. Cost-based rates facilitate proper role differentiation. However, if a firm cross-subsidizes an inefficient, money-losing service, it will persist in a niche that properly belongs to someone else.

If rates are cost-based, shipping firms position themselves to take advantage of the lower-priced, lower-cost service, and the entire transportation system becomes more efficient. By contrast, cross-subsidies reward firms for chosing higher-cost, less-efficient service. To 'discriminate' is to charge shipper X more than others, not because carrying X's goods involves higher operating costs but because X has less bargaining power than others – for example, because X is a 'captive shipper' totally dependent on rail. Extracting monopoly-type profits from X in order to grant other shippers heavily discounted rates commits many sins: discrimination, cross-subsidization, unreasonable rates for some shippers, non-compensatory rates for others. The argument thus far evoked wide support. Rail and truck lobbyists portrayed their own industry's rates as rational, cost-based, non-discriminatory; and each accused the other industry of cross-subsidization, discrimination, and ad hoc, arbitrary rate making. Beyond this point, however, the agreement, and the meaning of the terms, dissolved.

The railways carried the cost-based argument to a conclusion, and to a policy, that regional protestors thought 'discriminatory.' Carriers incurred lower operating costs on trips involving large shipments, long distances, or busy, intercity routes. Longer trips permitted carriers to spread terminal costs over more miles and thus produce lower per-mile costs; it cost more to handle ten small shipments than one large shipment of the same aggregate weight; and one secured more fully loaded trucks when operating on the main, intercity routes. On such trips, the railways argued, lower operating costs justified lower rates. Moreover, the railways should be allowed to provide special discounts to shippers sending most or all their goods by rail (the 'agreed charges' practice), because a more intensive use of existing rail capacity would maximize operating efficiency and thus reduce prices for all railway users. But Atlantic and Western shippers thought these rate discounts were illegal, certainly wrong, because they systematically discriminated against small-volume shippers, small towns, and areas outside central Canada. And agreed charges merely created more captive shippers, bound only to rail. It soon became clear that while everyone abhorred 'discrimination,' they disagreed on its meaning. Did the concept apply only to ad hoc, transaction-specific abuses, for example, favouring some individual customers over others; or did it, as the regional protestors insisted, also condemn a rates policy that consistently favoured some categories of shipper and some localities over others? Eventually the federal regulatory board decided that because the railways had based their differential rates on varying operating costs, they had created discounts for good reason and thus had not discriminated. (This was one of the more important transportation policy decisions of the twentieth century.) For decades thereafter, the debate focused on whether this decision had correctly defined 'discrimination.'

Although everyone favoured cost-based rates as a principle or symbol, there was no consensus on whether costs were to be the only criterion used in setting rates or how important this cost criterion might be in relation to others. Regional protestors insisted that rail rates should reflect not only costs but national policy, for example, the goal of fostering regional economic expansion through cheap rates. Many protestors argued that rates should be based on the shippers' 'ability to pay.' In this view, there is an upper limit to transportation rates, beyond which the shipper could not afford to send goods to market. Whatever a carrier's operating costs might be, rates should not be allowed to break through this ceiling. In reply, the railways, other carriers, and most policy professionals defended cost-based rates, producing an apparently clear split between defenders and critics of the cost criterion.

At this point the debate became more confused. Carriers were not prepared to live with rates based only on cost. In some circumstances, the carriers argued, rates should be based not on costs but on the 'value of service to the user,' which seemed little different from 'ability to pay.' High-priced goods tend to be relatively insensitive to transportation charges because such charges represent a small percentage of total costs or final price. In these cases, where demand for transportation services is relatively inelastic, shippers are willing to pay more than a cost-based rate, and carriers are able to earn above-average profits. Carriers viewed this kind of service – for example, non-fragile, manufactured goods, shipped in large amounts within urbanized Ontario and Quebec – as 'attractive' freight, as market cream. In the case of low-priced goods – for example the resource-based, unprocessed exports so essential to the Canadian economy – transportation costs constituted a larger portion of final price, and the carriers' ability to extract profits would be constrained by a highly elastic demand schedule.

Canadian conditions, according to carriers, demanded some departures from the cost-based principle. Because Canadian firms were smaller, because they must send goods long distances to markets, and because so many Canadian firms shipped inexpensive, resource-type goods, for which transportation costs would constitute a significant portion of the final price, many Canadian producers might be unable to compete in the world economy if they were made to pay cost-based transportation rates. Both the railways and truckers said they solved this problem by using above-average profits on the attractive freight to subsidize other users. This, of course, was the sin of cross-subsidization and a major departure from cost-based rates, but justified in this case by the attempt to preserve Canada's export capacity.

Going one step further, the carriers justified cross-subsidization as a means of protecting shippers in all unattractive markets. Here, cross-subsidization was legitimated by being linked to some powerful, positively charged symbols: the small town, the North, the small-firm shipper. Since carriers normally would avoid such unattractive markets, one needed regulators to impose these markets on carriers. And if regulation imposed a mix of attractive and unattractive routes on each carrier, the carrier could use the surplus profits derived from attractive routes to subsidize the others. For this reason, transportation regulation must be pervasive. If government regulated one mode and not another, or regulated some parts of a single mode but not others, the unregulated carriers would skim off the market cream, leaving regulated carriers to serve unattractive markets at high, unsubsidized prices.

Thus, the carriers were on all sides of the debate at once. The professionals as well consistently produced ambivalent statements. It was efficient, intelligent business practice, they said, for carriers to base price on willingness to pay and to charge higher rates in markets dominated by inelastic demand; but, at the same time, cross-subsidies, assuming they worked as the railways claimed, discouraged manufacturing and made Canada more dependent on resource exports. Cross-subsidization remained a good/bad thing, to be deplored on some occasions, and applauded on others. Added to this confusion was a long, inconclusive argument over who was cross-subsidizing whom, for example, whether central Canada was subsidizing the West or vice versa.

THE TURN TOWARD NON-INTERVENTIONISM

Although Canadian transportation thinking and debates largely involved a static recycling of the same old themes, the post-1945 period produced a growing emphasis on the culture's non-interventionist themes. No new ideas emerged, but internal priorities were substantially reallocated.

After 1945, many policy professionals, especially the economists, began to challenge the older assumption that transportation, especially in Canada, must inevitably be a heavily subsidized, closely regulated industry. It now seemed to many professionals that inter-modal competition was more healthy than destructive. Perhaps truck/rail competition had encouraged both sides to waste resources on lobbying and had sometimes produced pointless service duplication; but this competition also had pumped some new life into a lethargic railway management. The notion that the railways should be unleashed, deregulated, so that they could compete more effectively in the marketplace had been present from the early 1900s, but it now received added emphasis. If shippers could choose between carriers, they would have less need for the legal protections provided in classic regulation. Only in one area should regulatory powers be extended: in order to preserve healthy inter-modal competition, federal officials should block any transportation company's attempt to acquire companies operating in a different mode if that acquisition would have an anti-competitive impact. Subsidies had shielded the railways from invigorating market forces, protected the railway management from the consequences of its decisions, and preserved a railway management better able to lobby for more subsidies than to fight for market share. The evidence demonstrated that excessive importance had been attributed to subsidized, cheap transportation rates as a catalyst for regional economic development. (The studies also showed that targeted subsidies, designed to help specific shippers or specific goods, had more of an economic impact than sweeping, across-the-board assistance, like the Maritime subsidy.) Any subsidy had secondary, ripple-like, unwanted effects; and any subsidy created losers as well as winners. A truly multi-modal, system-wide perspective would help government see these secondary effects; a more serious commitment to even-handedness would lead government to avoid them. Rather than ask whether some shipping or carrying group deserved help in the form of a subsidy, the proper question was why this group deserved more help than others or why this group deserved help at the expense of others. Frozen rail rates for exports discouraged crop diversification among Western farmers, hurt the meat industry by diverting grain away from livestock, and undercut the emergence of a Western food-processing industry closer to the farms. Rail-only subsidies to Western grain growers and to the Atlantic provinces had stifled inter-modal competition in these areas. But, contrary to what the truckers demanded, the solution was not to subsidize trucking as well as rail. A subsidy, however broad, inevitably leaves some activities unsubsidized and winds up taxing these activities for the benefit of the subsidized interests. For example, the extension of the Maritime subsidy to trucking in 1970 helped commercial truckers but at the expense of private truckers, i.e., those shippers carrying their own goods. Whatever subsidies achieved, healthy truck/rail competition could achieve more effectively and efficiently.

The trucking industry endorsed, in fact had helped shape, this post-war, pro-market emphasis. It was in the truckers' self-interest to stress the damaging impact of rail subsidies, the desirability of deregulating railway prices so they might rise to their true market level, and the beneficial effects of having a healthy trucking industry challenge traditional rail dominance. CN and CP also liked this free-market emphasis because it meant more railway 'independence' from governmental scrutiny, controls, and demands.

There were some ambivalent elements in this new thrust, however. The professionals often said, in the 1951, 1955, and 1962 royal commission reports, for example, that they were not advocating less intervention, only that government undertake a careful cost-benefit analysis so it would fully understand the costs of intervention. But the underlying assumption was that, if we appreciated the full costs of intervention, there would be much less of it. According to this argument, intervention should always take a distinct, visible form, so that its costs and distorting impact on the marketplace could be precisely defined, preferably in dollar terms. If we first defined the true market price for a certain type of service, we could pinpoint the cost to the carrier and the subsidy to the shipper of any price-controlling policy, like the Crow. If government must use transportation industries as policy instruments, it should compensate those industries for the precise cost, including forgone opportunities, of their departure from market prices and business-like principles. The professionals were now increasingly and especially critical of cross-subsidies. Open, direct subsidies allowed us to determine the costs and debate the wisdom of intervention; in the case of cross-subsidization, and legally frozen rates that compel cross-subsidization, the subsidy is invisible, the costs are buried in the midst of a complex rate structure, and the losers cannot be identified.

The policy professionals and carriers who consistently pushed for this new non-interventionism had an appealing program: an elaborate, sophisticated, relatively consistent viewpoint, providing clear policy prescriptions, grounded in the prevailing culture, supported by 'the experts,' endorsed, at least in principle, by the MacPherson report in 1962, and consistent with the apparent post-1970 shift toward conservative thinking in Great Britain and the United States. Non-interventionist ideas and policies slowly worked their way throughout the policy system, culminating in the post-1975 move toward transportation deregulation. The ambivalence one finds in the cost-benefit argument, however, illustrated the central unresolved problem in this non-interventionist push. This push achieved precise, consistent policy prescriptions only by ignoring a large part of the historic culture: the view of transportation as a policy instrument, a public utility on which the economy depended, a key element in Canadian nation-building. Politicians could see a clash between this new emphasis and equally valid old commitments; but to many policy professionals these reservations were simply another example of the politicians' inability to confront the vested interests clinging to existing programs.

NON-INTERVENTIONISM: THE GAP BETWEEN RHETORIC AND POLICY

In attempting to describe federal transportation policy after 1955, one can begin by summarizing how cabinets officially characterized their policies in a long string of white papers and policy statements. At least at the level of expressive symbolism and general imagery, the official policy announced in these documents embraced much of the new non-interventionism.

Inter-modal competition, federal policy now acknowledged, is a healthy phenomenon that protects shippers, pushes each mode to perform efficiently, and eventually assigns each mode to its appropriate niche. Most of the controversies government is asked to resolve, like combined trips or railway ownership of trucking companies, will eventually be sorted out by market forces, although government may help carriers through the difficult transitional period. Because transportation is a policy instrument as well as a business, government may subsidize and regulate; but, to minimize market distortions, such intervention should be the least necessary to achieve a policy objective. Before intervening, however, government must assess all the harmful side-effects of its actions, must consider those hurt as well as those helped. If government uses any mode as an instrument of policy and compels it to depart from business-like practices, government should provide compensation, equal in magnitude to the extent of the departure. Similarly, any mode should reimburse the government for its use of facilities, like highways, built at taxpayer expense. If government remains strictly even-handed, each mode would try to outdo the others in efficiency, and the market will allocate its rewards accordingly. In place of the existing, rail-only subsidies, subsidies should be paid to the shipper, who could apply them to any mode and thus could select the mode most suitable to his needs. A cost-based rate structure is 'policy neutral' and reflective of market forces; by contrast, carriers who cross-subsidize artificially create winners and losers. Carriers in any mode should not be allowed to engage in service discrimination or to discontinue service without government's consent.

Although these statements claimed to identify the specific policies cabinet would pursue, they really concentrated on spelling out the cultural framework within which specific-level policy debates would proceed. Such ministerial statements did not so much announce new specific intentions as they expressed the correct, general-level values. As such, these statements gave official legitimation to much of the new non-interventionist thinking. In keeping with their expressive function, such statements also provided a carefully constructed, balanced allocation of symbolic rewards, designed to demonstrate federal even-handedness. Statements about compensating a mode for being required to depart from business-like principles represented a concession to the railways, who had long complained about being required to maintain branch lines and cheap grain rates without offsetting financial compensation. The truckers were pleased with the argument that a rail-only subsidy unduly distorted inter-modal competition. The notion that carriers should reimburse the government for their use of public facilities was a concession to the railways on the 'hidden highway subsidy' issue. The railways also were pleased with the statement about all modes acquiring the obligation to provide service because it presumably was pointed at the truckers' ability to pick and choose. But such statements, despite their non-interventionist rhetoric, did not announce any dismantling of programs. Federal politicians preached less government in the abstract but could not find existing policies they were eager to sacrifice. They still favoured using subsidized, cheap rates to spur regional economic development and still favoured preserving rail branch lines in order to preserve small towns. Thus, the classic disconnection between general-level symbolism and concrete policy decisions was reinforced by a gap between non-interventionist talk and specific interventionist commitments. White papers operating at such a high level of generality, moreover, could not provide new, specific guidance for federal regulators. Ministerial rhetoric was increasingly non-interventionist but was not translated into board decisions.

In fact, as new interventionist moves were approved, the gap between rhetoric and policy widened. In 1959, the Conservative government froze general rail rates and provided the railways with large annual operating subsidies to cover the gap between frozen and true market prices. (In supporting this move, politicians from all parties invoked the 'ability to pay' concept and warned that further rate increases would price many producers out of domestic and world markets.) Alarmed by rapid increases in the annual subsidy, annoyed that such massive subsidies failed to produce any visible improvements in service, and convinced that such subsidies merely whetted rail-employee appetites for more substantial salary increases, federal politicians later decided to phase out this subsidy. But they put in its place a new subsidy designed to compensate railways for the maintenance of unprofitable branch-line service, a subsidy that soon eclipsed in amount the discontinued general subsidy. Professionals had urged the politicians to cut back on the Maritime rate subsidy by making it applicable only to those specific goods that would most benefit from this subsidy. Instead, the 1969–71 revisions extended that subsidy to trucking, extended the subsidy to Maritime goods exported to the United States, and created new, additional subsidies for designated goods without reducing the across-the-board subsidy for all goods. When reforming grain rates in 1985, subsidies were expanded still further.

DEREGULATION: NON-INTERVENTIONISM ASCENDANT

Eventually, however, non-interventionist ideas would have more than a rhetorical impact; they would filter downward and alter specific policies, culminating in the National Transportation Act of 1987. But politicians applied these ideas selectively, to regulatory questions but not to subsidies, which continued to expand. Thus post-war non-interventionism became focused on deregulation, the dismantling of entry control and rate regulation. Since the cabinet, especially the Conservative government elected in 1984, continued to advocate sweeping, unselective non-interventionism, some of the old rhetoric/practice gap remained.

Although the cabinet officially endorsed transportation deregulation in 1976, the 1967 Transportation Act had already moved a good distance in this direction. That act had empowered the railways to alter their rates at will, within maxima and minima defined by federal regulators. The 1987 Transportation Act gave railways the authority to depart from published rates and to negotiate secret rate agreements with specific shippers, an authority and advantage that deregulated U.S. rail companies already had. The 1987 act dropped the requirement that railway rates be compensatory, although federal officials retained the authority to investigate cases of alleged predatory pricing. In line with the deregulatory thrust, and because only large-scale inter-modal acquisitions were considered a threat to inter-modal competition, the federal government henceforth would only review acquisition cases involving assets of $20 million or more. In place of the protections provided shippers by historic rate regulation, the federal government now provided conciliation mechanisms for rate disagreements between carriers and shippers.

The 1967 act had preserved historic safeguards against discriminatory or extortionate rail rates in the case of 'captive shippers,' who lacked access to modes other than rail. But, because a shipper who used both rail and truck would lose his captive status and the special protections involved, this captive-shipper clause had the perverse effect of cementing certain shippers to rail alone and thus inhibiting the emergence of a healthy trucking option. To encourage inter-modal competition, the 1987 act eliminated the captive-shipper clause. Instead the act tried to reduce the number of such shippers by encouraging more competitive use of existing railway tracks.

In 1984 and in the 1987 act, the government substantially deregulated airline service. The airlines were given almost full freedom to set their own rates; the controls on exit or discontinuance of service were eliminated; and traditional entry control, based on public-necessity and convenience criteria, was replaced with a modest fitness test, based only on an applicant's understanding of the airline business and commitment to maintaining safe vehicles. Airline regulation would no longer pursue economic objectives – for example, attempting to balance supply and demand on specific routes or ensuring the financial health of present carriers. However, because all Canadian airlines want access to u.s. cities, and because these access questions are defined by international agreements between the two governments, the Canadian government will always play a major role in deciding who flies to which cities and, therefore, a major role in defining the shape of the Canadian airline industry. Meanwhile, the act left maritime transportation unaltered and heavily regulated.

REFORMING GRAIN TRANSPORTATION, 1983

From roughly 1950 on, the professionals, the railways, and the trucking industry consistently demanded a reform of the Western Grain Transportation Act, 'the Crow,' which mandated frozen, low rail rates for Western grain growers. In a series of reports between 1949 and 1981, the professionals said that the railways were being used as a policy instrument without compensation, that farmers were receiving an inappropriately generous subsidy, and that other rail users were being taxed, through higher rates, to pay for this subsidy. The Crow subsidy also reinforced one-crop dominance in Western agriculture, hurt the beef industry, and had other negative, economic spillovers. Because the railways lost money on carrying grain and presumably lacked the funds to modernize grain-handling facilities, grain farmers paid for their frozen low rates by enduring poor service. According to these reports, the rates should be unfrozen, farmers should pay for the true costs of moving their grain, and the additional rail revenue should be used to modernize grain-carrying facilities. If government insisted on subsidizing grain shipments, it should allow rail prices to be set by the market and should pay the subsidy to farmers, so that government officials could specify the costs of this intervention and minimize the subsidy's distorting impact on market forces. Trucks could most efficiently move grain from small-town elevators to the railway's main-line terminals in major cities. If this were done, the railways could eliminate many unprofitable branch lines, and the federal government could reduce its massive branch-line subsidy. But the rail-only character of the Crow discouraged farmers from considering the trucking option. Therefore, if the government was determined to subsidize, it should replace a rail-only, hidden subsidy, i.e., the frozen rail rates, with an open subsidy paid directly to the farmers and usable by them for any transportation mode.

In its 1983 revision of the Crow legislation, the cabinet attempted to reconcile this non-interventionist argument with historic concerns about Canadian exports, regional development, and small shippers. In a manner typical of post-war federal responses to transportation problems, the cabinet fashioned this reconciliation by expanding the scope of subsidies. Grain rates were unfrozen and allowed to rise, but only very gradually and not to their true market level. Farmers would pay more to move grain and would help pay for the modernization of grain-moving facilities. The federal government would provide large annual subsidies to cover the difference between what farmers would pay and the true market price. Two major concessions were made to Western interests: the subsidy would be paid to the railways not to the farmers, and it would remain a rail-only subsidy, despite the government's long-standing rhetorical commitment to all-mode subsidies. The notion of extending the subsidy to truckers was opposed by the wheat pools, grain elevator operators, and the Canadian Wheat Board, all of which were heavily committed to a rail-based, grain-handling infrastructure. Also, many Westerners equated an expanded role for trucking with the abandonment of railway branch lines and the disappearance of many prairie towns. Paying the subsidy to the railways, rather than to the shippers, was one way to ensure that this subsidy would never be extended to trucking. Giving the money to the railways would increase the federal government's ability and inclination to closely monitor railway management decisions, precisely the reason why the railways had preferred to see the subsidy paid to shippers. What deregulation granted the railways in the form of less government scrutiny, government's growing role as subsidizer and financial overseer helped undo.

TRUCKING DEREGULATION

From 1925 on, most people assumed that pervasive, railway-type regulation must be extended to the trucking industry. With singular inconsistency, these same people were urging that rail be liberated from the stiflng hand of regulation. The post-1970 attack on trucking regulation was simply an attempt to bring trucking culture into line with post-war, non-interventionist transportation thinking. After sixty years of inconsistency, the case for railway deregulation was now being logically extended to all modes. If regulation had smothered the railways' entrepreneurial imagination, if inter-modal competition adequately protected shippers from railway abuses, were these not valid arguments against trucking regulation?

According to the original rationale, trucking regulation had been necessary to stabilize an excessively volatile industry plagued by chronic oversupply, destructive competition, insufficient profits, and excessive bankruptcies and turnover. But most professionals now decided that trucking, like the restaurant business, was merely competitive, risky, and unstable. Competition was truly destructive in industries with large infrastructures and high fixed costs, where short-run market fluctuations would push suppliers toward excessive caution and a less-than-optimum investment in long-term capital needs. This 'natural monopoly' rationale for regulation could not be applied to truckers, who easily adjusted daily operations in response to short-run market fluctuations.

According to this non-interventionist critique, provincial regulatory systems had turned licensed trucking into a legally privileged, legally protected cartel, which need not worry about competitors' efforts or customer complaints and which consequently provided poor service at high prices. Because an operator's licence authorized a firm only to carry specified goods on specified routes, the regulatory system created a large number of oligopolistic or monopolistic micro-markets. By restricting the number of suppliers, regulation made it easier for licensed truckers to collude, fix prices, and avoid competition on service quality. More than this, provincial 'rate filing' requirements actively encouraged collusion on price. And those provinces that set rates made collusion mandatory. With competitive pressures dampened and collusion either encouraged or required, no firm had the incentive or capacity to improve its operating efficiency and pass these gains on to shippers in the form of reduced prices. In a regulated trucking market, prices did not reflect costs, the more efficient carrier could not prevail by offering lower prices, and we could never determine any trucking firm's correct niche. Because the trucking licence was a legally protected right to secure above-average profits, it should be viewed not as a means of regulating the industry so much as a subsidy for the licence holder and a tax on all others. Truckers alleged that it was not difficult to secure a licence and that the burdens and obligations imposed on regulated firms were substantial when compared to the relatively modest privileges derived from a licence. But, according to deregulators, the high market value of such licences disproved this argument.

In addition, the detailed conditions of each firm's licence imposed a less-than-efficient pattern of operations on that firm. Licences often dictated that a firm take circuitous routes rather than seek out the most direct path between two cities. Trucks often travelled half empty because the firm was authorized to carry certain goods but not others. Many shipments had to be transferred from one firm's trucks to another's two or three times during the same trip, because no one company had the authority to provide 'through' service. The rigidities created by rate filing and rate fixing prevented a company from offering special, discounted rates in an effort to avoid empty return hauls. They also prevented a firm from offering service of varying quality at varied prices. A case could be made for performance regulation, for legal standards on vehicle maintenance or hours; but such standards could be imposed on trucking firms without resorting to entry control or rate regulation, as rules on work-place safety or minimum wage were.

The defence of trucking regulation was based largely on the original rationale. In addition, pro-regulators were increasingly worried about the intrusions of U.S. trucking firms into Canadian markets and were increasingly inclined to see regulation as a necessary protectionist barrier to such intrusions. Here, Canadian truckers invoked the Canadian theme. Because U.S. firms had the advantages of larger size, more capital, and an attractive, densely populated, inter-city home market in the United States, American trucking firms would always outcompete Canadian truckers, in either Canadian or American markets. For those same reasons, U.S. firms could make take-over bids that Canadian firms found too attractive to refuse. Moreover, Canada was more easily penetrated and thus more economically vulnerable. All major Canadian cities were within 100 miles of the border and thus easily reached by U.S. firms; but Canadian firms had to travel far more than 100 miles into the United States to reach most major U.S. cities. If allowed, U.S. firms would skim off the market cream, the profitable routes linking big American cities to big Canadian cities, and would leave the higher-operating-cost, lower-profit, small-town Canadian markets to be served (at rates much higher than present ones) by weakened, diminished Canadian firms. It was silly to argue that, if all protectionist barriers were eliminated, Canadian trucking firms would gain as many new routes in the United States as they lost in Canada. Given the initially unequal resources of Canadian and U.S. trucking firms, free trade would produce American dominance, not more competition but less. The Americans said that, when the U.S. industry had been deregulated in 1980, Canadian truckers had secured free access to U.S. markets, while continuing to operate from the safe haven of protected, regulated Canadian markets. In the Canadian view, however, this advantage gave Canadian truckers a much-needed equalizer and helped preserve competition between American and Canadian truckers.

Beginning in 1976, the federal cabinet committed itself to the eventual deregulation of interprovincial trucking, a commitment that later found legal expression in the 1987 Road Transportation Act that was tabled alongside the new National Transportation Act. Because trucking deregulation was an essential component of a more general policy design, because it made little sense to deregulate most modes but not this one, federal officials for the first time assigned a high priority to trucking issues. But the federal cabinet decided to make deregulation more important than federalization. It would leave interprovincial trucking powers with the provinces as long as they promised to implement deregulation; it would invoke federalization only as a threat, designed to hasten the provinces' deregulatory reforms. Thus, while moving immediately to reduce regulation for other modes, the federal government would pursue trucking deregulation through a protracted set of provincial/federal negotiations. In addition, even after passage of the 1987 act, the federal government's trucking position remained fuzzy. It was still unclear how far and how fast the provinces would have to move toward deregulation if they wanted to avert federalization. In the late 1980s, federal officials urged all provinces to model their reforms on an Ontario plan, which only partially dismantled trucking regulations. Here too there was a gap between the federal government's pro-market rhetoric, in this case, a sweeping endorsement of 'trucking deregulation,' and its more restrained, specific policies.

In summary, the post-war shift toward non-interventionist thinking has had a major although selective impact on specific policies. Perhaps this impact will become even more pronounced and less selective; perhaps future governments will consider desubsidization as well as deregulation. It is more likely, I think, that future governments will back away from this non-interventionist commitment and that the pendulum will swing back toward other elements in the transportation culture. The culture and the policy system are committed to many, inconsistent objectives. One can resolve this tension only through case-by-case trade-offs, not by a single, consistent dramatic reformulation of general principles. The non-interventionist formulation achieved consistency by excluding a large part of the culture and by ignoring many historic, legitimate concerns, like regional economic disparities, national unity, and the problems of an export-based economy, among others. By moving toward deregulation, we will discover how much a consistently pro-market policy sacrifices these other values and we very likely will recoil from such consequences.

3

The Canadian Trucking Industry

THE ARGUMENT SUMMARIZED

The prevailing transportation culture produced a standard descriptive account of the Canadian trucking industry. As everyone knew, the trucking industry was characterized by low capital requirements, easy entry, no significant economies of scale, small-firm dominance, chronic oversupply, intense, often destructive competition, and a high failure rate. For more than sixty years, debates on trucking issues were founded on this standard account. On the basis of this account, regulation was justified and launched. Regulation would dampen destructive competition and give some stability to this excessively volatile industry. Beneath this standard account, however, very little was known about the industry. Until recently, there were no serious, systematic studies of trucking. Cognitive or descriptive assertions about industry attributes were not summaries of evidence or experience but ritualistic reaffirmations of the conventional wisdom. Most economists 'described' the industry through a self-contained, deductive model, whose premises largely restated the standard account.

Given the reliable, empirical evidence that has been amassed since 1975, it is possible to construct a reasonably accurate picture of the industry. In the light of this picture, it becomes clear that the standard version is a partially useful, sometimes correct, but often seriously distorted account. Since 1925, the debates on trucking issues and the resulting policies have been based on this relatively inaccurate account, which creates at least some prima facie doubts about the rationality of these policies. And yet, despite much recent evidence to the contrary, the standard account has proved remarkably resilient, in fact, formed much of the cognitive foundation for recent deregulation debates. This standard account was another cultural trap, disconnected from and resistant to specific-level evidence. Policies based on such a distorted picture of the industry are likely to founder; policy critiques or demands for deregulation, if based on the same distortions, are unlikely to produce any better results.

To impose order on messy reality, any culture simplifies, selects, and distorts. At best one can hope for usable, adaptive rather than intolerable simplifications. It may be particularly difficult to find workable simplifications, and especially easy to over-simplify, if the subject-matter is especially complex and subtle, especially resistant to generalizations. The standard account of this industry mistakenly assumed that one could generalize as easily about trucking as one could about a simple, centralized, two-firm industry like rail. It assumed that the trucking industry was a reasonably homogeneous entity with clear boundaries and certain common, industry-wide features.

The term 'trucking industry' is little more than a useful rhetorical abbreviation, like 'Canadian public opinion.' Trucking is not an industry but rather an unintegrated collection of separate, segregated, non-competing sub-industries. There are many trucking markets or segments, each with its own distinctive texture and requirements. Primarily for market-based or economic reasons, although regulation reinforces the resulting pattern, truckers decide to operate in one or another of these separate segments. Because the segments are so different, crossing from one to another would involve one in a qualitatively different kind of trucking operation. Successfully adapting to the requirements of one segment often reduces one's ability to adapt or succeed in other segments. Because of this segmentation, the generalizations contained in the standard culture are not so much wrong as partial – applicable to some parts of the industry but not others. Truckers are people who carry goods in motorized vehicles somewhat larger than automobiles; little else can be said about all truckers. As I wish to show in this chapter, even generalizations about one segment, or about one firm, are risky.

Some of the system pathologies I describe occurred because trucking rather than some other industry was involved. The diverse, complex nature of the trucking industry made it difficult for the policy system to create a reasonably accurate picture of this industry. Those same complexities – for example, the problems involved in defining 'the trucking industry' and its 'interests' – made it difficult for trade associations to represent this industry and help explain why these associations often pursued irrational strategies. These same complexities make trucking a particuarly difficult industry to regulate and help explain the decidedly limited success of this program.

Given all the recent hard empirical data, why did the standard account stubbornly persist? Why this growing gap between culture and evidence? Five factors seem especially important. (1) The standard account persisted because it often served someone's political interests. For example, trucking associations, especially when talking to the minister, wanted to portray trucking as an organic, homogeneous industry, able to define 'the truckers' interests' and to formulate 'the trucking viewpoint' on most issues. The image of a fragile industry, easily torn apart by destructive competition, helped justify continued regulation. The alleged steady expansion in private trucking bolstered the arguments of both pro-regulators and deregulators. (2) Truckers adhered to the standard account because it served important expressive-affiliative functions. By portraying trucking as the last outpost of small-firm, highly competitive, risk-taking entrepreneurial capitalism, this account provided the industry with a clear, legitimate identity. (3) Wish-fulfilment sustained several aspects of the standard version, for example, the notion that regulatory systems protected small shipping firms, small trucking firms, and small towns. (4) People have substantial psychic investments, or sunk costs, in long-standing ideas, which gives these ideas great inertia and staying power. For example, convinced for more than fifty years that various segments battled over the allocation of a fixed aggregate trucking demand, truckers were not interested in evidence to the contrary. (5) A reasonably accurate account of the trucking industry would be based on carefully phrased, limited, undramatic generalizations, each subjected to many qualifications. Perhaps large-scale policy systems cannot work with such a subtle, complex image. If they have something simpler and more dramatic, they may resist complicating additions. Many people found it appealing, for example, to think of the trucking industry as divided into expansionist and defensive, protectionist firms, an illustration of our more general penchant for dichotomous, bipolar constructs. We return to this problem in the last chapter.

DIFFERENTIATED NICHES

When making business decisions, all truckers are heavily influenced by two central factors in transportation economics: the 'tapering effect' and the 'loading factor.'

In any single trip that moves freight from one place to another, by whatever mode of transportation, there are cost advantages involved in carrying larger loads for longer distances. Because the costs of loading and unloading goods (the terminal costs) do not increase with the growing length of a trip, a longer trip permits the carrier to spread these terminal costs over more miles and to produce lower operating costs per mile. Similarly, because doubling the size of a load does not mean doubling the operating costs for that trip (e.g., does not double the salary paid to the driver), larger shipments permit lower per-unit costs. All other factors being equal, the way in which operating costs taper off as the size of the load and the length of the trip increase, the so-called tapering effect, would encourage any carrier to seek a larger operating scale, for example, larger trucks operating over longer distances. In addition, by expanding the scope of goods carried and the routes served, the trucker can offer a wider array of services to any one shipper and thus become a more attractive carrier. The shipper might no longer find it necessary to have some goods carried by trucking firm A and other goods by B, or to have firm X carry a shipment part of the way with firm Y completing the trip. Contrary to the prevailing wisdom, then, there are some economies of scale in trucking, some advantages to being big, and some economic factors that push trucking firms toward larger-scale operations. Motivated by these natural, expansionist forces, trucking firms in regulated markets often press for expanded authority, both in the goods carried and in the territory served. However, other factors are not equal. Because the operating costs on a given trip are roughly the same whether the truck proceeds full or empty, firms can maximize their return on investment by operating with fully loaded trucks, both on the first leg, the 'prime haul,' and on the return leg, the 'back haul,' of each trip. A high load factor increases the efficiency of operations and generates maximum revenue in relation to a given set of operating costs. On routes connecting major cities, where there is a large volume of freight moving in both directions, truckers are more likely to find full loads for both the prime and back hauls. By contrast, uneven, predominantly one-way movement of freight – for example, many goods moving from large to small cities but few goods moving in reverse – creates the empty back haul, one of the banes of the industry. A firm's profit reflects its load factor more than the size of its operations. That a company may find itself unable to fill recently expanded capacity, that expansion may be accompanied by a lower load factor, counteracts the significance of various growth-inducing factors.

Many small trucking firms concentrate on a low-volume market but generate a decent profit rate by maintaining a high load factor. Because traffic volume in this market niche is too small to attract companies that have made a commitment to larger carrying capacity, this small firm may face few challenges from rivals. The smaller firm thrives in a sheltered niche because it dominates a market that few other truckers find attractive. Rather than say that the industry is decentralized because there are few economies of scale, it would be more accurate to say that, although there are some advantages to be gained from larger-scale operations, large and small firms seek out non-competing niches. Even when the standard cultural account recognized some internal differentiation among truckers, it misstated the nature of that differentiation. Smallness was a powerful, positively charged symbol. The culture assumed that small trucking firms operated smaller trucks, served small towns, and carried small shipments on behalf of small-firm shippers. All the various forms of smallness neatly correlated, so one could be in favour of them all, simultaneously. But this was more wishful thinking than accurate generalization. Firms of modest size do tend to establish themselves in smaller-volume markets, which often means a market serving one or more small towns. But small trucking firms may operate a small number of very large trucks. A small trucking firm may grow, may expand its gross operating revenue, by carrying goods on longer trips or by adding to the size of its fleet, not necessarily by buying bigger trucks. Nor is there a correlation between the size of shipment and the size of either the trucking or shipping firm. Many giant firms send goods through a very large number of small shipments. And some of Canada's largest trucking companies are specialists in the small, less-than-truckload shipment.

PRIVATE VS COMMERCIAL TRUCKING

A commercial or for-hire carrier hauls goods for a price; but almost half the trucking market consists of non-commercial, 'private' trucking, that is, goods carried in trucks operated by the company that owns the goods. This private-trucking sector stretches from the one-delivery-truck grocery store to large-fleet operations, for example, the breweries, the postal service, major newspapers, garbage-collection companies, the large retail chain stores, and the armed forces. Canadian provinces regulate commmercial but not private trucking.

The reasons why some firms chose to carry their own goods rather than hire a carrier, the factors that determined how private and commercial trucking divided up the market, were buried under mountains of wishful thinking, rhetoric, and myth. According to shippers and deregulators, more and more shipping firms were being driven to the private option by the poor service, inadequate competition, and excessive rates prevalent among commercial, regulated truckers. Instead of seeking government protection against this 'threat,' commercial truckers could diminish the private sector simply by improving service and/or reducing rates.

The commercial truckers' reply was an adaptation of early railway attacks on trucking. Commercial trucking was not only the more efficient sector, it provided that vital, core service even private trucking shippers wanted available on a stand-by basis. Private trucking was inevitably inefficient because it had a much lower load factor. Goods often were sent on a rush basis in half-empty trucks; and private trucks, such as delivery trucks, often returned empty. Private trucking units none the less survived only because government exempted them from the regulatory burdens it heaped on commercial truckers. Free to pick and choose, private trucking could skim off the market cream, large shipments moving over long distances from one origin to one destination. Commercial truckers were left to deal with the unattractive, low-profit markets and, denied the high-profit cream, could do so only through higher prices. Thus private trucking was expanding because it fed on a self-generated vicious cycle: shippers switched to private trucking because commercial rates were high, but each switch pushed commercial rates even higher.

The hard evidence rarely supports any of these assertions, on either side of the argument. Private trucking maintained a steady share of the total trucking market from 1957 to 1987. The great expansion of private trucking, welcomed by deregulators and deplored by regulated truckers, was myth. Although many shipping firms threatened to 'go private' if commercial carriers did not make better offers on service and price, thus feeding the myth of an expanding private sector, this threat was part of the shippers' normal tactics when bargaining with commercial truckers on the terms of specific trips. Carrying one's own goods was seriously considered only by those companies that frequently shipped relatively large, truckload (TL) orders. Thus, while trucking associations devoted themselves to this private-vs-commercial controversy, private trucking was a threat only to those trucking firms that specialized in truckload shipments. Because shippers engaged in private trucking most often cited rail not commercial trucking as their second choice, putting legal constraints on private trucking, as trucking associations advocated, would not have driven shippers back into the arms of commercial, TL truckers. Private trucking *did* have a smaller load factor and, assessed in these terms, was less efficient than commercial trucking; but many private units improved their load factor by securing a commercial licence and combining the two kinds of service.

A shipping firm typically resorted to the private-trucking option because it valued complete control over the movement of its goods and because it saw an advantage in having drivers perform sales- and service-related functions at the time of delivery. In other words, shipping firms were not driven away from the commercial option by regulation and would not have been lured back by lower rates or more prompt deliveries. Commercial carriers could never match the convenience and sales-and-service functions provided through private trucking. Although the culture and debates suggested otherwise, private and commercial trucking occupied differentiated, non-competing market niches.

SEGMENTATION WITHIN THE COMMERCIAL SECTOR

Market forces produced not only differentiation between private and commercial trucking but considerable differentiation or segmentation within the commercial sector.

The carrying of truckload (TL) shipments and less-than-truckload (LTL) shipments involves such different operating conditions that firms tend to specialize in one or the other. Truckers see the TL shipment as clean, simple, and attractive. In the typical TL trip, a fully loaded or almost fully loaded truck proceeds from the door of one shipper (consignor) directly to the door of one or more recipients (consignees). By contrast, the LTL business, in which one processes a great many small orders, is more complicated, demanding, and aggravating. If a single trip contains many small shipments from different shippers being sent to different consignees, there are more varied handling and delivery instructions to observe, a greater likelihood that goods will be delivered to the wrong place, more disagreements over whether shippers have properly crated goods, more disagreements about whether shippers have correctly itemized goods. LTL truckers, in train-like fashion, often provide regular, scheduled service between specified points; but TL truckers can adjust a trip's schedule to suit the one shipper's special needs. The extra handling involved in LTL shipments – for example, the time spent consolidating small shipments into larger ones – drives up operating costs and price. Yet, it seems to the LTL trucker that shippers always expect rush service on small shipments, at bargain rates. Because of the extra handling involved in LTL shipments, deliveries are more likely to be delayed, and goods more likely to be damaged, lost, or stolen.

Firms sending TL shipments at regular intervals often secure a minimum price by seeking competitive bids on long-term contracts. Thus, TL truckers subdivide into a single-trip, for-hire, and a contract segment. Some TL truckers specialize in short-trip, small-town service; others on long-distance, inter-city service. Firms sending large shipments are more likely to consider the rail and private-truck options, and firms sending goods long distances are more likely to consider rail. Thus, despite the great debates on 'road vs rail' and 'private vs commercial trucking,' it is only the TL truckers (and within this category mainly the contract carriers and mainly the long-distance truckers) who worry about the rail and private-trucking threats. By contrast, LTL truckers tend to compete against other LTL truckers. Because the sender of large shipments has so many options, he has considerable bargaining power, which he uses to drive down TL trucking rates.

For the firm that specializes in long-distance LTL shipments, efficient operation depends on the firm's ability to consolidate a number of small shipments going to the same destination, so that each truck departs with a full or almost full load. To do this, the LTL trucking firm must have a terminal in the place of origin and terminals in other cities in order to consolidate goods for back hauls. To make maximum use of this major investment in physical plant, the larger LTL firm typically offers storage or 'warehousing' services, even for firms that make no use of the company's trucking services. Thus, the traditional 'small firm, low capital requirements, easy entry' image of the industry applies to some segments but not others. LTL service between Canada's major cities requires a substantial initial capital investment and for this reason is dominated by large firms, usually based in Ontario or Quebec but operating across the country.

The LTL sector also subdivides into short-distance small-town and long-distance inter-city trucking. The short-distance LTL firms usually minimize the initial capital outlay by renting terminal space from other trucking firms or by doing without terminals and accepting a lower load factor. Because of this lower load factor and because short-trip truckers benefit less from the tapering effect, this small-town LTL market involves especially high operating costs and low profit margins. The many small firms ensconced in such markets are protected from competition by the unattractiveness of this segment to most other truckers.

ONE VS MANY PRODUCTS

Some trucking firms specialize in the hauling of one product or one family of closely related products; for example, petroleum, logs, gravel, milk, manufactured automobiles, oversized machinery, flammable or otherwise dangerous goods. The post-1950 emergence of trucks and loading equipment specially designed to accommodate these goods permitted truckers to move into a sphere long dominated by the railways; and this new technology spawned a large number of one-product firms, each occupying a small niche within the trucking market. Here as well, the 'easy entry' image falters. The beginning one-product firm must make a significant initial capital investment in specialized trucks and loading equipment, and the limited amount of goods available in a one-product market makes this a high-risk investment. One rarely seeks entry without first securing some contracts, guaranteeing a certain volume of business over a period of time. The difficulties in securing such contracts restricts entry far more effectively than any regulatory process does. The one-product trucker is a subset of the long-distance-contract TL carriers; he competes more against rail and the private-trucking option than against other commercial trucking firms. Because one is likely to carry logs from but not to northern British Columbia, livestock from but not to Alberta, minerals from but not to northern Ontario, the empty back haul is an especially difficult problem for one-product carriers. Empty back hauls and the seasonal nature of much specialized trucking encourage one-product truckers to think about diversification, but the specialized nature of their equipment and experience often confines those firms to their original niches.

Because each of these one-product markets is so different from the others, truckers tend to specialize in one and rarely try to straddle several. For example, firms that carry manufactured automobiles depend on landing contracts with one of the giant car-producing companies and compete mainly with rail. 'Express' companies, which resemble and compete with courier services and the federal postal service, specialize in carrying small parcels short distances; they respond to orders on short notice, provide fast delivery, and charge high rates, in line with their high operating costs. The dump-truck segment, specializing in the movement of sand, gravel, and other 'aggregates' to and from construction sites, consists of a very large number of one-person, one-truck companies that find work through a broker. Companies that move household effects, 'movers,' must deal with relatively small single shipments, each of which contains many fragile, uncrated, easily damaged items, having low market value but great personal value to the owner. Compared to truckers in other segments, the moving company provides a broader array of ancillary services, e.g., crating and uncrating of goods, storage, cleaning, installation of electrical appliances. And because movers often switch these uncrated items from truck to truck, the incidence of lost and damaged goods, and of customer claims, is very high.

GEOGRAPHIC SEGMENTATION

Trucking firms tend to specialize in certain regions or routes. Even in the absence of licences that confine firms to specific routes, and thus reinforce geographic segmentation, few trucking firms would choose to operate at large. Obviously, two firms that provide the same kind of service – e.g., general-goods LTL service – become segregated and non-competitive when they operate in different locales.

'Interlining' is a practice whereby two trucking firms agree to cover different portions of a specific trip and thus provide a long-distance shipper with 'through' service. Regulatory authorities gave virtual carte blanche to such agreements. And the emergence of the tractor-trailer combination permitted truckers to transfer the trailer, without having to unload and reload cargo. Interlining reinforced the small-firm, geographically specialized character of the industry. It was a way in which trucking firms could provide through service for long-distance shippers without having to extend the firms' geographic scope. Household movers, for example, are small, locally based firms that provide coast-to-coast service through their participation in the 'van line,' a nation-wide network of co-operating moving companies.

MICRO-MARKETS: HOW MUCH TRUCKING COMPETITION?

The 'micro-market' is the atom, the simplest unit, of the trucking market. For example, the movement of children's toys between Toronto and Ottawa on a for-hire basis and in LTL shipments would constitute a single micro-market. To carry the same goods between the same places but in TL shipments would mean operating in a different micro-market. Obviously, carrying different goods or operating in a different locale would also put one in a different micro-market. Although we follow the customary usage and refer only to the one-product carrier as a 'specialist,' every trucking firm is, in effect, specialized. It chooses between contract and for-hire service, between LTL and TL shipments, between a narrow range and broad range of goods; and it then selects a specific route or locality. Through successive specializing choices, each firm eventually confines itself to one or two micro-markets.

The way in which trucking firms sought out separate micro-markets, a process I will call 'segmentation,' helped give the industry its small-firm character and explained why there was less competition than met the eye. Only firms within the same micro-market competed. Two trucking firms often seemed to be competitors because they operated in the same locale or carried the same type of goods; but if the two firms carried different goods on the same route, or the same goods on different routes, or if one firm specialized in TL and the other in LTL shipments, the two firms occupied separate, non-competing micro-markets. The culture portrayed trucking as a small-firm, very competitive industry, but 'small firm' does not necessarily mean 'very competitive.' In the late 1980s, each province contained thousands of trucking firms, and more than 96 per cent of all trucking firms operated ten or fewer vehicles. Truckers were right to question whether one could have a cartel comprising thousands of firms; but deregulators were correct in noting that many micro-markets were two-firm oligopolies. If one or two small trucking firms saturated a small-volume micro-market, other firms saw no point in entering. Why split this small volume into even smaller, less-viable market shares?

Nevertheless, there was more competition than the deregulators alleged. Because each micro-market had its own grey and black markets, because shippers could so easily resort to quasi-legal, peripheral-sector trucking firms, there always was more de facto than apparent, de jure competition. In addition, although there was less trucking competition on the small-volume, small-town, 'unattractive' routes, there was far more competition on the major routes linking larger cities.

THE SEGMENTS AS POLITICAL RIVALS

Segmentation reduced competition between specific firms operating in different micro-markets. But each segment saw itself as an economic entity, struggling with other segments for shares of the total trucking market. It is not enough to say that there were few if any political issues on which all truckers agreed and not enough to say that industry was fragmented into a collection of diverse segments. Trucking also was divided into politically warring segments.

Truckers saw the various segments battling over how to allocate a fixed aggregate amount of commercial trucking demand. If some shippers decided to abandon their reliance on contracts, the for-hire shippers would expand their market share at the expense of contract carriers. If new one-product carriers appeared on the scene, the general-goods truckers that once had carried this product would lose ground. Thus, each segment organized and tried to secure legal restraints on the actions of other segments. If the regulatory system were to prevent contract carriers from engaging in interprovincial carriage, mixing the freight of two different shippers in the same truck, or exchanging trailers with other trucking firms, demand presumably would spill-over from the contract to the for-hire segments. Thus, when government set out to clarify terms like 'truckload shipment' or 'contract,' or to define categories of goods, like 'vegetables' or 'furniture,' each segment sought a clarification that gave maximum scope to its own operations and that restricted other segments as much possible.

Such battles rested on the dubious assumption that the aggregate demand for trucking was fixed and homogeneous, so that damming it up in one segment would cause it to flow into others. In fact, the evidence demonstrated that legal restraints on one trucking segment pushed shippers into rail or private-trucking options more often than into other trucking segments. But the warring segments had invested too much in these battles to consider such evidence; the war may have arisen from a dubious assumption but it also helped sustain that assumption.

CROSSING SEGMENTAL BOUNDARIES

The problem with the standard account of trucking was that it offered across-the-board, industry-wide generalizations, when in fact trucking is a collection of different, almost unrelated sub-industries. But even my 'segmented sub-industries' model, although largely accurate, requires some additional qualification.

While some market forces pushed firms toward segmentation, other forces encouraged firms to expand, diversify, and cross the boundaries between segments. The tapering effect encouraged firms to seek longer trips and larger shipments. Because the loading factor is so crucial to profit margins, any firm with underutilized capacity would seek additional freight, perhaps by reaching into new micro-markets. Underloaded trucks, especially empty back hauls, prompted private trucking units to seek commercial operator's licences. For similar reasons, truckers who were exempt from regulation – for example, carriers of exempt goods or truckers operating within a single municipality – edged into the regulated sphere through illegal or quasi-legal practices. Firms sometimes tried to make themselves more attractive to shippers by offering more varied, one-stop services; for example, a wider range of goods carried. A firm that experienced seasonal peaks and valleys sometimes sought entry into a new micro-market to keep itself busy during the slow months. Because the segments were so different, an economic slump in some segments might coincide with an economic upturn in others, a discrepancy that encouraged cross-overs from the depressed to the thriving segments.

The qualitatively different character of each segment remained a barrier to cross-overs, but the barriers surrounding various segments were of unequal importance. Some segments were easier to penetrate than others. A firm that specialized in TL shipments lacked the terminal facilities, the experience, and often the patience to solve the special problems associated with LTL shipments; but any LTL firm could accommodate a TL shipment on short notice. Similarly, a contract carrier could not enter the for-hire business without first creating marketing, billing, and credit operations; but, in the absence of legal restraints, any for-hire company could carry goods on a contract basis. And because contract work was a dependable source of regular, large shipments, any for-hire company would be keen to bid on contracts. Thus, if the industry were deregulated and the legal barriers to cross-overs eliminated, the economic barriers would leave contract carriers more vulnerable to cross-overs than for-hire carriers, TL truckers more vulnerable than LTL truckers. Before 1970 it was equally difficult for one-product carriers owning specialized trucks and loading equipment and general-goods carriers owning all-purpose trucks to cross the boundary between them, but the subsequent growth of leasing companies expanded the opportunities for cross-overs in both directions.

Individual firms usually moved from segment to segment over the course of their history. Most regulated trucking firms began as a small, one- or two-truck company, initially operating outside the regulated sphere. It usually was not difficult to gain some limited foothold in the regulated sphere, but the small, inadequate scope of this initial licence often pushed firms to seek additional authority, either by making new applications or by acquiring other licensed companies. Because expansion often occurred in a haphazard fashion, with the firm seizing on fortuitous opportunities, and because provincial boards usually granted applicants less than they demanded, the licensed authority and business operations of most regulated firms resembled a patchwork of disconnected, unintegrated activities. It was as if four or five disparate companies had been glued together. A firm might have authority to carry one product only on a contract basis on route X, general goods in TL shipments on a for-hire basis on route Y, and a limited range of stipulated goods in LTL shipments on route Z. The desire to turn this crazy-quilt pattern into an integrated, efficient network, providing similar service to a contiguous geographic area, was another factor pushing firms to expand.

Thus, sometimes it is difficult to generalize even about one trucking firm. For example, who are firm X's rivals? In one of this firm's micro-markets the competition might be other truckers, in another micro-market rail and private trucking, in another only the grey market. Although each segment formed its own association and tried to act as a unit on political issues, proceeding as if it were a united, discrete entity coming into conflict with other entities of this kind, most firms straddled more than one segment. Even statements about 'what the TL truckers wanted' or about 'conflict between contract carriers and for-hire carriers' are partially useful but over-simplified generalizations.

Boundary crossing by individual firms had a major dampening effect on inter-segmental political conflict. Crossing was an alternative to conflict. A firm that had begun in segment X and later acquired authority in segment Y obviously lost interest in imposing legal restraints on Y for the benefit of X. Even if a given firm were not part of segment Y at present, it might hope to spread its activities into this segment at some future point and would not support new legal constraints on Y. If a for-hire firm thought that contract carriers were granted too much legal scope and consequently were gaining too much market share, that firm might either seek authority as a contract carrier or seek additional legal restraints on contract carriers, but not both.

REGULATION

Because of the expansive pressures described above, most regulated firms sooner or later crashed into the limits imposed on them by the terms of their licence. Economic forces created segmentation, but licensing helped reinforce it. There would be somewhat more inter-segmental cross-overs in a deregulated industry. Each trucking firm had an ambivalent attitude toward regulation. When I wanted to expand into your micro-market, detailed licensing conditions were an irritating restraint on my freedom of action; when you wanted to encroach on my micro-market, these conditions were vital sources of protection and security. Deregulators sometimes portrayed the industry as neatly divided into conservative, protectionist firms, which used the regulatory regime for self-defence, and more aggressive, expansionist firms, who saw regulation as a restraint; but there is little evidence to support this portrayal. Rather than conflict between firms, there was ambivalence in the view of each firm. At many points in any firm's history, it invoked regulation as protection; on perhaps just as many occasions, the same firm found regulation an annoying barrier. A specific firm's attitude toward regulation might depend on whether it was in an expansionist or consolidating phase of its history. At any given moment, the firm's attitude might reflect whether it or its rivals had an application pending before the board. Such ambivalence made it difficult for trucking associations to represent 'the truckers' viewpoint' on regulatory questions.

THE PERIPHERAL SECTOR

One cannot easily define the shape or boundaries of the trucking industry. If we treat regulated truckers as the core, this industry had a vast, ill-defined periphery. Many thousands of largely invisible, small trucking firms conducted a for-hire trucking business without seeking licensed status. Most of these firms were one-person, one-truck companies, often operating out of the owner's private residence. The classic 'easy entry' generalization fits this peripheral segment more accurately than any other part of the industry. (This generalization can be applied to the entire industry in the sense that it is relatively easy to enter *some* part of the trucking business, for example, the peripheral sector.) Most peripheral-sector firms derived their revenue from some combination of three activities: (1) they legally operated in an area not covered by provincial regulation, either carrying those goods (e.g., garbage, junk) explicitly exempted from regulation or moving goods entirely within the boundaries of a single municipality; (2) they operated a black market, in clear violation of the regulations, by undertaking trips that were legally reserved for licensed, regulated truckers; and (3) they exploited loopholes or ambiguities in the law by engaging in possibly legal, possibly illegal, 'grey market' practices. In the grey market, for example, truckers bought goods from shippers, sold them to consignees, and thus claimed status as private truckers ('phony buy and sell arrangements'); or they provided for-hire trucking service under the fiction that they were merely leasing trucks and drivers to shippers ('pseudo leasing'). Undercapitalized and afflicted by short-run cash-flow problems, the peripheral-sector firm seized upon any available freight, offered any price necessary to close the deal, and roamed in opportunistic fashion among micro-markets and segments, restrained only by the limitations inherent in a small, poorly financed firm.

Much of the debate over this peripheral sector took predictable form. Trucking associations saw the reputable truckers being undermined and the shippers exploited by the shabby practices and cutthroat tactics of these fly-by-nights. Government should destroy the black market with more rigorous enforcement of regulations and should stamp out grey-market practices by clarifying ambiguities, plugging the loopholes, in regulatory language. Shippers and deregulators saw this thriving peripheral sector as a reflection of the high-priced inadequate service provided by regulated truckers and of the stifling inflexibilities imposed by licensing. As long as truckers and shippers alike had good economic reasons to evade these excessive legal restraints, government could never stamp out the peripheral sector; witness the ingenuity with which shippers and peripheral truckers devised new loopholes as soon as the old ones were plugged.

But this debate pointed to the existence of a larger, more crucial problem. That a great many small firms could thrive on the boundaries of the regulatory system was eloquent testimony to the failure of that system. The 'reliable' truckers had supported regulation as a means of protecting them, and shippers, from these irresponsible gypsy firms; yet, after fifty years of regulation, truckers were making the same complaints about gypsies and asking for the same protection. In fact, many truckers said, all regulation did was impose new burdens on the core and thus enhance the unregulated periphery's relative advantage. That the industry would always have a vast periphery, whose firms could not even be identified or located, let alone regulated, was an inescapable debilitating problem in all efforts at regulation. As long as this uncontrollable fringe retained the ability to do what it wanted, regulated truckers would never be content with the protection provided or willing to abide by regulations that rival truckers could ignore.

AMBIGUOUS ROLES, FUZZY BOUNDARIES

In the prevailing, cultural viewpoint, 'truckers' were business people, who managed a trucking firm and employed drivers and other staff. It was these truckers, this version of 'the trucking industry,' that trucking associations sought to represent. The basic unit in this market presumably was the transaction between a shipper and a trucker. On such images, regulation was based. But the growing complexities of the trucking scene challenged these images, created new definitional problems for trucking associations, and seemed to require some adjustments in the regulatory system.

The small, peripheral-sector firm clearly was a business enterprise and part of the 'trucking industry.' But there also existed a very large number of owner operators (oos), whose economic and legal status remained ambiguous. The oo owned a truck, usually the front, motorized portion of a tractor-trailer combination, and earned income by leasing his vehicle and services on short-term contracts to duly licensed trucking companies. He usually did not have an operator's licence, and the trucking associations did not see him as a 'trucker.' Legally, he was neither an employer nor an employee. The availability of oos permitted the regulated trucking companies to expand and contract operations on a short-term basis, and to do so without paying union wages or fringe benefits. For this reason, regulated truckers fought any attempt to clarify the legal status or strengthen the bargaining position of oos – for example, they opposed giving the oos operating licences and allowing them to operate as business enterprises but also opposed extending to oos the normal protection accorded employees by the standard labour legislation.

For regulated truckers, however, oos represented a threat as well as a resource. The oos were major suppliers of grey- and black-market services; and the existence of oos made it possible for shippers to experiment with private-trucking options without having to buy their own trucks or hire drivers. In response to this threat, trucking associations wanted the regulatory system to prohibit oos from leasing trucks or their services to private trucking units, on the grounds that oos, in such cases, were not leasing but rather engaging in for-hire transactions without the necessary licence.

The Teamsters' International organized a portion of the Canadian trucking industry during the 1960s and early 1970s, but the normal labour/management, collective-bargaining model was applicable only to the larger, formalized, for-hire firms, which accounted for a small percentage of the industry. The model could not be so easily applied to private trucking units, to the one-person, peripheral-sector firms, to the oos, and even to the many small regulated firms that consisted of three or four employees, all members of the same family. Given this pattern, the Teamsters became strong advocates of the regulated trucking sector, of regulation per se, and of stronger government efforts to stamp out the grey and black markets.

After 1955, the emergence of new intermediary roles added new complexities to the classic, bilateral shipper/trucker transaction. 'Freight forwarders' consolidated small shipments at a warehouse and arranged to have the goods carried by a TL trucker, thus securing the advantage of the lower TL rates for small-shipment consignors. The emergence of forwarders apparently narrowed the gap between LTL and TL rates; if the gap widened, more shippers simply would use forwarders to secure the lower TL rate. 'Brokers' assumed responsibility for providing trucking services to a shipper at a stipulated price. Sometimes the broker would shop around and negotiate the best trucking rates for his client; sometimes the broker would subcontract the work to a number of oos or small truck companies, either regulated or not. Many oos and small trucking firms, like the dump-truck operators, were heavily dependent on the broker's finding them assignments; in a sense, these truckers worked for, were employed by, brokers. It was difficult enough trying to decide whether forwarders and brokers were to be defined as 'truckers' and therefore part of the 'trucking industry.' To complicate things further, the new and old roles sometimes overlapped. Some regulated truckers served as brokers, undertaking to provide service to a specific shipper, carrying some of the goods themselves and subcontracting other portions.

Even more dramatic changes were brought about by the emergence of a major truck-leasing segment in the period after 1965. Again, it was difficult to draw clear boundaries between roles, to distinguish sharply between 'truckers' and 'leasors.' Regulated truckers increasingly supplemented their primary hauling function by making vehicles and drivers available on a lease basis, sometimes to shippers for private-trucking operations, sometimes to other regulated truckers seeking short-term expansions in capacity. There also appeared a growing number of companies whose sole purpose was to lease truckers and drivers.

In many respects these new developments reinforced the small-firm, decentralized character of the industry. Leasing permitted small firms to meet short-run increases in demand without having to make a long-term commitment to expanded capacity. By linking a large shipper to many one-truck companies (for example, a large construction company to many dump-truck owners), brokers helped this shipper cope with, and tolerate, highly fragmented trucking supply.

More generally, these new complexities, by greatly expanding the range of options open to all parties, made the trucking market more flexible, responsive, and efficient. For regulated truckers, however, these new trends represented both a gain and a threat. By enhancing any trucking firm's ability to adjust to short-term market fluctuations, leasing added to the flexibility and efficiency of trucking operations. And many regulated firms benefited from their role as leasors, as well as lessees. But leasing, whether by leasing company or by regulated truckers, also permitted more shippers to explore the private-trucking option with minimal, start-up costs. Brokers and freight forwarders facilitated transactions between shippers and regulated truckers, by, for example, often finding shipping clients for truckers; but they also helped shippers seek out the services of leasing companies, oos, or peripheral-sector firms. The oos and peripheral-sector firms gained ground from a growing shipper interest in leasing; and, as these marginal truckers became stronger, so did the grey and black markets. Leasing itself could easily be extended into a grey-market practice. In the regulated truckers' view, a leasing company or peripheral-sector firm that 'leased' truck and driver to shipper X for one leg of a trip and struck a similar agreement with shipper Y for the back haul really was providing a commercial trucking service without the appropriate licence. Furthermore, because leasing permitted more truckers to encroach into other truckers' micro-markets – for example, allowed general-goods carriers to bid for specialized one-product contracts and lease the special equipment needed to handle this product – leasing seemed to undermine the historic protections provided by legally enforced segmentation.

In assessing these recent trends, the truckers' inertia and fear of change eventually won out. The trucking associations decided that these developments were more threatening than helpful, that the new, emerging roles were not part of these associations' constituencies, and that the newer practices must be restrained by being brought within the confines of an expanded regulatory system. No one should be allowed to act as freight forwarder or broker or to operate a leasing company unless they had secured an operator's licence and satisfied a public-necessity test. oos must be prohibited from doing business with shippers. To prevent leasing companies from edging into a de facto for-hire business and to drive both oos and peripheral-sector firms out of this field, the law should prohibit anyone from leasing both a vehicle and driver to the same shipper. To prevent one-trip leases, the law should require that any lease have a minimum thirty-day period. At the same time, the law should not restrict the regulated truckers' access to oos or the regulated truckers' ability to act as leasor, lessee, or broker. Shippers and deregulators were right to argue that such proposals attempted to restrain innovation and preserve a less-flexible, less-efficient market, primarily in order to protect the interests of licensed truckers. Because these innovations were useful to many people, legal efforts to smother them proved futile. New roles, new market practices, and new, ingenious, grey-market evasions always seemed to develop faster than new legal restraints.

4

Interest-Group Rationality:
Trucking in Canadian Politics

THE ARGUMENT SUMMARIZED

Voluntary associations with an occupational or economic base are created to advance the market-related interests of their members. The various trucking associations created in the 1920s and 1930s were intended to foster the economic interests of trucking firms and to promote the continued vitality of trucking as a transportation mode. To play this political game rationally, an interest group must define a constituency it will represent, correctly identify the economic interests of that constituency, define goals that would advance such interests, and produce strategies designed to secure official approval of those goals. Doing all this well is difficult. In this game, as in any other, one often has insufficient, ambiguous information about complex, rapidly changing conditions. Mistakes are easy to make; political action is often less than rational.

This discussion of political rationality focuses less on the occasional, random mistakes and more on the aggregate pattern of an interest group's behaviour. What underlying structural factors produce more or less political rationality in this aggregate pattern? The Canadian Trucking Association (CTA), created in 1937 to defend the federal-level interests of the Canadian trucking industry, pursued a strategy that in the aggregate was not terribly rational or effective. But the major purpose of this chapter and of chapter 6 is to show that political and cognitive-instrumental irrationality have the same systemic sources. Just as the transportation-policy culture often was a maladaptive trap that inhibited a rational approach to policy formulation, so the CTA's political-game culture provided a simplistic picture of reality and inhibited the association's pursuit of political rationality. The same system pathologies that produce maladaptive policy ideas and inhibit our ability to devise effective solutions to policy problems also curtail our ability to play politics with the right amount of self-interested cleverness. Thus, the pathologies described in previous chapters are crucial to the following account.

POLITICAL CULTURE AND POLITICAL RATIONALITY

The truckers' political culture, the higher-level viewpoints that would dominate CTA behaviour for many decades, emerged mainly from the rail vs truck controversies of the 1925–39 period. The result was a simplistic, bipolar construct, based more on affiliative than rational-political perspectives. The transportation world was divided into two separate, warring camps. Truckers saw the two railway corporations as an unrelenting, politically sophisticated enemy, dedicated to the enfeeblement of the trucking industry. Whatever the railways favoured must be contrary to the truckers' interests. To 'prove' that proposal X would hurt trucking, one need only cite railway's support for X. If truckers were in doubt about what position to take on a given issue, they need only choose the opposite of whatever the railways were demanding. Other players must attach themselves, or be assigned, to one camp or another. One was either a friend or enemy of trucking. And a friend of trucking could not be a friend of rail. Because it was important to locate each player in one camp or another and because each act provided symbolic clues about this location, attention was shifted from the apparent meaning of actions to their underlying, affiliative-expressive significance. Each bloc coined its own terms, so that even the language a speaker used presumably told us something about the speaker's loyalties.

In applying this framework to Canadian federalism, the truckers arrived at equally simplistic, dichotomous conclusions. The provinces were allies. But federal officials were railway people, who neither understood nor sympathized with trucking concerns. The railways' major objective was to have legal, crippling restraints imposed on the spread of trucking. The railways favoured the federal assumption of trucking powers because only the federal government would impose such restraints. Thus, federalization was a railway idea. To endorse it was to betray one's pro-railway allegiance. By demonstrating some sympathy for this idea, during the 1936–9 period, the federal government had confirmed its membership in the railway bloc. If they acquired authority over trucking, federal officials would pursue punitive regulation, restoring trucks to a subordinate, ancillary role in order to revive the financial health of the railways. Thus, truckers were intensely committed to defending continued provincial jurisdiction. Mainly for this purpose, CTA had been created.

The CTA's adherence to this overly simple, intellectual framework often obstructed a rational, political defence of the industry's economic interests. Trying to fit everyone into a two-team framework blinded CTA to the gradations and subtleties that often characterized the players' real viewpoints. This simple, bipolar construct had great staying power, despite evidence to the contrary, because it performed important affiliative, boundary-defining, solidarity-generating functions. Fighting the railways was what united and identified truckers. Fighting the railways and federalization gave trucking associations much of their reason for being.

One can see a number of system pathologies at work: the framework was built largely on a strained, overattributed interpretation of symbolic messages; the CTA became excessively committed to this framework (fixation); the association carefully selected and interpreted evidence in a way that would confirm these images (self-closure); the CTA culture thus became disconnected from evidence and immune to challenge (vertical disjunction); the culture became more an object of loyalty and reaffirmation than an intellectual instrument designed to help one make the right political moves (ritualization); and the association pursued an inflexible, all-or-nothing fundamentalist strategy. Even in the 1930s, the high-water mark of road vs rail battles, the framework rested less on firm evidence than on symbolic overattribution, that is, on speculative, exaggerated interpretations of underlying messages. Truckers read too much into the simple fact that federal officials, like the railways, were sympathetic to federalization. Manifest obvious meanings and intentions were ignored in favour of strained interpretations of deeper meanings. When federal officials explicitly promised to promote and sponsor trucking, if acquiring jurisdiction, truckers discounted the significance of such remarks. Instead truckers fell back on their standard proof: if federalization would help trucking, why did the railways support it? In 1936–7, C.D. Howe said that wage and hour practices in the trucking industry should be improved, that the 'hidden highway subsidy' deserved further study, and that the railways should be allowed to compete against other modes by offering price discounts. Truckers found in such remarks further proof of federal hostility to trucking, even though Howe's comments merely reflected the cultural consensus of that day. (From the truckers' viewpoint, one of Howe's great sins had been to use a railway-coined term, 'hidden highway subsidy.') By contrast, when two provincial royal commissions in the 1930s portrayed the growth of trucking as a healthy market phenomenon and said that the public had a stake in the existence of a sturdy, efficient trucking industry – again matters of consensus, questioned only by the two railways – the truckers read into such relatively innocuous conclusions proof of a basic pro-trucking sentiment at the provincial level.

Admittedly, federal officials had spent decades worrying about how to repair the railways' sagging financial fortunes. During the inter-war period, federal officials had tended to assume a unimodal, rail-dominated perspective on transportation issues and only slowly came to appreciate the significance of the newer modes. The federal 1932 royal commission concentrated on solutions to the railway's financial problems and considered trucking only as a threat to rail and, therefore, as a major cause of those financial problems. If this was evidence of a federal pro-rail bias, however, it was evidence the truckers had helped manufacture. Federal officials and federal royal commissions viewed trucking as a peripheral concern, because the provinces and the trucking industry had demanded that federal statements and studies be confined to railway issues. All further CTA efforts would be marked by this same ambivalence: the federal government should adopt a multi-modal perspective, acquire more experience with trucking issues, and show more sympathy for trucking concerns; but truckers would denounce any federal attempt to study or comment on trucking matters as an encroachment on provincial jurisdiction.

The CTA's culture became even less accurate and useful after 1950, as the boundaries between road and rail become blurred through railway acquisition of trucking companies and as federal officials, shedding their historic preoccupation with rail, become more knowledgeable about and sympathetic toward all the various transportation modes. Federal officials correctly complained about the truckers' double standard. No matter what federal officials said or did, the truckers could always find some deeper, allegedly hostile meaning in federal conduct. By contrast, the provinces' pro-trucking label was less a performance-based, earned reputation than a static quality ascribed on a once-and-for-all basis to the provinces. The provinces did little to justify this label, but whatever they did was given a highly sympathetic, symbolic interpretation by most truckers. Rather than trucking support for provincial jurisdiction being based on provincial performance, the contrary process prevailed: the truckers strained to find some pro-trucking achievements they could attribute to the provinces in order to justify continued trucking support for provincial jurisdiction. Thus, in the post-1975 deregulation debates, the various trucking associations consistently but incorrectly attributed great positive achievements to the provincial regulatory systems.

Truckers allocated to the cause of continued provincial jurisdiction, not measured, conditional, wary support but sweeping, unreflective loyalty. That the truckers had such trouble finding solid provincial achievements to praise was partly a result of this fundamentalist attachment to the provincial cause. CTA could have secured far more results from the provinces had it adopted a calculating, opportunistic approach on jurisdictional issues, had it bargained with both levels of government in search of the best deal.

At the federal level as well, CTA's rigid commitment to a simplistic cognitive framework produced a fundamentalist and not very effective political style. The association dogmatically pursued a sweeping, excessively ambitious, anti-railway program; it ignored the lack of support this program commanded among other players and thus the unlikelihood of gaining official approval for this program. Because it defined the political contest in morally absolutist terms, CTA would not negotiate with the enemy or accept half-victories, even though there was little chance of the full program being adopted.

CULTURE, EXPERIENCE, AMBIVALENCE

Despite attempts to shield this culture from challenging evidence, there sometimes was an obvious, unmistakable tension between the two. CTA's experiences with federal and provincial governments sometimes severely tested its initial cultural framework. Ambivalence was CTA's major response to this tension. One can see this ambivalence at work during the 1940–54 period. No one questioned the federal assumption of wartime controls over trucking and other industries in 1940, but CTA feared that federal officials, and their railway pals, would use the war as an excuse to impose long-term crippling restraints on trucking and that Ottawa might never restore these powers to the provinces. In retrospect, however, CTA had nothing but praise for the federal government's wartime role. Federal officials had imposed only minimum, war-related constraints on the industry, had consulted more extensively with the industry than provincial officials had in the pre-war period, and had responded favourably to many industry requests, such as a request that the conscription process recognize truck drivers as 'essential' workers. Then, in 1945–6, the federal government had dismantled all controls over trucking and returned jurisdiction to the provinces, rejecting railway demands to the contrary. Jolted out of its traditional assumptions about federal hostility, and concerned about how well ten provincial systems could accommodate the likely post-war expansion in long-distance trucking, CTA, in the 1945–8 period, urged the federal government not to wash its hands too thoroughly of trucking matters. Clearly, interprovincial truckers did not want to live with the consequences of unalloyed provincial jurisdiction; but what they and CTA did want remained unclear. The federal government must maintain a 'presence' in trucking, it must secure more interprovincial co-operation and greater uniformity in the various regulatory regimes, but at the same time it must not intrude in any way on the provinces' trucking jurisdiction.

Such ambivalent flirtations with federal power came to an abrupt end in 1949, when the Canadian Supreme Court decided that interprovincial trucking was a federal responsibility. Faced with the federalization spectre once more, CTA suddenly switched back to its original premise: that trucking had to be protected from the hostile intentions of pro-railway federal officials. In an equally abrupt switch, the association now said that the provinces were capable of solving all interprovincial issues without any federal interference. Having decided to refight the 1936–9 campaign against federalization, CTA viewed the 1954 settlement, which left interprovincial trucking with the provinces, as a great victory for the industry. By 1955, however, CTA had returned to its case for a federal presence.

This ambivalent, approach-avoidance attitude also characterized CTA's lobbying in Ottawa. On the one hand, the CTA had been created largely to convince federal officials that they must keep their hands off trucking issues, that they should not try to study trucking problems or develop a trucking policy. On the other hand, it wanted the federal government to 'recognize' trucking as a major mode and to pursue more even-handed policies in road/rail issues. It also wanted elaborate federal restraints imposed on the railway's ability to offer discounted rates – for large shipments, for shippers in areas served by other modes, for shippers that agreed to send all their goods by rail – because such discounts allegedly crippled trucking and thus weakened inter-modal competition. But, of course, the minister was to approve such restraints without examining how crippled trucking had been. As a result of CTA's ambivalence, the minister was wrong if he commented on trucking and thus intruded on a provincial matter; but failure to comment was an obvious symbolic indicator of continued federal hostility to trucking.

MARKET CHANGES, POLITICAL AGENDA

In the 1950s two major trends transformed relations between the rail and truck industries. Having finally concluded that government was not going to block the continued expansion of trucking, the railways decided to participate in and profit from this expansion by entering the trucking business. Because it was easier to acquire an existing firm with its licence than to secure a new licence from provincial regulatory bodies, each rail corporation moved promptly to buy up well-established firms and to create a nation-wide trucking network. (As each of the two corporations became a holding company for diverse transportation divisions, they renamed themselves Canadian National [CN] and Canadian Pacific [CP], dropping any reference to rail in the name of the parent corporation.) Second, shifts in transport technology permitted several modes to co-operate on the same trip, while keeping the handling of goods to a minimum. By the early 1950s one could carry goods on the first leg of the trip by truck, disconnect the trailer and roll it onto a railway flatcar, and later link the trailer to another truck tractor. This multi-modal, combined trip, often referred to as piggy-back or 'trailer on flat car' (TOFC), captured the benefits of both truck and rail service. Trucks provided door-to-door service and lower loading costs at both ends of the trip; the railway provided lower line-haul costs on the middle leg. By the 1960s shippers were able to load sealed large containers, which could be transferred as a unit from one mode to another on a given trip. The scope for combined trips was expanded even further in the 1980s by the development of cabs mounted on rubber and steel wheels and thus capable of functioning both as a truck trailer and a boxcar. The two rail companies saw everyone – rail, truck, shippers – benefiting from this new technology and took the lead in offering combined trips.

As most observers realized, these newer developments made it increasingly difficult to see the freight market or transportation politics as divided into two discrete, contending camps. The railways were becoming part of the trucking industry; and, through combined trips, the two modes were becoming as much collaborators as rivals. But the trucking industry was determined to preserve the old culture and fit the new events into it. CTA attributed malevolent motives to the railways, assumed they would use combined trip and trucking-company take-overs to cripple the trucking industry, and concluded that the association must launch an all-out campaign against these market developments.

According to CTA, if the railways were allowed into the trucking business, competition between the two modes, and competition within the trucking industry, would soon be destroyed. CN and CP would keep acquiring trucking firms until a competitive, small-firm industry had been converted into a duopoly. Everyone now agreed that inter-modal competition was a healthy phenomenon; but how could there be genuine road/rail competition when both modes were dominated by the same two corporations? Neither CN nor CP would offer attractive trucking service on a given route where that service might reduce the freight carried by rail. On the contrary, the rail strategy was to subordinate the acquired trucking companies in order to promote the rail option. As the trucking option dried up, more businesses would find themselves 'captive shippers' Other shippers might think they had a road/rail choice but find they were negotiating with the same parent corporation. The federal government must stop such take-overs, especially because these take-overs, CTA said, were being financed with federal railway subsidies, diverted from their intended purposes. The railways also could use these federal subsidies to operate their trucking divisions at a loss, drive independent truckers out of business, and hasten the drift toward a trucking duopoly.

Based on speculation rather than evidence, CTA assumed that those customers attracted to combined trips were the ones currently using trucks alone, so that a growing use of such trips would shift market share from truck to rail. As proof, CTA invoked its traditional argument: if combined trips did not hurt trucking, why were the railways so eager to pursue them? Unless resisted and contained, combined trips would soon dominate the market, so that no trucking firm could refuse to provide this service. The railways might then co-operate only with peripheral-sector firms or might give favourable terms to their own trucking subsidiaries, thus excluding most regulated truckers from this vital service. Even if the railways were willing to negotiate with regulated truckers, the availability of these other trucking partners would give the railways undue bargaining power. Once a trucking firm had become dependent on combined trips, the railway, by threatening to cancel the combined-trip agreement, could dictate policy to that firm or even coerce the firm into accepting a railway take-over bid.

According to CTA, the federal government should prohibit CN and CP from operating trucking companies; or, failing this, the provinces should deny trucking licences to any railway-affiliated applicant and should block all rail acquisitions of trucking companies. Any trucking company that became a rail subsidiary would be ejected from the trucking associations and treated as if it were not part of the trucking industry. On the combined-trip issue, CTA called for vague, undefined 'legal restraints' and, in the meantime, urged its members to stay clear of agreements with the railways. But this CTA policy simply augmented the 'take-over threat.' If truckers would not co-operate on combined trips, the railways could provide this service only by acquiring more companies of their own.

DEFENDING 'THE INTERESTS OF THE TRUCKING INDUSTRY'

Although CTA tenaciously clung to these viewpoints, they were increasingly challenged by evidence, by events, and by the market behaviour of specific trucking firms. Research in the 1960s found that more and more trucking firms were co-operating with the railways on combined trips and that this trend, contrary to CTA's dire warnings, had slightly increased trucking's share of the freight market. By then it also was clear that combined trips were only useful in moving large shipments over long distances. Far from dominating the freight market, such trips could play an important but limited role. At roughly the same time, many trucking firms decided that they did not want to be protected from railway take-overs, particularly because the railways often paid a good price and allowed the acquired firm to retain a quasi-autonomous status. Also, the entrenchment of CN and CP trucking networks did little to alter the small-firm, segmented character of the industry. Trucking could never even approximate a duopoly.

The position of CTA and the provincial trucking associations on these issues remained unchanged, resulting in a growing gap between what these associations officially said and what their members unofficially did. This gap raised questions about exactly whom or what CTA was defending. Railway take-overs and combined trips were irrelevant to the great majority of trucking firms, who served small, isolated, micro-markets of little interest to the railways. And many other trucking firms apparently did not want to be protected from railway take-overs or combined trips. To clarify its position, CTA said it was defending trucking as a mode and 'the trucking industry' as a corporate entity. Thus, while specific trucking firms might benefit from rail take-overs or combined trips, 'the industry' would suffer. But was it suffering? CN and CP were more interested in maximizing profits than in stifling trucks or protecting rail. CN or CP was willing to curtail rail service if it could serve that same route at less cost with trucks, whereas, in the days prior to take-over, that same corporation would have fought to retain these customers for rail. The take-overs expanded trucking's market share. The industry seemed to benefit in political terms as well. CN and CP now behaved as if they were part of the trucking industry, abandoned support for legal restraints on trucking, and began to advocate the trucking viewpoint on issues like the gas tax and limits on truck size. None the less, the trucking associations insisted that the railways and railway-owned trucking companies were not part of the 'trucking industry' these associations were trying to defend.

It is inherently difficult to define the boundaries and interests of such a diverse and fragmented industry as trucking. Trucking associations have special problems in defining what constituency they are fighting to defend. CTA tended to resolve these questions in a conservative, restrictionist manner, by defending the status quo and refusing to treat new elements as part of the industry. Throughout the post-war period, the trucking associations fought to defend the kind of trucking industry that had existed around 1948, an industry without combined trips or railway ownership. They seemed guided partly by inertia, by a strong preference for the kind of industry these truckers had known for most of their working lives. They also fought to preserve the notion of a political/economic sphere divided into two discrete, warring camps. In pursuit of these objectives, CTA mounted a long, hopeless campaign against inevitable market developments and pursued a political program that no one outside the industry could support.

THE TRUCKERS IN FEDERAL POLITICS

CTA often complained that it was an ineffective pariah in federal politics, mainly because of federal anti-trucking attitudes. But CTA's political ineffectiveness was largely its own doing. Aside from its inability to say clearly whether it wanted federal officials to consider or ignore trucking, the CTA's major problem was its inflexible commitment to a program that everyone else strongly opposed. The CTA's post-war campaign against combined trips, discounts in railway rates, and railway take-overs of trucking companies obviously was doomed from the start; yet the association persevered for over thirty years.

Truckers entered the post-war period with a great deal of political credit. In the 1920s and 1930s the truckers had seemed the more progressive, entrepreneurial force, while a sleepy, quasi-monopolistic rail industry had begged government to protect it from this new competition. As well, post-war thinking coincided with what truckers had always maintained: that truck/rail competition could protect shippers more effectively than regulation, that subsidies to rail stifled the growth of a trucking option, and that healthy inter-modal competition could occur only if rail prices were allowed to find their true market level. By concentrating on a post-war program mainly designed to restrain the market behaviour of railways, however, CTA destroyed this credit and alienated everyone. For decades the railways had been urged to solve their financial problems by developing market-based solutions rather running to government; now, by pursuing rate discounts, by entering the trucking business, and by experimenting with combined trips, the railways seemed to be taking this advice. If the railways could secure profits from trucking and become less dependent on federal hand-outs, if transportation politics could be less dominated by the 'financial ill health of the railways' issue, everyone, except the truckers, would be delighted. Moreover, what rational politician would oppose lower railway rates or order the railways to cancel discounts? To most observers, it seemed as if the pre-war roles were now reversed; the railways were pursuing market innovations, the truckers seeking legal restraints on competition and change.

Both combined trips and railway take-overs of trucking companies acquired widespread, positively charged symbolic importance. In attacking them, the truckers wounded themselves. The ability of road and rail to co-operate on specific trips buttressed the classic assumption that there was a natural harmony of interests among the various modes, that each mode performed a specialized, complementary function. In addition, if the CN or CP conglomerate assigned to each of its modal divisions the kind of service that division could most efficiently provide, such intracorporate planning would help us achieve a rationalized, differentiated transportation network.

From the outset, as early as 1948, both federal and provincial politicians rejected all CTA's program in strongly worded, unmistakable terms. At the federal level, politicians, civil servants, and royal commissioners urged the association to pursue less-sweeping, more-realistic objectives, to identify and seek limited restraints on those specific railway abuses truckers most feared. (Many of these proposed restraints later became part of the 1967 Transportation Act.) But the association seemed unable to contemplate partial victories; it persisted with a fundamentalist, all-or-nothing, largely futile campaign.

TRUCKERS AND WESTERNERS: AN ANTI-RAIL ALLIANCE?

In the immediate post-war period, the CTA briefly considered forming an alliance with Western interests, based largely on a common hostility to the railways. Both CTA and the Westerners often accused the railways of incorrectly blaming their financial problems either on trucking competition or on federally imposed requirements, like the Crow and the maintenance of branch lines. Both. Westerners and truckers accused the railways of overstating their financial need to justify subsidies they did not deserve. Truckers, Western shippers, and Western provincial governments disliked the railway's practice of offering discounted rates to those who shipped only by rail because such discounts created captive, easily exploited shippers.

Despite some common grievances against rail, however, a CTA/Western alliance proved unworkable. Westerners blamed the trucking industry as much as the railways for the spread of cheaper, competitive rail rates in central Canada. Truckers said that the emergence of a healthy trucking option in the West would pull rail rates down and effectively achieve Western objectives, but Westerners preferred more immediate, tangible action, like a freeze on rail-rate increases or major increases in federal subsidies to rail users. Moreover, better trucking service in Western Canada might be used as an excuse to shut down railway branch lines. As Westerners became more insistent on the need for special subsidies to compensate regional victims of cross-subsidization, the CTA began to argue that differences in rail-rate schedules from one region to another were fair and non-discriminatory because cost-based – the same argument urged by the railways and by the Ontario and Quebec governments. Thus ended CTA's brief flirtation with the regional protestors.

TEN ECONOMIES OR ONE?

Post-1945 advances in truck technology and highway construction promoted the growth of long-distance, interprovincial trucking; but the existence of ten different regulatory regimes created obstacles to the free movement of goods across provincial boundaries. In principle, everyone favoured freer interprovincial trade and greater uniformity ('harmonization') among the various regulatory regimes. The provinces said they could achieve all this through interprovincial diplomacy and began this negotiating process in 1953, mainly to convince the federal government that it should leave interprovincial trucking in provincial hands. But almost thirty-five years of negotiations produced virtually no results. CTA remained ambivalent, torn between its fear of federalization and its disappointment with the results of interprovincial diplomacy. According to CTA, trucking must remain a provincial responsibility because only varying provincial regulatory systems could take due note of the significant differences in provincial market conditions; but, at the same time, these system variations allegedly were strangling long-distance trucking. When the federal government demonstrated little interest in trucking questions, the CTA deplored the futility of interprovincial negotiations and urged a stronger 'federal presence.' But if the federal government showed too much interest in trucking questions, CTA insisted that the provinces were making great progress and required no outside assistance.

In a manner typical of this transportation sphere, the debate over interprovincial uniformity was a largely expressive game, conducted in a grand, rhetorical style and disconnected from specific evidence or policy outcomes. The choice was 'ten economies or one,' the goal was to create a 'Canadian common market in trucking,' the enemy was 'balkanization' or sometimes 'provincial parochialism.'

The debate suggested that there were great variations in provincial programs, that an interprovincial trucker would need a battery of lawyers to understand and ensure compliance with such varied rules. In fact, the regulatory regimes were remarkably similar, largely because the later regimes were based on the ones established in Ontario and Quebec during the 1930s. All provincial regulatory systems required truckers to secure a licence from a regulatory board, and all boards issued licences in line with a vague 'public necessity' or 'public interest' criterion. (The only exception was Alberta, which regulated interprovincial trucking as all other provinces did but allowed unregulated access to the intraprovincial trucking market.) All systems defined performance standards, for example regarding hours or cargo insurance; and the substance of these standards, the precise minima required, varied little from province to province. All systems required rates to be fair, compensatory, and non-discriminatory; all required standard-form bills of lading; and all required truckers to report regularly on business operations. Some provinces, like Saskatchewan and Manitoba, authorized the regulatory board either to set trucking rates or to disallow the rates submitted by the truckers; other provinces, like Ontario and New Brunswick, required only that truckers file rates with the board and thereafter adhere to those rates in specific transactions. But even this one important variation was more significant in law than in practice. Because rate-setting provinces usually accepted without question the rates submitted by truckers, these provinces pursued a de facto policy little different from that of the rate-filing provinces. It seems that all regulatory systems were poorly enforced, so that what small variations existed could not have posed serious obstacles to long-distance truckers.

Although it knew better, the CTA helped propagate the notion that lack of uniformity among provincial regulatory systems was the key barrier. The CTA issued a uniform model system and urged all provinces to adopt it, but in fact the CTA model more or less described existing provincial practices. This was a classic example of 'sublimation.' The association recognized the real, more serious obstacles but had no useful ideas about how to eliminate them. Unable to address the real obstacles, but unable to remain silent on so important an issue, CTA emphasized the harmonization problem, not really a problem at all, or instead fell back on ritualistic affirmations of general 'free trade' principles.

CTA could not directly address the more serious obstacles, partly because of internal splits within the trucking camp. For the smaller intraprovincial firms in many provinces, 'free trade' meant that large, Ontario-based, interprovincial firms would be allowed to dominate the attractive, intercity routes, while local firms would be left to deal with small and remote communities. Because no one could openly dissent from a sacred value like interprovincial free trade, the intraprovincial firms, often supported by their provincial trucking association, could only work behind the scenes to preserve all obstacles, major and trivial, to long-distance trucking. Long-distance truckers accused many provincial regulatory boards of favouring local trucking firms and imposing unduly confining conditions on out-of-province firms; but, to avoid airing internal quarrels, CTA refused to discuss provincial protectionism as a possible obstacle.

Where some differences in regulatory regime existed – for example, the difference between rate-filing and rate-setting provinces – the truckers in each province favoured retaining their own province's distinctive way of doing things. Inertia, a preference for the familiar, set each provincial trucking association against the others. The Manitoba and Saskatchewan truckers insisted on rate setting, the Ontario and New Brunswick truckers on rate filing. In each province the trucking association endorsed the CTA goal of uniform regulatory systems, but each association believed that its own province's system should become the model for all other provinces. Thus, where real, small variations existed, CTA's uniform model either was vague or allowed any province to opt out, which made the model not a very powerful harmonizer.

In one area, the statutory limits on truck size and weight, there *were* significant variations in provincial requirements, and these variations *did* restrict the actions of interprovincial truckers. A trucking firm moving goods across four provinces would have to meet the size and weight limits of the province with the lowest limits, unless that firm wanted to incur the cost of switching freight from larger to smaller vehicles before entering the more restrictive province. But truckers lived happily with such variations. Nation-wide uniformity on weight and size limits might be secured on the basis of the lowest common denominator, that is, by allowing the most restrictive province to retain its low limits and levelling the other provinces downward. By contrast, the existing lack of uniformity permitted truckers to pursue a levelling-up strategy, in which one urged the low-limit provinces to align themselves with their less-restrictive neighbours.

The single most-important obstacle to interprovincial traffic was the mere existence of ten separate regulatory systems. Long-distance truckers had to make separate applications to three, five, or eight provincial boards. A firm securing a licence in one province could provide interprovincial service only through interlining agreements with firms in other provinces. Even when a firm secured licences in many provinces, the terms of those licences varied. If authorized to carry all furniture in New Brunswick but only new furniture in Quebec, an interprovincial trucker would be limited by the terms of the more restrictive licence. If the terms of two provincial licences lacked any common features, e.g., goods A and B in Ontario, goods C and D in Quebec, one lacked authority to move any goods interprovincially. A firm might be unable to move new furniture from Toronto to Saskatoon because, although it had received authority to move such goods in Ontario and in Saskatchewan, it lacked authority to travel in Manitoba.

The CTA's solution to this multiple application problem was to have interprovincial licensing applications heard by a joint board, consisting of representatives from those provinces concerned with each case. The firm would make one application to one board and would receive one clear definition of the firm's total interprovincial authority. Despite CTA's official stance, most truckers could see some advantages in working through multiple regulatory systems and had serious misgivings about the joint-board solution. If each province could add its own distinctive terms and conditions to any licence, the authority granted by this joint board would vary from province to province, and truckers would be no better off than under the existing system. If the terms and conditions granted a trucker were to be uniform across all the relevant provinces, any one of the participating provinces would have a veto; and the trucker-applicant stood to lose everything. Moreover, considering the impressive immobility displayed by interprovincial conferences on trucking, most truckers thought that a joint board would take ages to arrive at decisions and that one could get faster results through multiple applications to separate provinces. By the 1960s, therefore, CTA dropped its demand for a joint board. It had no other solution to the multiple-application problem.

Having the federal government issue interprovincial licences would eliminate the need for multiple applications, but CTA was unalterably committed to continued provincial jurisdiction. Many interprovincial truckers disliked federalization because, like the joint board, it compelled the firm to stake everything on one application. There were some merits in having the licensing power fragmented and decentralized. Although no trucker dare say it openly, 'balkanization' was not all bad.

The debate suggested that each province had a different entry or licensing policy, when, in fact, no province had a perceivable entry-control policy of any kind. The behaviour of provincial licensing boards was uniformly capricious and unfathomable. Each board applied some undefined, undefinable 'public necessity criterion'; each issued decisions without reasons; and no board built a case law to which truckers could refer. All truckers objected to such unpredictable, quirky decision-making processes; but interprovincial truckers, dealing with six or eight separate processes, found it a special problem. CTA could not directly attack this problem either. To dwell on the arbitrary nature of provincial boards would anger board members, who held great power over the future of individual trucking firms, and would give fresh ammunition to the advocates of federalization. CTA had no useful solutions to offer. According to CTA, more clarity and predictability would be introduced into licensing if the various provinces provided detailed definitions of the controlling, public-necessity criterion. But CTA's model definition, which it urged provinces to adopt, was a string of the usual clichés: stabilize the industry, protect shippers, conserve fuel, maximize efficiency, serve small towns, promote exports, develop the North, and so on. Such a list, if adopted, would have added little to the predictability of board decisions.

The interprovincial trucking negotiations never even considered most CTA proposals. Although they claimed to be marching toward freer interprovincial trade, the provinces focused on harmless, low-stakes issues, which had little to do with obstacles to free trade. And little agreement was attained, even on these secondary issues. In the early 1920s, the provinces had agreed that automobile owners need only register their vehicles in their home provinces and that all other provinces would recognize the home-province licence plates; but not until 1987 did the provinces agree to extend this same 'reciprocity' on motor-vehicle registration to trucks. (Of course interprovincial truckers must still secure an operator's licence in each province; there would be no reciprocity on this.) By the late 1980s, after thirty-five years of negotiation, the provinces had approved this vehicle-registration reciprocity plan, a standard, nation-wide format for bills of lading, common definitions for key terms, and a system for categorizing goods – nothing more. Because the tax rate on gasoline varied from province to province, and because truckers would exploit these variations by 'filling up' in the lower-tax provinces, the interprovincial conferences spent decades trying to agree either on a common tax rate or on a system that would pool all provincial gas tax revenue and reallocate these funds in some equitable manner. But no agreement was reached.

What modest achievements there were can be attributed almost entirely to the threat of federalization. When Ottawa showed interest in assuming more power over trucking, the provinces felt they must respond by demonstrating the effectiveness of interprovincial diplomacy. Only then did some agreement on a trucking issue emerge. In trying to exert influence over interprovincial diplomacy, the CTA's only weapon, but a none-the-less formidable one, was the federal threat. Had it behaved in a politically rational manner, the association would have adopted a conditional, pragmatic approach to jurisdictional questions, would have bargained with both levels of government and played one off against the other. Instead, CTA remained cemented to the provincial cause. And in response to the new, post–1975 federal threat, CTA provided its usual defence of interprovincial diplomacy, which allegedly had made major strides toward freer trade in trucking.

SECTION III: BREAKTHROUGH OR BETRAYAL?

In 1967 both CTA and federal officials made a serious attempt to establish a closer, more structured relationship. In section III of the proposed National Transportation Act, the federal government would reassume the interprovincial trucking authority it had delegated to the provinces in 1954. Rather than prepare for the expected dispute with CTA, the federal minister, Jack Pickersgill, invited the association's leaders to help draft section III. By involving the association in this way, and by addressing many of the truckers' substantive concerns in various parts of this act, he hoped to provide symbolic indicators of federal good faith and to transform the truckers' traditional assumptions about hostile federal intent. The federal government, he said, would take over trucking regulation in order to promote, not stifle, the industry. After many years of futile lobbying, the CTA also seemed eager for a fresh start. CTA leaders worked on and then endorsed section III, a dramatic turnabout for an organization that had spent its life defending provincial jurisdiction. To justify this turnabout and sell CTA members on federalization, both CTA and ministry officials portrayed many features of the 1967 act as concessions to the trucking industry, which had emerged from CTA/ministry bargaining sessions and which would form the basis of a more co-operative long-term relationship between the two sides. In fact, these efforts to negotiate and to build a stable relationship had met with little success. On one side, the minister was only somewhat eager to placate the truckers. He was not sure he would proceed with federalization and, therefore, not sure he would need the truckers' support. Those parts of the act imposing new restraints on the railway's anti-competitive behaviour, although portrayed as concessions to the trucking industry, were part of the post-war cultural consensus; they commanded very broad support and probably would have been enacted in any case. The 1967 act said only that rail subsidies *could* be extended to other modes. In 1970, the cabinet extended the Maritime subsidy to trucking, not to placate CTA but because all the provincial officials and interest groups in Atlantic Canada favoured such an extension. When the grain transportation subsidy was redefined in 1985, Western representatives opposed extending this subsidy to trucking because they feared the phasing out of rail branch lines; and the cabinet, responding to this regional consensus rather than to CTA, left the subsidy as rail only.

A more serious obstacle to some CTA/ministry rapprochement was CTA's fundamentalist style. Because the association remained rigidly committed to its older program – banning railway take-overs, eliminating railway discounts, legally restraining combined trips – it had little interest in bargaining. And because they were unaccustomed to horse-trading, CTA leaders found it difficult to assess the significance of what was being offered. They overvalued some concessions, undervalued others, and afterwards remained uncertain about whether they had secured a good or bad deal.

For many years, federal officials and interest groups had urged CTA to seek limited legal protection against specific railway abuses rather than blanket prohibitions. This advice, although rejected by CTA, became the basis for the 1967 act's new restraints on railway behaviour. Under the act, railway behaviour would be more carefully scrutinized for signs of coercion, predatory pricing, or other unfair, anti-competitive tactics. The CTA did not win a ban on railway acquisitions of trucking companies, but the legislation authorized federal regulators, the Canadian Transport Commission (CTC), to prohibit any acquisition likely to reduce significantly the extent of road/rail competition. The railways still would be allowed to invoke a variety of rate discounts but not in a manner designed to cripple other modes and thereby weaken inter-modal competition; and the railways were prohibited from offering non-compensatory rates. In arriving at negotiated agreements on combined trips, the railways would not be allowed to discriminate between one independent trucker and another or between independent truckers and a rail-owned trucking subsidiary (e.g. giving the subsidiary better terms than it was prepared to offer the independent). A financial wall of separation would be established between the rail and trucking divisions of CN and CP so that neither corporation could cross-subsidize its trucking operations either with rail-derived profits or federal, rail-related subsidies. Both corporations were prohibited from using federal subsidies to support their small-package or 'express' service, a service that the truckers thought a part of their niche. Someone who made limited use of trucking but shipped a 'preponderant' portion of goods by rail still would be defined as a 'captive shipper' and would retain the protection accorded to this category. Perhaps most important of all, on railway-related cases coming before the CTC, truckers now would be defined as an 'interested party,' would have legal standing to challenge specific railway requests or practices, and thus could help enforce the new restraints on railway behaviour.

These new restraints were not concessions, extracted by a hard-bargaining CTA. They had to be thrust upon, sold to, CTA officials. CTA undervalued these restraints because they fell far short of the association's blanket, post-war program. In contrast, CTA overvalued the minister's decision to base the new federal trucking regime on the model the association had been urging interprovincial conferences to adopt. Perhaps CTA had to exaggerate the importance of its own plan; but because this plan described what provinces already did, there was little remarkable or new in it or in the federal government's proposed trucking system. At the same time, CTA underappreciated the extent to which the minister tried to re-assure truckers on future licensing procedures. The minister promised that all existing licences would be honoured, that no currently licensed trucker need reapply for authority already held. Because the CTC would work through specialized, unimodal subcommittees, all trucking applications and issues would come before a trucking subcommittee, presumably sympathetic to the industry's concerns. To ensure such sympathy, the subcommittee could co-opt provincial board members with experience in the trucking field. (But assigning different modes to autonomous subcom-mittees undermined the minister's claim that federalization would move us toward multi-modal, comprehensive transportation planning.) One other aspect of the act was insufficiently appreciated by CTA: since section III stipulated that truckers could file rates through a tariff bureau, the act gave unambiguous federal consent to such bureaux and therefore exempted them from anti-combines, unfair-trade-practices legislation.

It had not been smart politics for CTA to remain unquestioningly riveted

to the cause of provincial jurisdiction. It would have been more ration[...]
the truckers to adopt a more pragmatic, bargaining relationship with [...]
levels. By the late 1960s, some truckers seemed ready to reassess [...]
traditional pro-provincial commitment and at least debate the pros and [...]
of federalization. (For one thing, federal regulators probably would bu[...]
case law and act far more predictably than provincial boards did.) But [...]
CTA leadership's sudden leap into the federal camp, its abrupt reversal [...]
long-standing commitments, left much of the membership confused and
sceptical. Most truckers could not so quickly abandon the forty-year-old
assumption that federal officials were anti-trucking and that federalization
would produce punitive regulation. Compared to the association's apoca-
lyptic warnings about the threat posed by certain railway practices and
CTA's all-out political campaign to prohibit these practices, the new
restraints on railways seemed to many truckers unimpressive victories, and
thus not very convincing symbolic indicators of a new federal attitude.
Therefore, what emerged in the trucking community was not a thoughtful
reassessment of previous commitments but the truckers' characteristic
inertia. Suddenly confronted with federalization, uncertain about what to
expect from such a major change, most truckers opted for the known evils
of continued provincial jurisdiction. Truckers could not enthusiastically
defend the status quo, but they at least understood it and had learned to live
with it.

The federal government, once again incapacitated by provincial
opposition, at first stalled and then, in 1972, officially abandoned its
attempt to federalize trucking. The reaction of CTA leaders to this federal
indecision was abrupt, exaggerated, and morally self-righteous, in line
with their traditional political style. CTA seemed incapable of pragmatic
small moves or measured responses. Having leaped into the federal camp
in 1967, it now flopped back to its previous unquestioned support for
continued provincial jurisdiction. CTA also seemed unable to appreciate the
significance of recent gains, such as the extension of the Maritime subsidy
to trucking and the new legal restraints on railway behaviour. Despite such
gains, CTA said that the ministry had betrayed the association, failed to
negotiate in good faith, had never intended to federalize trucking, had used
section III merely to build more support for the entire act. This betrayal
seemed to confirm CTA's traditional assumptions about the untrustworthi-
ness of federal officials and their indifference to trucking concerns.

In addition, there had always been a basic misunderstanding about how
the future CTA/ministry relationship was to develop. CTA saw the 1967–70
talks as an opening round, to be followed by more concessions. In the

ministry's view, the CTA, having been granted standing to appear before CTC, should now pursue its concerns before this body on a case-by-case basis, rather than expect new policy commitments from the minister.

THE CAMPAIGN FOR CONTINUED REGULATION

After 1972, most of CTA's previous concerns were thrust aside by the appearance of new, even more serious dangers. After 1970 an increasing number of American-based or American-owned trucking firms began operating in Canada. Here, as in the earlier railway-take-over case, the trucking associations decided to define 'the industry' in historic, more-restrictive terms. U.S. trucking firms operating in Canada would be defined as threats to, not as parts of, the industry, even though some well-known Canadian trucking firms had become subsidiaries of these U.S. companies. To CTA, the provincial regulatory systems now seemed the only barrier to this American threat; these systems had become legitimate, crucial instruments of Canadian protectionism in the trucking industry.

In 1975–6, the federal cabinet endorsed trucking deregulation and threatened to federalize trucking unless the provinces moved on their own to deregulate. After the U.S. government had partially deregulated its trucking industry in 1980, American officials began arguing for 'mirror reciprocity,' that is, an equally deregulated trucking market on both sides of the border. In CTA's view, while the provinces were protecting truckers from Americanization, the Canadian federal government was mainly, excessively, interested in preserving good relations with Washington and would sacrifice the interests of Canadian truckers to achieve that objective. Thus, CTA could mount one campaign against the three big threats: deregulation, federalization, and Americanization. The federal government wanted to assume authority in order to deregulate trucking; it wanted to deregulate Canadian trucking in order to weaken this industry and thus pacify U.S. interests. Only continued regulation at the provincial level would prevent a massive U.S. invasion of Canadian trucking markets.

Like earlier assumptions about provincial sympathy and federal hostility to trucking, 'protectionist' and 'pro-American' were affiliative, ascribed qualities, unrelated to the specific actions of either federal or provincial officials. There was nothing protectionist about provincial regulatory practices. No provincial system treated the nationality of trucking firms as a relevant factor; Canadian and American firms appearing before provincial boards were treated alike; no province had impeded the movement of U.S. trucking firms into Canadian markets. Moreover, the argument that the federal government wanted trucking deregulation in order to appease Washington ignored the entire post-war shift toward non-interventionist values. On federal/provincial questions, CTA still operated with a double standard, with self-confirming assumptions. The provinces were always given the benefit of the doubt, although they did little to earn it, while CTA consistently read underlying hostile intent into any federal action. During the later 1980s, CTA blamed much of the continued American intrusion into Canadian trucking not on the permissive, nationality-blind practices of provincial licensing boards but on the federal government's 1983 agreement with the United States. In 1982, to intensify its pressure on behalf of mirror reciprocity, the American government had banned all further permits for Canadian trucking firms seeking to operate within the United States. A year later, the U.S. and Canadian governments signed a trucking accord, in which the United States agreed to lift this ban and both sides agreed in principle to free trade, open borders, and fair competition in international trucking. To CTA, this accord was a sell-out of Canadian trucking interests, a definitive rejection of protectionist principles, proof positive of CTA's earlier fears about federal intent. But, as federal officials correctly pointed out, this accord erased the U.S. ban on new permits, made no reference to mirror reciprocity – the preferred U.S. solution – bound Canada only to some general principles, subject to varying interpretations, and merely restated the principles that Canada had agreed to in GATT and many other international trade agreements over the previous thirty-five years.

5

Regulating the Industry

What is the substance of regulatory policy in the various provinces, and what impact do these policies have on the trucking industry? Just as the transportation culture produced a standardized description of the trucking industry, so the recent debate over deregulation proceeded on the basis of a commonly accepted, standardized view of what regulation had achieved. In this chapter I describe the results and impact of trucking regulation in one province, Ontario. Because there is prima facie evidence of great similarity in provincial trucking regimes, the Ontario findings very likely have broader applicability, although province-by-province research is obviously required.

Trucking regulation in Ontario has been a frail, porous, minimal system, which achieved almost none of the objectives attributed to it in the deregulation debate; in fact, it achieved very few identifiable objectives of any sort. The deregulation debate in Ontario and elsewhere in Canada was seriously marred by vertical disjunction and overattribution. Both the supporters and critics of the existing regulatory programs assigned excessive effect and importance to these programs and proceeded with highly inaccurate cognitive images of what regulation had achieved. They debated the merits of a hypothetical, pervasive, well-enforced regulatory regime rather than what really existed.

Why did the debators badly misread the programs being assessed? Why commit so much energy to debating a relative inconsequential system? Why should regulated truckers tenaciously defend a system that gave them few real benefits, and shippers complain so bitterly about a system that imposed such minimal restraints?

Ontario staged a great debate on trucking deregulation because it was expected to. This issue was being debated throughout North America.

Ontario was home base for much of Canada's trucking industry and had been the first province to institute trucking regulation. As a result, Ontario's debate emerged from, and was based on, the larger cultural context rather than indigeneous problems or evidence. Because the early Canadian transportation culture had viewed trucking regulation as a badly needed corrective for certain market inadequacies, the Ontario debate assumed that trucking regulation did have this intended impact. The original mandate presumably had been fulfilled; only the validity of the mandate was in question. This debate also projected United States ideas and experience onto the Ontario case, without reflecting on the validity of this transference. Ontario wound up debating not its own trucking regulatory system but the far more pervasive system that had prevailed in the United States before partial deregulation in 1980.

REVERSE MOBILIZATION

Some processes are pathological because they reverse what seems to be the rational sequence of steps, because like the Queen in *Alice* they start with the verdict and then proceed to the evidence. In a rational sequence, conclusions follow from evidence, policies are attempts to solve problems, interest-group demands reflect some prior decisions about what would best serve the group's interests, and we allocate attention and resources by first determining what is important. But when such outcomes take the form of public commitments, the sponsor must justify, bolster, or sustain that commitment. In a pathological process, which I call 'reverse mobilization,' we may casually, unreflectively, make a commitment and then engage in elaborate post-facto rationalizations, finding evidence to support generalizations, problems to justify solutions, interests that would be served by demands. Overattribution, assigning excessive truth, importance, or remedial powers to one's commitments, is a common product of this justification process. The CTA's elaborate efforts to find evidence of federal hostility and provincial sympathy, described in the preceding chapter, was an example of reverse mobilization. Ontario's entire regulatory effort is another example: a program structure was casually created and an elaborate effort subsequently made to discover some rationale or purpose for this program. The deregulation debate is still another example. Having initially committed great attention and resources to this debate, because the larger context seemed to call for it, Ontario debaters, on both sides of the fence, had to justify this commitment, both to themselves and to their constituents. They did this by vastly overstating the program's impact on market phenomena. The resulting debate was mainly expressive, ritual combat, disconnected from specific evidence about Ontario's program.

THE TWO CULTURES

Truckers and shippers operated with two separate levels of belief; they were carriers of two different, disconnected cultures. As participants in their trade associations and in public debates over policy issues, truckers and shippers adhered to the official, legitimate, idealized version of reality, derived in good part from the prevailing transportation culture. As I have argued, this culture was dominated by, and burdened by, overstated rhetoric, condensed symbols, and standardized but inaccurate descriptions of the trucking industry and trucking regulation. This culture functioned in a predominantly expressive arena, often disconnected from specific-level experience and action: for example, disconnected from the way in which shipping and trucking firms engaged in everyday market transactions. These transactions were more accurately described and more effectively guided by a less-visible, inside-dopester's, underground culture. The official culture permitted one to say the right things and engage in dramatic 'great debates'; the underground culture contained practical rules of thumb on how to survive in the trucking market. The latter culture was more realistic and more easily changed because subjected to daily testing. But, because practices coincided so little with official values, this more realistic culture could not be brought to the surface, fully legitimated, or integrated with the official culture.

A gap, a cultural schism, resulted. The official culture and the trade associations often presented a picture of the world – e.g., the standardized image of the trucking industry, the CTA's fears about railway take-overs and combined trips – that each trucking and shipping firm knew to be inaccurate. No firm would base its daily decisions on the ideas it endorsed when participating in its trade association. Thus, truckers and shippers endorsed the overattributed version of regulation described above; but when acting in the marketplace, truckers and shippers knew how ineffective the regulatory system was and they acted accordingly. When trucking or shipping executives appeared before a public body, they began with the standard, trade-association, official-culture line; but if asked to talk about their specific firm's problems, strategies, and environment, these witnesses made a qualitative leap in role and culture. The gap between these two cultures helped produce the ambivalence so characteristic of these groups. At the official-culture level, truckers wanted rigorous enforcement, formalized transactions, and industry-wide rate schedules; but at the underground-culture level they thought and acted otherwise.

REGULATION TO WHAT END?

In the policy-oriented, cognitive-instrumental game, governments devise programs to cope with public problems. Knowing what problems the program is designed to solve helps one assess its achievements. But trucking regulation in Ontario was a hollow shell. The province created a licensing structure but never indicated what purpose this structure was designed to serve, what goals it was supposed to pursue. This was reverse mobilization: one did not begin with a problem and then devise a program; the program was created, and there ensued an interminable debate over why it had been created and what direction it should take.

In the 1926–32 period, Ontario officials had created a regulatory system for trucking in a casual, almost unthinking manner. During the inter-war period it was unquestioningly assumed that trucking should be regulated. The structure created in Ontario closely paralleled that model regime approved by the provinces and the federal government in 1932 and subsequently praised by all relevant groups. But in Ontario, and elsewhere, there was agreement only on a label, not its meaning. Behind this apparent consensus on the need for 'trucking regulation,' there were different versions of how one should regulate and exactly what objectives such a program should pursue. Municipal councils, ratepayer associations, fiscal conservatives, and railway allies thought that trucking regulation meant subjecting the truckers to new taxes and thus compelling them to pay for a greater share (presumably their fair share) of highway construction costs. Shipping companies said regulation was mainly designed to protect them from the disreputable trucking firms that failed to meet commitments, lost or damaged cargo, refused to process claims, or literally disappeared, went out of business, before claims could be filed. Regulation would screen out unfit truckers, would create a registry so shippers could locate and assess trucking firms, and would suspend the licences of firms engaging in unscrupulous practices. According to the Ontario Trucking Association (OTA), regulation would restrict entry, reduce the number of trucking firms, curtail destructive competition, and thus help rationalize an otherwise unstable industry.

In initiating a regulatory system, the minister hoped to appease these groups, all of which demanded trucking regulation, but he carefully avoided committing the province to any specific version. Only the structural shell was clearly defined. The Public Commercial Vehicles Act (PCVA), both in 1926 and in its later versions, created a licensing procedure but neglected to say why and failed to indicate what purposes this structure would serve. Any firm wishing to engage in commercial trucking must secure an operator's or PCV license from the minister responsible for highways. Exempted from this requirement were private truckers and the carriers of certain, exempt goods, like unprocessed farm products. Truckers operating entirely within a single municipality were subject to municipal jurisdiction. The 1932 PCVA amendments stipulated that no applicant could secure an operator's licence from the minister unless the Ontario Municipal and Railway Board (OMRB) first found that the proposed service constituted a 'public necessity or convenience (PNC) and then issued a PNC certificate. Although an OMRB negative finding would be final, the minister was not required to issue a licence in all cases where a PNC certificate had been granted. Licences were to be granted for a fixed term, normally one year, and the minister had authority to renew, revoke, or temporarily suspend licences. In 1955, the power to issue PNC certificates was shifted from OMRB to the Ontario Highway Transport Board (OHTB), a body that heard only trucking applications.

The act gave the minister sweeping authority to issue regulations on any aspect of trucking; but, since the act said nothing about the intent of such regulations, it left the minister free to regulate the industry as he saw fit. Moreover, the act empowered but did not require the minister to issue these supplementary regulations. Because the minister issued very few regulations, one was left with little more than the basic licensing framework described in the act.

In contrast to Canadian railway regulation and American trucking regulation, which were dominated by strong, independent boards, Ontario had created a 'strong minister, weak board' system. The minister, not the board, was authorized to issue supplementary regulations and to enforce all aspects of this program. In subsequent practice, the minister made it clear that he, not the board, would make policy. If the minister saw some larger policy-issue implications in a specific case, which admittedly was seldom, he would tell the board how to resolve the case or would remove the case from the board's hands and decide it himself. Because this was a minister-centred system, the relevant interest groups assumed it was up to the minister to clarify the rationale and aims of this program.

In his infrequent, cryptic comments, however, the minister failed to provide such clarification. In part, the cabinet had viewed licensing as a means of identifying truckers so that they might be subjected to a new weight-distance tax. But this tax was abandoned in 1928, and the financial rationale for licensing disappeared with it. In the OTA's version of history, the government originally had intended only to identify or register truckers; but in 1932, by adopting a PNC criterion and authorizing an independent board to implement it, the government had embraced restrictive, tough entry control as the major purpose of trucking regulation. In fact, the minister had given OMRB a role in licensing only because he found it an irritating, growing burden to deal with thousands of minuscule trucking cases. He invoked 'public necessity' as a criterion for licensing decisions, only because the term had been endorsed in recent federal/provincial conferences on trucking, had been widely used in other regulatory settings, and was an accepted part of the culture. Both then and subsequently, no one could define the term, and few tried. He created OHTB in 1955 to placate the truckers, but he provided no rationale for this move.

A program without a purpose was an embarrassing void and, therefore, a ripe subject for overattribution. Each interest group filled this void by reading into the act its own preferred version of regulation and then deploring the minister's subsequent failure to implement this initial, real intent. OTA's account of what the 1932 amendments really meant was a good example of such misattribution. Each group wanted the minister to fill this void by producing a definitive trucking policy for Ontario that they assumed or hoped would mean ministerial endorsement of that group's preferred version. At the very least, the minister and the board should clarify what PNC meant and what criteria would determine specific licensing decisions.

MINIMALIST REGULATION

Despite the cryptic quality of official statements, the minister did have a de facto policy, one that might be called 'minimalism.' He wanted to stabilize a fragile trucking industry but to achieve this with the least amount of regulation possible. Market forces must be given maximum play. Having a regulatory program would permit the government to keep an eye on the industry and occasionally issue advice or warnings, but little more. The minister had secured sweeping authority to issue regulations mainly for bargaining purposes. By threatening to invoke this power, he could pressure shippers and truckers to find private, voluntary solutions for most market problems. Usually, he threatened but did not invoke. The performance standards on cargo insurance, processing of claims, wages, and hours, which shippers and other groups had seen as the program's raison d'être, were few, undemanding, and largely unenforced. The minister often threatened to require the periodic examination of all vehicles if the truckers did not take steps to improve their vehicle-maintenance record, but he never implemented this authority.

The minister was determined to resist the imposition of a pervasive, highly restrictive, railway-type, or U.S.-type trucking system; and he was impressed with the manner in which even small program expansions acquired a momentum of their own and dragged one, willy-nilly, into such a pervasive system. Some observers have called this the 'tar baby' effect: touch one part of a regulated industry and one soon becomes glued to all parts. If truckers regularly submitted records for provincial scrutiny, the inspectors would soon see a need for even more documentation and for more regulations to cope with the problems revealed in such documents. Enact a regulation and one must follow this with three or four additional regulations clarifying the intent of the first and 'closing the legal loopholes.' In order to determine whether the rates submitted by truckers were fair, government would get drawn into deciding how efficiently specific trucking firms were run, what constituted a fair rate of return in trucking, whether specific managerial moves in specific firms had been wise or not. To avoid the tar-baby effect, the minister would resist even modest system extensions (for example, instituting regular reporting by trucking firms). The minister adopted rate filing in 1963 to appease the truckers and keep them loyal to continued provincial jurisdiction, but he adamantly opposed having the province review substantive rates to determine whether they were fair, non-discriminatory, or compensatory.

The resulting minimalist system, then, would consist of little more than entry control, little more than the bare-bones licensing procedures described in the original PCVA. But even licensing, although the core of the program, would pursue minimal, unclear goals. Licences should provide some degree of security and protection to truckers, and thus some degree of stability to the industry, but must not become a burdensome, inflexible 'straitjacket,' unduly restricting business decisions. Beyond this vague hostility to pervasive regulation, the minister could see no policy issues involved in detailed licensing cases and had no wish to be drawn into them. For this reason, he almost invariably confirmed a favourable board decision, which meant that the board became the de facto licensing body. For the same reason, he automatically renewed all licences, which meant that a licence, once secured, became the unchallenged, permanent property of the holder. He consistently rejected demands that he make licensing a policy instrument for the pursuit of certain objectives. In the early years, the railways had wanted the licensing board to engage in inter-modal planning, for example, refusing trucking licences for micro-markets already well served by rail; but the minister rejected this idea. Later, he ignored OTA's request that railway companies be prevented from either securing trucking licences or acquiring trucking firms. More recently, he refused to have the board treat the national home-base of applicants as a relevant factor and thus refused to make licensing a device for excluding American truckers from Canadian markets. Although the act, as amended in 1932, empowered the board to set limits on the size of a company's fleet, the minister refused to make it an instrument for fighting concentration of ownership and ensuring small-firm dominance in trucking, so that, in practice, licences never included such limits.

It was easy to compile a list of all those objectives regulation did not attain, objectives the minister did not want it to attain. The problem with minimalism was that it clearly defined what the minister opposed – a more pervasive, suffocating regulatory system – but not what he thought the existing, minimalist system should achieve. Before the deregulation tide, most trucking and shipping groups complained about how little regulation achieved. In the long-awaited, definitive trucking policy, they hoped the minister would be drawn into a more aggressive, ambitious brand of regulation, which would provide more 'protection' for shippers and truckers. The minister refrained from issuing such a statement precisely to avoid creeping interventionism, and to avoid, as well, having to choose among the various, conflicting versions of what regulation really should be. To deflect pressures for a definitive statement, the minister often invoked the prevailing culture, referred such demands to the board, deplored 'ministerial interference' in board matters, and deferred to board 'independence and impartiality.' Often he simply denied there was a problem: everyone was in favour of 'trucking regulation,' the existing system worked well, so obviously no system extensions or policy clarifications were needed.

REGULATION PURSUED FOR TOO MANY ENDS

Only in the late 1970s, and then as a response to the deregulators' assault on the entire regulatory system, did the government feel compelled to tell people why this system existed and what objectives it was supposed to attain. Although his statements provided a post-facto rationalization of what had been a largely content-free structure, the minister insisted that there always had been a deliberate, precise intent and that the objectives he now articulated had characterized this program from the outset. As the deregulation tide swelled, the minister responded by attributing more and more objectives to the system, presumably demonstrating how essential it was to preserve regulation. According to these statements, trucking regulation in Ontario provided for a healthy, efficient trucking industry, guaranteed shippers adequate trucking service, protected shippers from service discrimination and other possible trucking abuses, ensured that there was neither an oversupply nor undersupply of trucking services, protected the small shipper, promoted maximum efficiency in the use of fuel, promoted economic development in small towns and in northern Ontario, helped keep Ontario goods competitive in extra-provincial markets, ensured a decent but not excessive rate of return in the trucking industry, provided for fair, non-arbitrary, non-discriminatory, and rational (cost-based) trucking rates, ensured that trucking remained an industry of small firms, and so on. In making specific licensing decisions, OHTB presumably took all these factors into account. Here then was the long-awaited 'trucking policy,' the long-awaited definition of PNC.

Faced with a need to justify continued regulation, the minister had invoked a familiar solution: the long list of vague, legitimate platitudes. The minister's statements were primarily ritualistic exercises, reaffirming the correct, standard values – and legitimating regulation by linking it to those values. When the minister said that regulation achieved objectives X, Y, and Z, all he meant to say was that X, Y, and Z were 'good things,' of which he approved. He set out to embrace all the correct values, to endorse all possible versions of regulation, and thus to provide some symbolic pay-offs for each group. Of course, this minimal program really did not, could not, achieve such sweeping objectives. For example, the minister said that rate filing guaranteed fair, cost-based, compensatory, non-discriminatory rates; in fact, the law required each regulated trucker to hand OHTB a copy of his rate schedule, nothing more. Nor could such statements provide a clear direction for the future. Each item on the list – protecting small towns, conserving fuel, and so on – was a vague aspiration, not a precise goal. Such a laundry list of every conceivable aspiration, without any indication of priorities or trade-offs, could not provide a licensing board with clear guidelines and could not produce more predictable board decisions.

As the deregulation debate gathered momentum, protagonists on both sides of the issue increasingly assumed that Ontario's program in trucking regulation had precise, substantial consequences. Forgotten were the forty-year complaints about the system's minimal, aimless character. Many groups were now prepared to accept the minister's compilation of symbols as a definitive 'trucking policy' or as an accurate summary of the program's achievements, whose merits one could now debate. The deregulation debate began by overloading the program with fake achievements; it proceeded on the basis of inflated, dramatic rhetoric, which poorly described the modest, relatively ineffective practices.

NORTHERN DEVELOPMENT

The case of trucking in northern Ontario neatly illustrated the enormous gap between legitimate, overblown rhetoric and casual, aimless decisions. The 'North of North Bay rule,' approved in the 1940s without any stated or apparent rationale, said that a trucking firm might be licensed to serve southern or northern Ontario but not both, and that consequently all freight moving to and from the north would have to be transferred at some junction, like North Bay. Moreover, only a restricted number of firms would be allowed to operate in the north. A rule limiting the number of available carriers in the north, and requiring at least one transfer of freight on all north-south movement, resulted in inadequate and expensive service for northern shippers. It proved so restrictive that, by the 1970s, the rule was widely ignored by shippers and truckers alike. Although the government had given up on enforcing the rule, although a state of de facto deregulation existed in northern Ontario, the minister still fabricated a defence of this rule in the late 1970s, arguing that such limits on trucking competition were necessary to compensate northern truckers for the otherwise unattractive aspects of this market. Soon after, however, the minister, with no explanation other than a general remark that the cabinet was trying to 'loosen up' regulations, announced the abolition of all previous rules relating to northern trucking.

LICENSING AS 'POLITICS'

One of the truckers' long-standing goals was to ensure that licensing would not be, even in part, a political game. If 'political' perspectives prevailed, the issuing authority would view the licence as a reward or pay-off, to be granted in exchange for support or gratitude, perhaps to be granted to persons with the most influential friends or the right partisan affiliations. Applicants could be easily exploited – for example, required to demonstrate tangible support for the party in power before receiving serious consideration. A patron/client pattern might emerge, in which truckers applied for licences as humble supplicants, with no rights to assert or legitimate claims to make; and the licence would be granted as a favour, an act of discretionary generosity. In this political context, licensing cases would not be assessed on their economic merits, nor could one conceive of licensing as an instrument for achieving policy objectives. According to OTA, ministers tended to base licensing decisions on political factors, while an independent board would base such decisions on the substantive merits of each case. The formal procedures and case law such bodies normally developed would produce rule-governed, predictable outcomes and would convert the trucker from an exploitable supplicant to a party with legal rights to assert. Consider the initial, 1926–32 period, when the minister alone made licensing decisions. Because most businesses, the municipal councils, and the provincial legislators in a given region favoured more trucking service for that area, there tended to be more people supporting a specific trucking application than opposing it. Therefore, on politically rational grounds, the minister was motivated to grant rather than deny licences; and the result, it seemed to OTA, was an excessively liberal, easy-access policy. The 1932 shift of de facto licensing decisions to an independent board presumably would result in decisions based on the economic merits of each case and thus would produce tighter, more restrictive entry control.

The problem was that, in fact, 'political' factors played an important role in board decisions. Members of OHTB were party faithful, until recently, Conservatives, rewarded for service to the party with a well-paying, undemanding job. Board members developed ad hoc, particularist preferences for some firms and antipathies toward others that seemed to play a major part in board decisions. Certain trucking lawyers established close rapport with the board, sometimes assisted the board in preparing its final decisions, and often defended the board's actions; it was thought advisable for a firm to be represented before the board by one of this inner clique. Many of these favoured trucking lawyers were prominent Conservatives; some were ex-members of Ontario Conservative cabinets. It also was considered smart politics for a larger trucking firm to name some of these trucking lawyers or prominent Tories to its board of directors. Some firms regularly gave generous Christmas gifts to board members. But above all, because one would have to appear before this board in future cases, it was bad politics to criticize either specific board decisions or general board behaviour. Of course, no one really knew why the board behaved as it did; but because trucking firms thought these 'political' factors important and acted on that basis, they *were* important.

No one was prepared to talk openly about these well-known political factors, and so most discussions about the board remained disconnected from reality. In the late 1970s, deregulators and shipping groups argued that, although the initial purpose of Ontario's regulatory program had been to police carrier abuses, truckers had captured the board and turned licensing into a means of cartelizing the industry. This view wrongly attributed some single, clear objective to the initial program. Moreover, it made little sense to portray the board as an industry puppet, eager to do the truckers' bidding. Truckers felt they were vulnerable humble petitioners in the grip of a powerful, quirky, unpredictable board – but could not say this lest they antagonize board members. Meanwhile, because OTA remained rigidly committed to the virtues of a strong-board/weak-minister system, because it consistently defended an idealized version of how independent boards behaved, the association was not eager to air realistic accounts or criticisms of OHTB behaviour.

LICENSING AS MICRO-MARKET PLANNING

If the purpose of trucking regulation was micro-market planning, licensing boards would be 'expert,' economics-oriented, investigatory bodies, mainly concerned with balancing supply and demand in each small unit of the trucking market. For each micro-market, the board would ensure that there was sufficient but not destructive competition, enough competition to protect shippers but not so much that the market was broken into excessively small, non-viable shares. Regulation advocates all favoured 'licensing as micro-market planning.' And everyone, both the critics and defenders of continued regulation, agreed that this, in fact, was what OHTB did. The board's procedures seemed to confirm this claim. Applicants were expected to provide evidence on existing service inadequacies in a given micro-market, while opponents would try to demonstrate that service was adequate or expandable and that demand in this micro-market could not sustain another trucking firm.

But this was rhetoric without reality, as any shipping or trucking firm that had appeared before the board knew. The board was not a proactive, investigative body, whose staff undertook independent analyses of supply and demand in each micro-market. OHTB had no staff, except for routine clerical functions, and the board took no initiatives of its own. The board confined itself to a passive, judicial role, making decisions only in response to cases brought before it, and deriving its conclusions about the state of a micro-market entirely from the evidence submitted by contestants. The board, without even looking at economic data, automatically granted all unopposed applications. Thus, the board might have contributed to oversupply in those micro-markets where licence holders were not alert enough to protest.

While the board sometimes portrayed itself as micro-market planner and sometimes as a court, in fact it operated according to no obvious ground rules or apparent design. The board never defined PNC, never gave reasons for specific decisions, did not build a case law, and never cited precedents. In contested cases, the board never indicated what kinds of economic evidence it was looking for; it allowed any and all evidence to be submitted in hearings; and in announcing its decision, the board never summarized the facts or indicated what evidence it had found convincing. Firms could only speculate about possibly discernible regularities or tendencies. Some firms thought the board was impressed by quantity and thus accumulated as many testimonials as possible; some thought the board was especially impressed by testimony from 'big names' in municipal, provincial, or federal politics. The board appeared to give more weight to evidence presented in person than submitted in writing. The board appeared to put the onus of proof more on the applicant than on the opposition. An applicant apparently could help his cause by demonstrating that, when shippers previously had voiced explicit complaints about service, the current licence holder had ignored these complaints. Board members, it appeared, approved applications in order to remedy service inadequacies but not to lower trucking rates in a specific micro-market; so trucking lawyers discouraged applicants from presenting complaints about 'excessive rates.' An applicant could discredit opposing firms by demonstrating that they had violated regulations or the terms of their licences. The board sometimes but not always sympathized with a licensee trying to knit a crazy quilt of disconnected authorizations into some integrated pattern. In some cases, applicants were asked not only to show inadequate service but also to demonstrate that currently licensed firms were *incapable* of providing the additional, needed service, a demonstration applicants found impossible to provide. And sometimes, to make things more confusing, the board's decision seemed completely unrelated to evidence submitted on the adequacy-of-service issue. The model OHTB more consistently followed than any other was that of a mediation board. Its aim was to produce agreement among conflicting trucking firms, not to ensure that the right level of service was provided to a micro-market. In cases where currently licensed firms opposed only some parts of an applicant's request, the board usually granted the unopposed parts of the application but not the opposed parts. The board seemed favourably disposed to those applicants who tried to meet the opposition half-way by submitting modest rather than extravagant applications in the first place. The board always encouraged the contestants to seek a negotiated compromise and would automatically endorse any settlement arrived at. Shipping groups, who had hoped for more competition among truckers and had supported an application for additional service, often felt betrayed by a subsequent deal between two trucking firms; but the board was not willing to overturn settlements because of shipper complaints. The board's task, it seems, was to mediate between truckers, not between trucker and shipper.

THE IMPACT OF ENTRY CONTROL

Working primarily with American evidence, deregulators portrayed entry control in Ontario as a formidable barrier and Ontario's regulated trucking industry as a closed club of privileged, protected, heavily subsidized monopolists. Rising to the bait, truckers defended tough, restrictive entry control as a necessary device for stabilizing an overly competitive idustry. The subsequent debate, which focused on the merits of restrictive entry, was largely irrelevant to the Ontario system.

The debate proceeded as if the entry of new firms into the regulated trucking sector were the central question before OHTB, as if the major purpose of regulation were to keep new members from joining the cartel. In fact, over 80 per cent of the applications considered by the board in any given year were initiated by already licensed firms seeking some extension of authority. The board spent most of its time not policing entry into the regulated sphere but rather settling jurisdictional contests among already licensed truckers.

More important, licensing in Ontario was a weak, porous barrier, easily penetrated by persistent applicants. As practised in Ontario, entry control was incapable of turning the regulated trucking sector into a cartel of privileged carriers, systematically exploiting shippers and consumers. In any given year, about 10 per cent of the applications were unopposed and were approved by OHTB in toto; about 15 per cent of the applications were totally rejected; and the great majority of applicants, about three-quarters, received approval for some portion of their initial request, usually by negotiating a compromise with those firms opposing the application. Thus, roughly 85 per cent of applicants secured all or some part of what they asked for. Deregulators correctly noted that this 85 per cent success rate failed to consider the firms that voluntarily withdrew an application rather than fight opposing firms and failed to consider the firms deterred by this process from applying in the first place. Because the great majority of successful applicants received only part of what they originally asked for, one might question whether they really had been 'successful.' In contrast, many unsuccessful or partly successful applicants eventually secured most or all of what they wanted through a process known as 'board harassment.' These applicants would reapply again and again, clog the board's agenda, and eventually wear down both opposing firms and OHTB members. For firms seeking authorization, the licensing process was less a definitive obstacle than a time-and-resource-consuming nuisance. But it was the same costly nuisance to the licensed firms fighting back new entries. Entry control tested the resolve of both sides and often rewarded the one with more staying power. Since persistent applicants eventually won out, licensing in Ontario provided regulated truckers with very little long-term protection against new rivals.

For the firm with a bit of capital, whatever expanded authority one could not achieve through the application route was attainable through company acquisition. OHTB gave unquestioning, pro forma approval to all acquisitions of licensed firms, apparently proceeding on the assumption that, if the service provided by the company to be acquired was once deemed to have met the PNC test, the service would be equally 'necessary or convenient' when provided by the acquiring company. It allowed the acquiring firm to 'split' the licence of the firm being acquired and purchase only the more attractive portions. According to the prevailing culture, companies should not be allowed to sell a licence if they no longer provided the service in question; but OHTB regularly allowed the sale of 'dormant' licences, even in cases where the seller had acted contrary to law and had discontinued service without first seeking the board's approval. For a trucking firm with sufficient capital, then, acquisition was a fast, dependable means of breaking into the regulated sphere or expanding one's authority within that sphere.

OVERATTRIBUTION CONSIDERED FURTHER

One can easily compile a list of all those objectives that both critics and defenders attributed to this program but that the program neither achieved nor seriously pursued. The board made no attempt to assess the 'fitness' of applicants, and, consequently, regulation in Ontario did not screen out those financially shaky, irresponsible, inexperienced firms that threatened both shippers and reputable truckers. Regulation presumably reduced the chronic oversupply and cutthroat competition in trucking, but OHTB policy on new entrants was far too easy-going to achieve this aim. Regulation allegedly protected shippers from exploitation by requiring all truckers to pursue reputable practices regarding the processing of claims, the insurance of cargo, the fulfilment of promises made in written bills of lading; but there were few rules on these subjects, and those that existed made minimal, substantive demands on truckers, and even these minimal rules were poorly enforced. Regulation presumably protected shippers from service discrimination; but as the evidence presented to OHTB so clearly demonstrated, truckers often refused to carry less-attractive freight (e.g., fragile goods, short trips), although licensed to do so.

Sometimes the system achieved exactly the opposite of those objectives attributed to it. As noted earlier, the minister's policies inhibited rather than encouraged the emergence of adequate trucking service in northern Ontario. The minister said that rate filing permitted the government to ferret out possible cases of collusion; but in fact filing encouraged firms to have a tariff bureau file a common rate on their behalf. Regulation allegedly helped preserve the deconcentrated, small-firm character of trucking; but real practices, by making it easier to acquire new authority through the acquisition rather than the application route, did just the opposite.

SEGMENTATION: GOOD OR BAD? NATURAL OR FABRICATED?

The trucking industry was divided into qualitatively different, non-competing segments; and each segment was further divided into many small specialized micro-markets. The standard cultural view on this segmentation had always been ambivalent. On the one hand, because each trucking firm appeared to be searching for its distinctive, specialized niche, the one to which it was uniquely suited, the resulting market-wide segmentation should approximate that efficient, role-differentiated network the culture had always advocated. On the other hand, shippers and policy professionals often argued that the typical trucking firm behaved in an overly cautious, conservative manner, carved out too small and specialized a niche, and inertly clung to its current niche rather than seek out a more efficient mix and scale of activities. If this latter view was true, the trucking market was excessively fragmented, localized, and specialized; it contained too many firms, too many inefficient firms, too little competition, too many sheltered, insular niches.

Once the deregulation debate had been launched, most shipping groups and policy professionals decided that segmentation was (a) unambiguously bad and (b) almost entirely the product of a licensing system, which confined truckers to specified micro-markets. Ministerial claims to the contrary notwithstanding, regulation was legally mandated inefficiency. Licences often required a firm to use a circuitous rather than more direct route between two places and often reduced a firm's load factor by restricting the type of goods that firm might carry between two locations. By allowing a firm to deliver certain goods to city X but forbidding it to pick up those goods in city X, perhaps forbidding it to pick up any goods in city X, licences often mandated empty back hauls. Limited geographic authority meant that long-distance freight would have to change hands several times on a single trip and that many firms could not benefit from the tapering effect. And licensing imposed on many firms a crazy-quilt pattern of unrelated authorizations. The pro-regulation case, however, remained ambivalent on the segmentation issue. In reply to the above criticisms, truckers and other regulation advocates offered the following, inconsistent arguments. (a) Segmentation is a good thing because it produces an efficient, role-differentiated network, with each firm occupying its appropriate niche, and because it permits each trucker to offer expert, specialized service to appropriate shippers. Because segmentation is the result of market forces, of individual trucking firms freely adjusting to economic factors, critics of segmentation should not blame this pattern on regulation. (b) Segmentation is a good thing but is not a product of market forces. Rather it is one of the beneficial consequences of regulation and one of the reasons why we must retain regulation. Deregulation would result in extensive crossing-over and a near-dissolution of the segments. Larger firms would invade niches previously held by smaller firms, destroy the smaller firms, and produce an industry marked by concentrated ownership and large-firm dominance. (c) Segmentation is a bad thing, because it produces insufficient service for unattractive (small-town, small-shipper) markets; but fortunately regulation protects us from too much segmentation. By imposing on the licensed firm a mixture of inter-city and small-town service, regulatory boards not only guarantee service to unattractive markets but allow the regulated firm to cross-subsidize these markets with profits earned on the inter-city routes. In a deregulated industry, most trucking firms would avoid unattractive markets. Without cross-subsidies, prices in these markets would rise. And some unattractive markets would have no service at all.

Each argument, on both sides of the issue, was a mixture of fact and fancy. Segmentation was encouraged by regulatory practices but largely resulted from the many market-based factors described above. Had regulation never been approved, most firms would, nevertheless, have confined themselves to one or two small micro-markets. Deregulators were right to point out how detailed licensing terms often imposed inefficient operations on the licensee. However, persistent firms, willing to harass the board, could get these terms extended. Rather than lock firms into specific micro-markets, Ontario's licensing system accommodated most expansionist demands; otherwise there would not have been so many firms straddling micro-markets and segments. OHTB might be more correctly criticized for granting extensions in an ad hoc, random manner, which left most firms with a disparate, unintegrated, inefficient pattern of operations. However, given minimal enforcement, a point discussed below, neither the licensing terms nor any other aspect of this regulatory system could have been terribly confining.

Because trucking firms did not seek a mix of big-city and small-town routes, and OHTB never imposed this mix on any firm, there was a great deal of segmentation and virtually no cross-subsidization between small-town and inter-city routes. The culture remained ambivalent about the merits of cross-subsidization; but, whether the practice was good or bad, it was not one of the Ontario regulatory system's products.

By allocating firms to segregated micro-markets, segmentation did greatly reduce competition among truckers, as deregulators alleged. But this reduced competition, like segmentation, was more the product of economic factors than a legal fabrication. Here, as elsewhere, both critics and defenders attributed too much to the program and overestimated the market changes that would result from deregulation. In a deregulated trucking industry, there probably would be somewhat more crossing of segmental boundaries but not intense, destructive competition, as the standard view assumed. The fact that other truckers found the market in question unattractive protected most trucking firms far more effectively than OHTB. In a deregulated industry, these same unattractive markets very likely would be served by these same firms, offering much the same service at very similar prices. By contrast, on the busy, more-attractive, intercity routes, great pressure for entry had combined with the usual OHTB liberality to produce healthy competition, even under regulation.

ENFORCEMENT: DE FACTO DEREGULATION

In addition to those laws that apply to all business enterprises in Ontario, two statutes were especially relevant for trucking firms. The PCV Act required for-hire truckers to acquire an operator's licence, abide by the conditions of that licence, and observe some requirements (e.g., rate filing, insurance coverage) imposed only on PCV-licensed truckers. The Highway Traffic Act (HTA) defined the conditions under which any motorized vehicle might operate on Ontario's roads and highways and imposed some special requirements on trucks, such as weight and size limits. By and large, HTA was well enforced. A large cadre of provincial and local police was assigned to this task. Municipal councils, ratepayer associations, motorist associations, and members of the legislature strongly supported HTA enforcement, especially against trucks. Moving violations were easily spotted. And roadside inspection stations were effective means of checking the structural adequacy of trucks and enforcing the weight and size limits.

Enforcing PCVA was an entirely different story. It was far more difficult to detect PCVA violations: for example, exceeding the terms of one's licence, failing to maintain the required cargo insurance, exceeding the daily limit on driving hours. The groups demanding tough HTA enforcement showed no interest in PCVA violations. A truck with defective brakes was serious; a trucking company charging less than its filed rate was not.

The major push for tougher PCVA enforcement came from the regulated truckers and sometimes from shippers' associations; but their real attitude on the issue was ambivalent. Shippers wanted continued access to grey- and black-market truckers. Both truckers and shippers valued the freedom to negotiate deals that pushed a trucker beyond the terms of his licensed authority. 'Tough enforcement' was a pseudo-demand, more a symbol to be regularly reaffirmed than a goal to be achieved. Neither trucking nor shipping firms were prepared to accept the concomitants of real enforcement. The minister could have enforced PCVA if he implemented those parts of the act requiring trucking companies to maintain detailed records and submit them for ministerial scrutiny at regular intervals, if he invoked that part of the act allowing provincial inspectors to enter the premises of any trucking or shipping company in order to observe practices and examine records, if he took seriously the PCVA requirement that the terms of all transactions must be fully described in a standard-form bill of lading. But truckers and shippers intensely opposed such moves. And the minister, from the outset of the program, decided against them.

Having ruled out all these enforcement methods, one could only rely on roadside inspections, in which a small staff of PCVA inspectors was expected to cover a vast province. Because trucks rarely carried the appropriate documentation, like a copy of the company's licence or the bill of lading, how could roadside inspectors determine whether filed rates had been adhered to, whether the terms of the licence were being observed, whether the company carried the necessary cargo insurance, whether the limit on daily driving hours had been exceeded, and so on? Even if produced, the licence usually was a complex document, containing multiple, unintegrated authorizations and comprehensible, if at all, only to the most experienced trucking lawyer. Should one verify the contents of a shipment by unloading it, and thus further infuriate both driver and trucking company? Trucking firms were enraged at the time and money lost; shippers and consignees complained about delayed shipments; drivers and the Teamsters Union complained about harassment of drivers at roadside kangaroo courts. The roadside inspection created great conflict yet achieved little serious PCVA enforcement.

One of the key enforcement problems was the unassimilated periphery. As long as grey and black marketeers could operate so effectively outside the regulatory system, regulated truckers were reluctant to be bound by the system's requirements. In OTA's view, enforcement should be aimed entirely at this peripheral sector. As long as this sector 'roamed the province at will,' the minister should not be harassing decent truckers with trivial, nit-picking charges, like exceeding the terms of one's authority or failing to produce proper documentation. (Portraying such PCVA violations as trivial further demonstrated OTA's ambivalence on regulatory issues, a problem examined further in the next chapter.) But these peripheral firms were difficult or impossible to locate. Often the firm consisted of nothing more than one person, a leased truck, and a telephone in that person's home. The peripheral firms might be better located if government inspectors entered business premises; but neither the minister nor OTA wanted to see the enforcement effort cross this crucial threshold. When the minister intensified roadside inspections, he flushed out fewer illegals than licensed truckers violating some part of PCVA. OTA would then deplore this assault on honest truckers; trucking firms served with a violation would complain to their provincial legislator, who would raise questions in the House about harassment; and the minister then would quietly terminate the short-lived crack-down. Because the act was so poorly enforced, any trucker charged with a violation understandably felt that he among thousands had been selected in some capricious manner.

Ministers, truckers, and shippers seemed eager to deflect attention from the real reasons for ineffective enforcement. The problem, they said, stemmed from certain inadequacies in the PCV Act: the fines imposed on violators were too modest, the minister had to press charges in court to secure these fines; and the OHTB, which received many complaints about violations in the course of its hearings, had no enforcement authority. Of course, had there been a serious commitment to enforcement, these statutory obstacles could have been removed. Moreover, the minister commanded a sanction far more potent than fines: the ability to suspend or revoke licences. But he never used this power as an enforcement weapon, and the regulated truckers strongly urged him not to.

Ontario's real enforcement policy was based mainly on industry self-policing, egged on by occasional threats from the minister. The Teamsters sometimes could be relied on to flag violations of the rules on maximum hours or vehicle maintenance. OTA and the various tariff bureaux campaigned to secure better voluntary compliance among their members; and OTA also maintained its own highway patrol, which issued friendly warnings to offending firms. The minister threatened to name certain firms and thus punish with publicity, but rarely did. The minister's most formidable weapon was the two-week, intensified roadside inspection campaign, which he often threatened to invoke and which he actually instituted roughly once a year, mainly in order to spur on the industry's internal, self-policing efforts.

The regulatory system was very poorly enforced. As OHTB proceedings clearly revealed, shippers and truckers freely violated the conditions of specific licences and the system's more general requirements. Here was another reason why licensing failed to produce the stifling restraints deregulators alleged. The disappointed applicant often proceeded with his initial plans, despite his failure to secure authorization. The deregulation debate rested on a tacit agreement to ignore the enforcement problem, to assume that what the system required was really observed, to attribute achievements to the system that might have existed only if the act had been seriously enforced. At the underground level, each firm knew how little the system was enforced but this was not a legitimate phenomenon that these firms or the minister were eager to talk about in public.

Given this enforcement context, the great debates over closing loopholes and extending the scope of the system were largely ritual combat, with purely symbolic pay-offs at stake. Truckers and shippers argued over new legal restraints on leasing activities, but at the underground level everyone knew that the new rules would be no better enforced than the old. In the later 1970s, there was a great battle over whether shippers, as well as truckers, should be held liable for illegal trucking transactions; and the 1979 amendment, which made shippers liable only if they 'knowingly' participated in illegal transactions, was a carefully constructed compromise. Despite the considerable resources committed to this issue, everyone knew that the minister was not going to examine the records of transactions, and no one believed that shipper liability would or could be enforced through roadside inspections.

In summary, the, critics of Ontario's program in trucking regulation, rather than attributing major, harmful effects to this program, should have asked whether it was worth committing considerable time, attention, and resources to a program that had no apparent purpose and achieved so little of substance. Rather than defend Ontario's system as if it were an effective one, pro-regulators should have said that trucking regulation in Ontario could not be assessed because it had never been seriously attempted. Pro-regulators should have suggested that a more effective, enforced system would achieve those good things incorrectly attributed to the present system. The resulting deregulation debate would have been less elaborate, dramatic, or interesting, but it would have been more relevant to the Ontario experience.

6

Interest-Group Rationality:
The Ontario Trucking Association

THE TRUCKING-GROUP PROBLEM

It is extraordinarily difficult for any trade association to represent the interests of so diverse and fragmented an industry as trucking. What are the boundaries of this industry? Should a trucking association try to represent the many thousands of barely visible, peripheral-sector firms, which often consist of little more than a person, a leased truck, and a telephone? Are owner operators, freight forwarders, or brokers to be considered 'truckers' and thus part of the association's constituency? Does 'trucking' include private trucking units, which really are shippers in disguise?

The different segments of this industry also have very different interests. Any association's attempt to present a 'trucking viewpoint' or to identify 'the issues that concern truckers' is bound to be an over-generalization, applicable to some segments but not others. Some truckers, but not all, worry about truck vs rail competition, concern themselves with commercial vs private trucking issues, see rate softness as a central problem, think barriers to interprovincial trucking a key issue, and so on. The various segments not only worry about different things, they often clash head-on. All regulatory issues pit regulated truckers against private and peripheral-sector truckers. Even within the regulated camp, as noted in chapter 3, there was political conflict between for-hire and contract carriers or between general-goods and specialist carriers over how each segment would be legally defined and regulated. On only two issues, opposition to gas-tax increases and hostility to legal restrictions on the weight and size of trucks, could one find something approximating a common industry-wide trucking viewpoint. But even here, only some firms pushed against, and felt confined by, the weight and size limits; and some of the better-established firms thought that a higher gas tax might not be all bad if it forced some marginal firms out of business.

An association that tried to speak for all truckers, even in a single province, would be immobilized by internal disagreements on almost every issue. The more a trucking association strived for all-inclusive representation, the less able it would be to formulate any clearly defined viewpoints. A trucking association might try to solve this problem, and emerge with sharply defined policies, by carving out some subconstituency within the industry, by representing certain truckers but not all. To some extent, this was the solution adopted by the Ontario Trucking Association (OTA). Although OTA claimed to speak for 'the Ontario trucking industry,' it mainly represented regulated truckers. After 1974, deregulators and shippers were increasingly critical of OTA's protectionist, guild-like defence of the regulated truckers' legal privileges. None the less, the guild strategy represented a reasonably rational solution to the problem of representing a very divided, diverse industry.

To an extent, OTA behaved like a politically rational guild. The reasons why it often departed from this guild-like strategy, its inability to find an alternative mission or strategy, and the resulting irrationalities in its lobbying efforts provide the substance of this chapter.

INTEREST-GROUP RATIONALITY: AMBIVALENCE

On many of the key regulatory issues, OTA was ambivalent. Ambivalence, both wanting and opposing X, both urging X but criticizing the minister if he adopts X, is a major obstacle to the pursuit of political rationality. Because the group does not know what its goals are, it cannot formulate rational, goal-maximizing strategy and it cannot later assess how successful it has been. Although other players know that the demands of an ambivalent group cannot be taken at face value, they do not know how to negotiate with or placate such a group.

Ambivalence often results when players cannot resolve some contradiction in their individual viewpoints. On most regulatory issues – the distribution of powers between the board and minister, for example – OTA experienced tension between aspects of the prevailing transportation culture and the truckers' everyday experiences, between the correct values and those moves that would best serve the truckers' economic interests, between the official and underground cultures. In some cases (program enforcement, attacks on concentration of ownership), regulated truckers wanted the end but not any of the means, the goal but not its concomitants.

Ambivalence resulted on all the above issues because the truckers felt they must endorse the correct values in public, expressive settings, even though not prepared to see these values implemented. Sometimes, ambivalence reflected a clash between two opposing, equally valued objectives and an ability to make trade-offs between these objectives. Thus, OTA wanted to 'rationalize' the industry but also retained a legitimating industry self-image running counter to that goal. Macro-level, trade-association ambivalence also had its roots in each regulated firm's view of regulation as both an irritating constraint and a welcome source of protection. And, often, OTA ambivalence mirrored a comparable inability of the larger transportation culture to decide whether certain things, like segmentation or cross-subsidization, were good or bad.

RATIONALITY: FINDING A CONSTITUENCY

OTA presented itself as the authoritative voice of all Ontario trucking, as an industry-wide, umbrella-type organization. It was politically important to OTA that all other players see it in these terms. Within OTA, this image performed affiliative, identifying, and legitimating functions. For both reasons, the association was not prepared to write off much of the industry, to link itself only with one subconstituency, and to accept a role as one among many specialized trucking groups. In fact, OTA spoke primarily for regulated truckers. Even within this regulated sphere, it tended to speak more for LTL, general-goods carriers, the so-called A category, than for other segments. OTA leaders tried to reconcile these practices with their all-embracing self-image by insisting that regulated truckers constituted the essential but highly vulnerable core of the industry and that A-category truckers were the core within the core. This argument worked only as long as the under-represented truckers gave it tacit assent. After 1970, when these under-represented truckers began to organize and issue their own policy viewpoints, OTA had to decide whether to preserve its earlier ecumenical legitimacy by drawing in these new groups and adopting fuzzier positions, or to preserve its earlier precise demands but accept a more restricted role as one among several trucking associations. OTA tried to retain the best of both options: it embraced the new groups but made only small changes in previous OTA policy. Thus, after 1970, it was less clear exactly whom the association represented. The small policy changes that did occur made OTA look less like a guild, made its positions somewhat more ambivalent or fuzzy. And perhaps these recently absorbed groups eventually will push the association to make even more policy changes.

In addition, how could OTA have consistently or rationally pursued a guild-like strategy, or any strategy based on the representation of a subconstituency, when so many trucking firms straddled internal boundaries and when firms so frequently redefined their location? Many private trucking units were also licensed, commercial carriers. Many A-category, general-goods, LTL carriers were also part of other segments. Because of OHTB's liberality, new firms were constantly being admitted to the regulated sphere, and regulated truckers were always shifting into new micro-markets. How could one defend the inner club of privileged licensees, in guild-like fashion, when new members kept pouring in? Even within the regulated sphere, the location of specific firms and the boundaries of each segment kept shifting. Because specific firms straddled the various segments, or hoped to as result of their subsequent efforts, no firm could unambiguously support an OTA strategy based on representing some segments rather than others.

INTEREST-GROUP RATIONALITY AND SYSTEM PATHOLOGIES

OTA thought it important to produce a clear, not very complex, relatively stable summary of 'what the truckers wanted.' Other players in the Ontario system demanded such a statement. It was important to OTA that other groups internalize an image of the trucking viewpoint, so they could anticipate truckers' reactions to various potential moves and thus avoid OTA's hostile reactions. To provide a stable, unmistakable message, which other players could easily internalize, OTA groups reduced its position to a shopping list of demands, presented in order of priority. Each demand was summarized, telegraphed, through a short identifying phrase like rigorous enforcement, board reform, or rate regulation. OTA's list changed remarkably little over many decades, partly a reflection of OTA's view that stable messages tended to be most effective, but also an indication of OTA's inability to resolve certain immobilizing contradictions in its own position. On many regulatory issues, OTA was boxed in, unable to move forward or backward, or was locked into place by its own ambiguity. Like many elements of the transportation culture, OTA's demands had a timeless, static, excessively familiar quality.

But the analogy with the prevailing transportation culture does not end there. OTA's program was transformed by some familiar, pathological processes: loss of meaning, ritualization, fundamentalism, fixation, reverse mobilization. Sometimes, in references to 'rigorous enforcement' or 'rate regulation,' the demand was deliberately kept vague because OTA was unable to formulate something more precise. In other cases, however, an entropic process occurred: an initially meaningful demand was given an identifying label but over a period of years the meaning behind this label diminished, so that it was increasingly unclear both to OTA and to others exactly what the association wanted. None the less, OTA became increasingly committed to these labels, increasingly prone to attribute vast importance and curative powers to them. Once put on OTA's official list, a demand was never reassessed, revised, or dropped. To a great extent, the demand became detached from its initial rationale, intent, and supportive evidence; it became a positively charged, not easily defined end in itself.

OTA often pursued less than rational strategies because affiliative and expressive factors became more important than political ones. Such intrusions help explain the above pathologies. When a group like OTA publicly commits itself to some idea, it establishes ownership or possession. Inevitably the group's self-esteem and reputation become linked to that demand. The group must engage in post-facto justification to bolster this commitment. In this reverse process, one's support for an idea follows from one's being publicly committed to it. If we cling to this commitment over a period of years, our support for it may grow, as we assign increasing importance and validity to it. How others respond to this demand becomes an important affiliative-symbolic indication of their attitude toward the demand and the group. Winning ministerial approval becomes a great expressive-affiliative victory, a demonstration of the influence and respect this group commands in the larger policy system. Whether the approved demand will solve problems or produce important market changes now seems less important. In fact, most of OTA's demands, had they been accepted, would not have dramatically altered the regulatory system or the trucking market, as the experience with rate filing demonstrated.

Nor can one say that all OTA's demands, even at their point of origin, were precise, well-considered defences of trucking interests. On private trucking, program enforcement, rates, and other regulatory issues, OTA had nothing to say, either because it had no useful solutions to propose, because it was ambiguous or boxed in, or because its preferred solution had been decisively rejected by government. Rather than remain silent on such important questions, the association focused on lesser, often irrelevant issues. Although initially broached for want of anything better to say, the demand subsequently became caught up in the normal evolutionary process, becoming increasingly important and valid, in OTA's view, with each succeeding year. Similarly, regulated truckers are supposed to fight private truckers, the railway, and other industry enemies. If one cannot find important differences, one must stage a fight over inconsequential issues. Thus, because of sublimation and ritual combat, attention often was diverted to unimportant, secondary issues.

CARTEL AND GUILD

Deregulators portrayed regulated trucking as a legally created cartel of licensees, protected from competition by the regulatory system and thus able to provide inadequate service at high prices. The trade association representing such an industry was seen as a guild, attempting to protect the special advantages and exclusive status of this inner clique. To protect this inner group from new competitive challenges and to preserve the scarcity, and hence the economic value, of licences, a guild would oppose allowing new members into the cartel. A guild would take the position that a licence, once issued, should become the property of the licensee, not a privilege held for a fixed period, subject to certain conditions, or capable of being revoked. A guild would want government to impose the fewest possible burdens (e.g., performance standards) on the licence holders, so that licensing would become more the allocation of a valuable good than part of a policing effort. Thus, a guild defines regulated truckers as its constituency and rationally defends the vested interests of these truckers.

To some extent OTA behaved like a guild. The association favoured a tough, restrictionist, entry-control policy, which would minimize the number of new firms allowed into the regulated sphere. It favoured a regulatory system based primarily on entry control rather than on performance standards or on government review of substantive rates. According to OTA, unless entry control reduced chronic oversupply and weeded out fly-by-night truckers, the reputable firms, despite their good intentions, would be compelled by the cutthroat competition to cheat on performance standards and on officially filed or approved rates. By contrast, rigorous entry control would curtail destructive competition and eliminate the incentive or need to cheat. Moreover, official rates and performance standards simply imposed additional burdens on the reputable firms, thus giving additional market advantage to the non-complying marginal firms.

In guild-like fashion, OTA wanted the licence to be the property of its holder, held in perpetuity and disposed of as he saw fit. Thus, OTA applauded the minister's pro forma renewal of all licences and the OHTB's willingness to approve the acquisition of any trucking company by another. A licensee could engage in long-term planning and maximize operational efficiency only if he felt secure about his long-term legal authority. If OHTB were to become more selective in its approval of acquisitions, if the board even delayed acquisitions through prolonged investigations, or if the minister merely announced he was considering the possibility of a more restrictive acquisitions policy, the capital value of all licences would be diminished. This would mean taking the truckers' property without compensation. It would be especially unfair to those licensees who had secured their present licences, and had paid dearly for them, through the company-acquisition route. (To an extent, one opposed new entrants in order to maintain the capital value of one's licence. There were many cases in which a trucker successfully opposed entry by an applicant and later sold his company, and its licence, to that same applicant.)

Because no one could publicly oppose tough performance standards, OTA usually endorsed such standards in principle but could always find some reason why the principle should not be implemented or the standard enforced. In principle, the minister should deal severely with licensees who violated regulations or traffic legislation; but, at the same time, a serious review of each firm's application for renewal might open the door to arbitrary or 'political' decision making on the minister's part. Compelling drivers to submit to periodic medical examinations made sense, but it might inhibit the trucker's ability to find additional drivers during peak seasons. In principle, OTA did not oppose a regulation requiring all trucks to be inspected every six months; but government inspectors might remove vehicles from the road during busy periods on the basis of trivial faults; or the governing party might exploit the patronage possibilities of such an inspection program by insisting that all trucks be repaired by cabinet-designated companies. Tougher performance standards were desirable, OTA said, but not if they applied only to PCV licensed truckers, thus exempting and thus giving new market advantages to private truckers.

As a guild, OTA consistently wanted the law to protect regulated truckers from various external threats. Restrictive entry control was pointless unless one also adopted a tough stance on grey- or black-market practices, otherwise rejected applicants simply would proceed with the unauthorized activity. The minister must clarify legal language and close legal loopholes so that firms could not carry on a commercial trucking operation by pretending to be lessors or private truckers. To shrink the peripheral sector, the source of much grey- and black-market activity, OTA wanted the minister to reduce or eliminate the list of exempt goods and to assume jurisdiction over intramunicipal trucking. The minister must control or stifle many of the newer roles and practices – freight forwarders, brokers, leasing – where these permitted shippers to circumvent regulated truckers; but this should be done in a way that did not inhibit the regulated trucker's ability to invoke these newer practices or roles for his own purposes.

RATIONALIZING THE INDUSTRY

The trucking industry was developed, in the years before the Second World War, by a group of free-wheeling, rugged individualists, who scrambled for customers in an aggressive, not always scrupulous manner. The early trucking firm relied much more on the intuition and drive of its founder than on formal management techniques or written records. Rather than have trucks sit idle, these early truckers grabbed at any freight, freely undercutting the rates charged by other truckers and often making extravagant, unattainable promises on delivery time. The terms of specific transactions, which emerged from shipper/trucker negotiations, were jealously guarded secrets, rarely committed to writing. Shippers and truckers both emphasized the importance of particularist ties to reputable firms and long-time customers; both sides emphasized unofficial links based on trust, reputation, and personal rapport. Basing transactions on informal, secret negotiations was important to both sides because it permitted truckers to retain loyal customers with special concessions (which if revealed might be considered 'discrimination'); it permitted shippers to bargain down rates by playing one trucker off against another; and it permitted the trucker to exceed his licensed authority or violate some aspect of provincial regulations if this were necessary to order to close the deal. Such informal agreements, however, produced frequent shipper/trucker conflict over what had been agreed to and left the shipper defenceless against irresponsible trucking practices. For many decades, the major trade associations, the trade journals, and later the tariff bureaux – trade associations that specialized in rate definition – sought a greater professionalization and 'rationalization' of the industry. This viewpoint was both prescriptive and descriptive; it urged more rationalization but also claimed that the industry, in fact, was moving rapidly toward this goal. Although one would need regulation – for example, rate filing and mandatory bills of lading – to help rationalize the industry, the trade associations hoped to achieve much of this goal through private, intra-industry effort. One had to change the thinking and practices of each trucking firm.

The old buccaneering tactics and 'seat of the pants' decison-making must give way to sophisticated management techniques and formalized trucker/shipper transactions. The old trucking firm was preoccupied with daily crises and short-term survival; the new firm must take the longer-run view. The new firm must keep accurate, detailed records, adopt proper accounting and auditing procedures, carry adequate cargo insurance, and promptly process shipper claims on lost or damaged goods. It must realize that small investments in regular vehicle maintenance save money in the long run, while running vehicles into the ground constitutes a false economy. Rather than grab any and all available freight, each firm should use cost data to decide what kind of service that firm could best offer, that is, should seek out and occupy that firm's proper market niche. Segmentation presumably was evidence of each firm's more sophisticated pursuit of such niche-seeking strategies, that is, evidence of growing industry rationalization.

Instead of quoting prices in an ad hoc manner or negotiating price commitments with shippers on a case-by-case basis, each trucking firm should issue a written rate schedule and should consistently adhere to that schedule in specific transactions. Thus, shippers would be given a large amount of information in a condensed format and could engage in intelligent comparative shopping with minimum effort. Although the shipper lost the ability to secure special deals, he would be spared negotiation costs; he would know what his rivals were paying; and he would know he was not being discriminated against. If the full details of each transaction were embodied in a written, standard-form bill of lading, gypsy truckers would be less able to make unrealistic promises, all truckers could be more effectively held to their promises, and there would be much less shipper/trucker conflict over what had been agreed to.

In the early years, truckers had set rates in an ad hoc, intuitive manner, responding to whatever specific rates shippers would tolerate, sometimes responding to what the railways were charging. After 1945, truckers simply applied increments to these traditional rates in line with increases in operating costs. The trade associations and tariff bureaux wanted trucking firms to replace these historic, 'unscientific' rates with more 'rational,' cost-based rates. With access to good information on his own operating costs, no trucker would inadvertently carry goods at less than compensatory rates. And truckers must be made to understand that deliberately carrying goods at non-compensatory rates, while producing immediate revenue, was ultimately suicidal. As the transportation culture had always insisted, if rates reflected the firm's operating costs in providing that service – not the historic, irrational rates, and not the shipper's bargaining power – each trucking firm would arrive in its proper niche, driving out of this niche the higher-cost, less-efficient firms. Because the operating costs for a given kind of trip would not vary enormously from one firm to another, and because all firms should be basing rates on costs, various firms should be able to arrive at a common price for each trip and thus produce a single industry-wide rate schedule. To erase the offer-any-price tradition and to stabilize the 'soft' or falling prices this tradition produced, the tariff bureau would recommend the rational, cost-based rate for each type of service and would urge trucking firms to adopt this common rate schedule.

This rationalization objective seemed largely compatible with a guild-like strategy. Rationalization presumably meant an industry made up of fewer, larger, more-formalized, more-professionalized firms; it would squeeze out those undercapitalized, dad-and-son firms that allegedly created so much of the industry's volatility and destructive competition. To deregulators, rationalization simply meant less competition and more price collusion among regulated truckers, made possible and encouraged by the regulatory framework. The intent of the tariff bureau, it seemed, was to fix prices at artificially high levels and to exert pressure on trucking firms that might want to offer lower, more defensible prices. Because all provinces required trucking firms to submit a rate schedule and allowed a tariff bureau to submit a common schedule for many firms, regulation strengthened the bureau's position and thus abetted collusion.

In fact, the Ontario trucking industry did not consistently and unambiguously advocate or practice industry rationalization. For one thing, rationalization ran counter to the industry's self-defining, self-legitimating imagery. In an economy increasingly dominated by giant firms and administered markets, trucking presumably was one of the last refuges of the independent entrepreneur, the small firm, and truly competitive capitalism. In the post-war period, OTA and the national association had devoted most of their resources to a fight against railway acquisitions of trucking companies, primarily to preserve the decentralized, small-firm character of this industry. In this imagery, the one-truck, dad-and-son firm emerged as the 'Canadian small businessman' and a hero, rather than a rate chiseler, fly-by-night, or gypsy. But this was only one source of ambivalence on the rationalization question.

RATIONALIZATION AND THE TWO CULTURES

It was tactically convenient for OTA to portray the industry as one rapidly evolving toward greater professionalization, because one could then deflect all the shippers' criticisms onto those old-fashioned, disappearing firms. But this was an inaccurate picture of the industry. Even in the later 1980s, the Ontario industry still was dominated by the small, unprofessionalized firm and by the earlier, aggressively individualist ethos. Regulated truckers, who formed OTA's primary constituency, saw the rationalizing recommendations as legitimate, grounded in the transportation culture, and probably serving the long-term best interests of the industry. As participants in OTA, as 'good citizens' within the industry, individual trucking firms felt they must provide strong, expressive-rhetorical support for such recommendations. But in their daily operations and transactions, they clung to traditional, pre-rationalized practices. Truckers could see the dangers of unbridled competition and believed in the need for more interfirm co-operation, but each firm insisted on preserving a completely free hand in its own market transactions. Most firms preserved an informal management style, kept few records, believed that written records invited scrutiny and that scrutiny led to more outside interference. Feisty, independent truckers often were as suspicious of trucking associations as of government, as little inclined to have their records seen by tariff bureaux and other truckers as by bureaucrats. The result was a vertical disconnection between rhetoric and practice, between an official and underground culture. OTA members preached but did not practice rationalization. And one could not be sure they really wanted what they preached.

All truckers officially favoured a formalization of shipper/trucker transactions, which meant each trucker's adherence to filed rates and the mandatory use of an all-inclusive bill of lading, as required in the PCV Act. At the same time both shippers and truckers wanted to preserve their negotiating freedom and the secrecy of their dealings. And formalization, although the correct value, was important to some segments but not others. Written bills were especially useful for listing each item in a heterogeneous shipment or in cases involving unusual handling or delivery instructions; but the bill was less important to TL truckers carrying bulk freight, like oil or milk. OTA argued that written bills would help government hold shippers liable for overloaded trucks, but this liability could not be fixed on LTL shippers. For all these reasons, written bills were not consistently used; and, when used, they often excluded certain verbal understandings.

A comparable truckers' ambivalence on rate-setting seriously undermined any attempt to secure the kind of interfirm co-operation that tariff bureaux favoured and deregulators deplored. Truckers officially endorsed but did not practice such co-operation. About one-third of the regulated trucking firms refused to join any bureau. Firms that were bureau members often opted out ('flagged out') of the bureau's common schedule and published their own instead. Although it tried to discourage such opting out, the bureau's only weapon was peer disapproval, which meant very little to the independent-minded truckers. Furthermore, even those bureau members that officially adopted the bureau's common rate schedule freely departed from it in practice. Official adoption was more a reaffirmation of correct values, 'being a good citizen of the trucking community,' than a binding promise about the firm's future conduct. Whenever the Ontario industry attempted a co-ordinated, general rate increase, some firms would seek a market advantage by clinging to the old, lower rates, and, under pressure from the shippers, other trucking firms would eventually break ranks and retreat to the old rates, at least for a while.

Although regulated truckers preached the virtues of rigid adherence to filed rates, the published rate schedule of any trucking firm was little more than a useful beginning point for negotiations. In trucking, where one is not selling a standard item, adherence to filed rates and to common rate schedules is especially difficult to monitor, by either government, trade associations, or participating truckers. Even if the published rate was adhered to, truckers could provide rate reductions in the form of service concessions – for example, concessions on delivery time or the provision of free ancillary services, like storage, crating and uncrating, installation. If excluded from a written bill of lading, these reductions would remain hidden. Furthermore, no regulated trucking firm would be bound inflexibly to its filed rates, whether part of a common schedule or not, as long as it had to compete against non-filing peripheral-sector firms, able to offer any rates they wished.

In addition, no trucker would be bound to his filed rates because many shippers had great bargaining power, expected something better than the official rates, and could shop around until they secured it. The image of a cartelized industry exploiting defenceless shippers, while sometimes appropriate to rail, simply did not fit trucking. There were too many trucking firms, both legal and illegal, for shippers to select from. Many shippers had rail and private-trucking options. And many small trucking firms were dependent on the orders of a few large shippers. Contrary to the rail experience, when trucking rates discriminated, when truckers gave some shippers a much better deal than others, it was usually because large shipping firms had been able to intimidate smaller, weaker trucking firms.

There was a dual culture at work in the shippers' camp as well. As participants in their trade associations and in the deregulation debate, shipping companies portrayed themselves as the victims of price collusion by a trucking cartel; but in finding a trucker to move its goods, no shipping firm would be foolish enough to take a trucking firm's filed rate as the last word, to think truckers capable of maintaining a united front on a common rate schedule, or to underrate the shipping firm's considerable ability to bargain down trucking prices. Because of this bargaining power, the shippers, like the truckers, preached but resisted the formalization of transactions.

In short, the deregulators' price-collusion model was fantasy. The deregulation debate proceeded on the basis of an unreal, idealized version of market transactions partly because the real version involved illegitimate and sometimes illegal practices, which cast very little favourable light on truckers, shippers, or government officials. Trucking prices, which were supposed to be cost-based and non-discriminatory, in fact were very responsive to the shipper's bargaining power. Truckers often exceeded their licensed authority or violated some regulation in order to meet shipper demands. Neither shippers nor truckers were eager to talk about the extent to which they departed from a trucker's filed rates; nor did the government want to discuss why it freely allowed these and other violations.

RATIONALIZATION AND REGULATION

Deregulators said that OTA wanted to use provincial regulations as an instrument of industry rationalization. For example, if the government adopted OTA's policy of tough entry control linked to carte blanche on company acquisitions, firms would seek entry or expansion mainly through the acquisitions rather than the licence-application route, with a resulting trend toward fewer, larger firms. Many of the stronger, larger, more-professionalized trucking firms did, in fact, favour using higher performance standards (e.g., on vehicle maintenance or cargo insurance) as a device to impose new, perhaps intolerable operating costs on the small marginal firms and thus to drive them from the market. Some of these firms said that, in place of OTA's traditional emphasis on tough entry control as a solution to the chronic oversupply problem, driving out disreputable firms through higher standards was a far better solution.

But, because OTA and most of its members did not unambiguously favour industry rationalization, they were similarly ambivalent about using government to achieve that aim. Trucking must be rationalized but it must also be preserved as an industry of loners and independents, an industry where one person with a bit of capital still could succeed. OTA could not decide whether these small marginal firms were rate chisellers, fly-by-nights, and dispensable victims, as suggested in the rationalization model, or whether they were the last stand of competitive capitalism. OTA's position on performance standards differed markedly from that taken by many large firms. To preserve the small-firm character of trucking, OTA urged the minister to adopt very modest standards, which even the most frail, most marginal trucking firm could meet. OTA advocated rationalization but it also strongly opposed 'concentrated ownership' in trucking; it insisted there were dangerous signs of growing concentration, and it urged the minister to halt this frightening trend.   .

Apart from its ambivalence on the rationalization question, OTA also had difficulty telling the minister exactly how he was to fight concentrated ownership. OTA favoured the end but not any of the means; it wanted an anti-concentration policy, but any of the specific steps one might take to achieve this objective seemed to create new, unwanted restraints on truckers. The minister might discourage increases in firm size by restricting one company's acquisition of another, but such restrictions would interfere with the licensee's property rights and deflate the capital value of current licences. OHTB could actually use the authority it had to write limits on fleet size into each firm's licence; but such limits would compel each firm to seek board approval every time it wanted to buy a truck.

WHAT KIND OF REGULATORY SYSTEM?

Ambivalence also marked OTA's stand on the central concept of 'regulation.' The association, of course, favoured regulation and usually advocated more of it. Like many other groups, OTA assumed that the program had begun with some clear, elaborate intent but had yielded minimal, disappointing results. Extending this system, providing for more regulation, would give better protection to both truckers and shippers and would help fulfil the initial objectives. On just as many other occasions, however, OTA portrayed the Ontario industry as over-regulated, smothered in red tape, harassed by snooping bureaucrats, burdened with demands not made of other truckers. One must avoid stifling, railway-type regulation in which government would define a fair rate of return on investment and wind up second-guessing the truckers' daily operating decisions. Like the minister, OTA seemed worried about the tar-baby effect. Bureaucratic surveillance, if encouraged, generated its own momentum and inevitably led to all-pervasive regulation. For this reason, regulated truckers vehemently resisted any attempt to activate the PCV Act's 'regular reporting' clause. So strongly did truckers feel about this issue that many opposed OTA's campaigns to improve record keeping, on the grounds that, if a firm kept better written records, the government would be more likely to examine them.

Thus, expanded regulation meant better protection but it also was a dangerous opening wedge for pervasive, railway-type regulation. The truckers wanted more effective regulation but at arm's length, better protection but without any of the legal restraints or government surveillance necessary to secure that protection. The minister was wrong to remain content with so frail and minimal a system; but, if he expanded the system, it would not be long before he would be looking over the shoulder of every Ontario trucker.

OTA decided to fight every application coming before the board and to assist any member firm fighting any application. Where regulated firms were fending off applications from firms seeking entry into the regulated sphere, such a blanket opposition to favourable board action was consistent with a guild-like role. The deregulation debate proceeded as if this type of case dominated the board's agenda. But the great majority of cases involved already-licensed truckers seeking expanded authority, involved questions about how micro-markets should be allocated within the regulated camp. Thus, in most cases, the OTA fought against an application submitted by a regulated trucker, often an OTA member. OTA had difficulty defining a policy position on this type of case because each trucking firm held inconsistent, ambivalent goals: 'freedom to expand' when that firm was making the application, 'protection and security' when others were applying. The association opted for a policy of blanket opposition to all applications, apparently in order to protect smaller, weak firms from being swallowed up and to preserve the boundaries separating the industry's various segments, on the assumption that segmentation had produced a highly efficient, role-differentiated industry. OTA would fight all applications in order to resist growing concentration of ownership and to preserve the segmented, small-firm character of the industry, even though this approach ran counter to its emphasis on rationalization. OTA's pronouncements never clarified whether trucking still was a volatile if not chaotic industry, very much in need of rationalization, or whether segmentation had already achieved much of this rationalization. Nor was it clear whether rationalization meant fewer, larger firms or each small firm in its appropriate small niche.

Ambivalence also characterized OTA's repeated, high-priority demand for 'better enforcement.' As OTA accurately alleged, the freedom with which black and grey marketeers operated throughout Ontario critically undermined the effectiveness of the regulatory system. But the truckers were not prepared to have their records examined or government officials visit their premises. And intensified roadside examinations were less likely to catch illegals than regulated truckers exceeding the terms of their licences. In this respect, OTA was an odd guild. Although alarmed about the threat posed by leasing, brokers, freight forwarders, or grey- and black-market practices, regulated truckers could not bring themselves to accept the degree of 'government interference' required for effective regulation of these elements.

Moreover, how could a licensing system provide security or protection to any regulated truckers unless licensing conditions were enforced on all other regulated truckers? OTA said that licences with detailed, confining terms provided regulated truckers with essential protection; but in the next breath OTA would accuse the minister of nit-picking if he charged a trucker with exceeding his licensed authority; or OTA would tell the minister that regulated firms often exceeded their authority because the terms of licences were unreasonably confining. In cases coming before the board, OTA often helped an applicant and an opposing firm work out a carefully constructed compromise, designed to minimize the new applicant's intrusion on the licensee's present authority; but the following week OTA would argue against any ministerial attempt to enforce the terms of this negotiated agreement. Of course, OTA said, a firm that repeatedly violated the law did not deserve to have its licence renewed; but initiating a policy of selective licence renewal would open the door to arbitrary, political decision making on the minister's part.

OTA wanted to protect licensees from unlicensed firms seeking entry into the regulated sphere. But, because of the board's permissive practices, most applicants won some portion of what they wanted, and the regulated sphere steadily expanded. For OTA, yesterday's applicant-opponent became today's licensed trucker and OTA member. The association would oppose the admission of new entrants or might help arrange a compromise that allowed them into the club only under highly circumscribed conditions; but, once admitted, the new firm became a full-fledged member, fully covered by OTA's insistence that all licences should be renewed automatically and that no serious effort be made to enforce the limiting terms of any licence.

Because it opposed all applications but embraced all successful applicants, OTA had difficulty phrasing its description of trucking service. Generally, OTA said, the industry had always been characterized by 'oversupply.' But, when talking about a specific micro-market, OTA always said that the present level of service was 'just right.' To say there was oversupply in a micro-market would imply that some of the firms now in this micro-market should not have been given licences, which was contrary to OTA's policy of defending every licensed firm, including very recent entrants. Having fought an application on the grounds that existing service in a given micro-market was just right, and having lost the battle, the OTA then had to say that the new level of service, with the new entrant admitted, also was just right.

BOARD REFORM

OTA consistently advocated a 'strong-board/weak-minister' plan. It applauded the early decision to make the board the de facto licensing body. It wanted to go further and have the minister transfer to the board his authority to issue regulations and enforce the PCV Act. The OTA position was derived largely from the prevailing culture's preference for independent boards. The decisions of such boards were viewed as 'fair and impartial,' ministerial decisions as 'political,' that is, particularist, exchange-based, patron/client oriented. OTA's assumptions about ministerial decision-making were so framed that they could never be challenged by evidence. If there was no sign of 'politics,' the *potential* always remained. Thus OTA wanted OHTB to acquire the power to renew licences because the minister, even though he automatically renewed every licence, *might* activate his discretionary power some day and use it for patron/client purposes.

But, as we noted in the previous chapter, the truckers found the board to be mysterious, arbitrary, and 'political.' By contrast, the Minister more consistently supported OTA positions on regulatory issues, like highway finance or closing regulatory loopholes; and on all issues his behaviour was more patterned, more easily interpreted, more predictable. Somehow the truckers had to reconcile their culture with their specific-level experience, their strong-board preference with evidence of the board's disappointing performance. One solution was to blame the board's shortcomings on the minister, more specifically on his failure to issue a definitive trucking policy, to define the 'public necessity' criterion, or to impose a restrictive entry-control policy on the board. Another solution was to hedge one's demand for a full transfer of ministerial powers. Because the board was thought to be too generous in granting applications, OTA did not want to strip the minister of his power to refuse a licence in the face of a favourable board decision. But neither did OTA urge the minister to use this power.

Still another solution was to urge that the minister transfer his power not to the present board but to a new, reformed one. 'Board reform,' although it became a high-priority OTA demand, was one of those multivalent, impossible-to-define symbols; it was a pseudo-demand, less a request for some precise ministerial action than an expression of OTA's unhappiness with the existing board. It never was clear what direction reform should take. Sometimes OTA said that the board should become more of an aggressive, expert, fact-determining, micro-market planner. At the same time, OTA urged the board to behave more like a court, emphasizing fair procedures, impartially hearing evidence, giving reasons for decisions, and basing decisions on written precedents. But a court-like board would become more a passive, non-expert recipient of evidence than an economic planner; in fact, OHTB used judicial imagery as an explanation of why it did not make more of an effort to investigate or plan. After 1975, it became clear that, if there were to be any research or economic planning related to trucking, it would emerge from the ministry's new office on trucking policy; but OTA still insisted that this should be OHTB's job, not the ministry's. On still other occasions OTA said that OHTB need not be court or planner. Because everyone knows that trucking is characterized by excessive capacity, OTA said, the board should assume the existence of at least adequate service in any micro-market. An applicant should be required to prove that currently licensed firms were *unable* to remedy any existing service inadequacies or to prove that the granting of an application would inflict *no* substantial economic harm on currently licensed firms. Because such assertions would be impossible to prove, the board could skip the judicial formalities, skip the expert fact finding, and just provide quick rejections.

'RATE REGULATION'

OTA's position on rates, like many of its other stands, was characterized by approach-avoidance, a wish to achieve a certain objective but an unwillingness to accept any of the specific measures that would bring one closer to that goal. Because the industry seemed unable to co-ordinate rates through private, voluntary action, most truckers thought that some legal enforcement of collectively established rates, especially of rate floors, was a necessary solution to the rate softness problem. But no trucker wanted the government to begin reviewing the substantive rates proposed. To judge whether rates were fair, compensatory, or non-discriminatory, government would have to define fair-profit levels in trucking and would soon be assessing how efficiently specific firms were run. It was apparent from other provinces that rate review did not lead government to engage in pervasive second-guessing, that government would not even attempt a serious review of private rate setting in such a decentralized, small-firm industry. None the less, OTA's fears remained.

For OTA the solution to the rate softness problem was to have the industry prepare its own rates and have the minister enforce, but not review, these rates. As early as 1932, however, the minister roundly rejected this plan as an improper delegation of public authority to a private body. With its key demand rejected, OTA had great difficulty finding a second-best solution. Unable to pursue its central goal but unwilling to remain silent on so important an issue, OTA at first disguised its difficulty by issuing a vague call for 'rate regulation' and then, in the late 1930s, adopted a demand for rate filing. By binding truckers to an observance of their own published rates, filing would eliminate the informal, shipper/trucker bargaining that so often extracted below-standard rates from truckers; but filing would not involve government in rate review. As it renewed its rate-filing request for each of twenty-five years, OTA assigned growing importance, curative powers, and urgency to this proposal. Still, when the minister officially adopted filing in 1963, many OTA members denounced the move as wholesale, unconscionable government intrusion into the daily lives of trucking managers.

The subsequent experience with filing, however, demonstrated that it achieved too little, not that it intruded too much. The filing requirement did not prevent any trucker from submitting an official schedule that undercut other firms. It bound a trucker to his original schedule for no more than the thirty-day period needed to process an amendment. Moreover, filing was no better enforced than other parts of the regulatory system. To compete against the peripheral-sector firms, who retained their anonymity and did not file, the filing truckers freely departed from their filed schedules. Having spent thirty years attributing vast importance to the adoption of a filing requirement, OTA leaders felt obliged to treat the new requirement as a great success; but, by the late 1960s, many truckers admitted that filing had failed completely to solve the soft rates problem. In fact, by imposing one more burden on the 'reputable,' regulated truckers, filing merely augmented the market advantages of peripheral-sector firms. To go beyond filing, however, meant involving the government in rate review, a move most truckers strongly opposed. Although the association continued to call for 'rate regulation,' it no longer had a policy or set of demands on the rates issue.

THE THREAT OF PRIVATE TRUCKING

In its attempts to defend regulated truckers from the threat of private trucking, OTA fought its major campaign in the 1930s, lost in a resounding manner, and then, in line with its experience on the rates issue, had great difficulty finding a plausible fall-back position. According to OTA, private trucking units should be required to secure an operator's licence and to meet a 'public necessity' test, and they should be subjected to the same burdens regulation imposed on commercial truckers. Virtually every business association and every business firm in Ontario opposed this plan. They were aghast at the notion that a board might deny some shippers the authority to transport their own goods, which seemed to them one of business's inviolable rights. The minister agreed and promised that Ontario would never impose constraints on private trucking, a position confirmed by many ministers thereafter.

Private truckers often sought commercial, PCV licences, usually as a means of filling trucks on the back haul. OTA urged the province to reject all such applications, to establish a wall between private and commercial trucking. It was unfair to have private truckers compete against commercial carriers in a commercial market, OTA said, because the private unit was subsidized by its parent, shipping company or at least was not required to generate a normal return on investment. This battle also was won by the private truckers. The minister told the board to treat private-trucking units seeking commercial licences like all other applicants – in effect, to ignore the private vs commercial distinction in hearing any application.

Convinced it could not remain silent, and after groping about for something to say, OTA eventually decided that private truckers at least should be registered, listed, identified. Such a plan would allow government to spread the same burdens, mainly the licence fees and the performance standards, on both commercial and private truckers; and it would help PCV inspectors flush out the black- or grey-market truckers who disguised themselves as private truckers but who probably would not register as such. OTA became increasingly enthusiastic about the registration solution, the shipping associations eventually accepted OTA's exaggerated view of its importance, and a dramatic twenty-year debate ensued. Although registration was never approved, its adoption probably would have had a negligible effect. Neither the PCV Act's minimal, unenforced performance standards, nor the PCV operators' licence fee, about $1000 per vehicle per year in the late 1980s, were a serious burden on regulated truckers; and it is unlikely that a registry of private truckers would have

spurred on the government's lack-lustre enforcement efforts. The registration plan was important not because it would have had real market
consequences but because both sides needed an issue to contest, because
OTA's overattribution invited a response in kind, because this issue
provided a suitable arena for ritual combat.

The great 1970s debate on 'intercorporate trucking' also was ritual
combat. Suppose one firm carried the goods belonging to another firm and
received payment for this service, but the two firms were subsidiaries of a
common parent or there were a significant overlap, say 50 per cent, in the
ownership of these two firms. Shipping associations said such trucking
transactions should be treated as intracorporate, private ones; OTA would
concede private status only where there were a 100 per cent overlap in
ownership between the two firms; and the minister settled on a compromise
90 per cent overlap rule. But the whole issue affected only a very small
number of firms in Ontario. This was largely a Canadian re-enactment of a
recent American debate on the same issue.

While these great debates raged, OTA quietly won a far more significant
victory over private truckers: a PCV Act amendment that restricted the
shippers' ability to lease vehicles and drivers or draw on the services of
owner operators. Of course, this OTA victory would have been far more
important if the government had any intention of enforcing the amendments. None the less, the high drama involved in ritual combat distracted
the shippers' attention from this less exciting but more important issue.

LICENCE CATEGORIES AND MARKET SEGMENTATION

In response to pressure from truckers, the regulatory system spawned a set
of licence categories, designed both to reflect and strengthen the segmented
character of the industry. Each successful applicant received a licence of a
certain type: for example, category A for LTL, general-goods carriers;
category C for TL, for-hire carriers; category D for TL, contract carriers.
Beginning around 1950, a new letter was added for each of the emerging
specialties, for dump trucks, movers of household effects, cement mixers,
truckers specializing in dangerous goods, in dairy products, petroleum,
and so on. Segmentation presumably produced an efficient, rational pattern
of specialization, and letter categories were justified as a way of giving
each segment better protection against cross-overs. With the category
system in place, regulated truckers pressed for more-precise definitions
of each category, so that trucking firms could not exploit ambiguities or
nibble away at boundaries. For example, a contract carrier who relied on

a large number of short-term contracts was edging into the for-hire segment, and a TL trucker carrying goods from one shipper to different consignees was edging into the LTL segment, all of which had to be stopped through tougher legal language.

Regulated truckers greatly overstated the importance of this category system and devoted an inordinate amount of attention to its development. If the goal were to minimize cross-overs, the specific terms of each licence did this far more effectively than a category system. OTA said a category system would be an efficient way for the minister to issue regulations covering an entire category, rather than write restraints into each licence; but the minister had shown little interest in using his regulatory powers and he issued very few category-related regulations.

Regulated truckers assigned high priority to the category system partly because it was a way in which the various segments could engage in political conflict. As noted earlier, the various segments saw themselves battling for aggregate trucking demand and thought that restraints on one segment would produce demand spillover into other segments. Thus, each segment wanted the legal boundaries drawn in a way that gave more scope to its category and less to others. Because OTA, and to an extent the minister, viewed the A-category, LTL, general-goods carriers as a particularly important, versatile segment, providing the more essential service and often serving unattractive, small-shipment, short-trip markets, this A-category segment proved particularly effective in securing legal restraints on the operations of other categories and in winning jurisdictional arguments. But because the basic demand-spillover assumption was refuted by most of the hard evidence, this intersegmental conflict and the resulting restraints on various categories probably had little impact on market share.

The categories also were important for affiliative-symbolic reasons. A separate letter status conferred recognition, legitimacy, and respect on that segment. To deny this letter status or to permit encroachments was to suggest that any inexpert trucking firm with idle capacity could drift into this segment and adequately serve it, an insult to all the experienced, specialized truckers operating in the segment.

But the regulated truckers' attitude toward this letter-category system, like their attitude toward segmentation, was ambivalent. Having justified the system on the grounds that one must confine truckers to separate spheres, most truckers then urged that the board grant multiple-category authorizations to firms, in effect allowing firms to cross or straddle segment boundaries. (Multiple authorization was most strongly supported by the general-goods LTL carriers, because, as we noted in chapter 3, they were better protected by natural economic barriers and thus had less need for legal restraints on cross-overs.) Many truckers argued that allowing only one letter category to a firm would produce an excessively fragmented or segmented market, would produce inefficient, insufficiently large trucking firms. Moreover, multiple authorization would allow a firm to straddle attractive and unattractive markets and to cross-subsidize the latter. Thus segmentation was both good and bad; one needed a category system to reinforce it but also needed multiple authorization to weaken it. Once the board began to issue multiple-category licences, the letter categories lost most of their capacity to reinforce segmentation. None the less, OTA praised the great achievements of this category system; while the deregulators, equally off target, emphasized how these categories created excessively fragmented, inefficient micro-markets.

NEW DEPARTURES?

For more than fifty years, OTA's program, like the larger transportation culture, had a static, timeless, unquestioned character. This frozen quality was partly the product of a ritualization process that turned precise, useful demands into vague, charged, ends in themselves. As well, regulated truckers were boxed in and unable to move, unhappy with the minimal protection provided by a frail regulatory system but unwilling to accept the concomitants of a seriously enforced, more intrusive system. After 1970, demand for trucking levelled off, and profit margins waned. In response, regulated truckers became increasingly alarmed about the threats posed by grey and black marketeers and American truckers; and they became increasingly unhappy with a regulatory system that provided so little protection against these threats. By the mid 1970s, regulated truckers seemed ready to break with the past and accept a more intrusive system. To resist American encroachments, the association now seemed ready to have OHTB use discretion in approving acquisitions. Perhaps the board should ban the sale of dormant licences. OTA now argued that truckers should be allowed to challenge another trucker's filed rates, presumably for being too low, even if this meant empowering government to review the substantive fairness of filed rates.

But any rethinking of prior positions was brought to a sudden halt by the deregulation challenge. In response to this challenge, OTA switched back to an uncritical, all-out defence of the existing program, attributing sweeping, unreal achievements to that program. Those people who tried to reform regulation during the 1980s, an effort described in the following chapter, wondered why truckers should cling to such an ineffective system. The reformers hoped that OTA would endorse a new, less ambitious but more seriously enforced program, one that promised less protection but delivered what it promised. Although helping to define this new system, the association eventually decided to fight it, mainly because of the truckers' usual inertia or 'conservatism.' Confronted with change and uncertainty, regulated truckers again fell back on the familiar, again opted for the known evil.

7

The Structure of a Policy System

People who regularly interact on matters relating to a given policy will tend to form a structured system. By identifying those parties whose interests, demands, and reactions should be taken into account, the players give this system a boundary. The behaviour of key players will be shaped into identifiable roles; interaction among the key players will take on a stable, patterned form. A policy system usually develops its own insiders' language or jargon and its own distinctive rituals. Such a system also develops its own policy culture, a set of common, standard beliefs about the nature of the policy problem and the usefulness of various solutions. Systemness of this sort produces not consensus but rather clarity and predictability. Conflict is a major component of these policy systems, but conflict is channelled, patterned, processed. In fact, the system facilitates conflict by helping us appreciate the stakes, players, moves, and outcomes.

A policy system, any social system, consists of visible events and actions, a process level, which occur within the controlling context of higher-level, stable understandings. In cybernetic hierarchies there is a two-way flow of influence between structure and process. In other words, a policy system is in part an individualistic, aggregative structure, built from the bottom up, and in part an organic or solidary system, in which higher-level structures regulate individual, specific-level conduct in top-down fashion. The system's outcomes, the policies pursued, result from both bottom-up and top-down forces.

To clarify the argument, let us assume for the moment that systems result only from aggregative, bottom-up forces. Under such circumstances, players enter the system in order to pursue extra-systemic, self-interested objectives, work the system to their own advantage, and expect the system to produce useful pay-offs for its member players. The system is an arena, playing-field, or market. System outcomes – e.g., policies – are the unplanned, aggregate result of many individual moves; and the system often is a neutral, accurate registrant of these moves. Higher-level structures are intentional creations, the outcomes of bottom-up influences and process-level moves. In the political game, for example, we deliberately construct alliances, reputations, rapport, obligations, credit. Structures exist because they serve the interests of system members; and as system members we adopt a cold, calculative view of such structures, supporting them when they serve our interests, changing them or exiting from the system when they no longer do so. As long as the structures do serve our interests, however, we recognize the need to maintain some differentiation between levels; for example, we avoid destroying a long-term relationship merely to gain some temporary tactical advantage.

At the same time, as system members we come to value the standard rules, culture, and patterns as more than merely means to our individualistic ends. We form attachments and diffuse loyalties, invest in preserving the structure, resist changee, and repel outsiders. The higher-level culture is not merely a convenient set of rules regulating a contest – no hitting below the belt, no use of poison gas; the culture defines for us what objectives are worth pursuing, what our 'real' needs and interests are. To an extent we play the game in order to realize personal, self-interested objectives defined outside the game; to an extent our objectives emerge from the game's higher-level structure. As well, there are certain distinctive problems involved in organizing any game, certain macro-level functional problems that have to be solved. The following discussion, for example, considers some of the macro-level problems involved in organizing complex interest-group interaction. The rules often reflect these systemic needs and thus represent more than convenient instruments for the pursuit of personal advantage.

Process-level power is the ability to get other people to do what we want in specific situations. We make gains or score victories while playing the game. Structure-level power is the ability to define or change the conditions under which the game is played. At the process level, players' successes may reflect the extra-systemic resources and commitment, the 'purchasing power,' they bring to the game and how cleverly they use these resources; and the system registers these varying degrees of player commitment or skill. But the system also creates and allocates structure-level power, the ability to define or change the ground rules and basic assumptions. The ability to define the premises on which others proceed – for example, the ability of the policy professionals to shape the transportation culture – is formidable power, far more important than the ability to offer inducements, threats, or arguments in specific situations.

The problem with the deregulators' micro-economic approach to policy failure, with a great deal of political realism, and with most narrative, story-like accounts of policy making is that they get too close to events, over-emphasize the process, and perceive little more than process-level power. As a result they overstate the amount of conflict, the unpredictability of outcomes, and the extent to which power is dispersed; they often miss the latent understandings that give these events an underlying pattern and fail to appreciate the power of those who can shape such understandings. This type of approach, if it deals at all with higher-level structures, treats them solely as the outcome of bottom-up aggregative forces.

THE ONTARIO SYSTEM: THE ARGUMENT SUMMARIZED

Ontario has processed trucking issues within the framework of a highly structured, relatively insular policy system, whose basic ground rules emerged in the 1920s and 1930s and changed very little thereafter. A stable system occurred partly because the key interest groups and government officials valued stable relations, predictability, a clear understanding of what people wanted, and what specific actions meant; in other words, they valued 'systemness.' Where events or actions were difficult to interpret, the system developed distinctive rituals, patterned communications, or performances designed to provide the correct meaning. A stable, insular system emerged because, for the larger Ontario political system, trucking was a low-priority, low-visibility issue, a political backwater into which outsiders rarely intruded. From 1926 until the post-1974 deregulation debates, no political party in Ontario took a stand on trucking issues; these issues were never part of an election campaign; and each new minister invariably adopted his predecessor's position on trucking issues. The existence of a 'minister's policy,' one pursued by all trucking ministers regardless of which party or premier was in power, helped give this system much of its structure and continuity.

To some extent this system was a market-like political arena, in which policy outcomes emerged in bottom-up fashion from contests among interest groups defending their market-based interests. The minister, standing at the centre of this system, was obviously a political actor, trying to placate or avoid trouble with these various groups. The closer one gets to specific events, the more it appears that the minister was merely a passive political mediator, responding to interest-group initiatives. If one takes a longer-run view, however, it becomes clear that the minister exerted crucial structural, pre-process power. He largely decided the overall shape of the system. He defined what questions were to be addressed, what premises would be assumed, what aspects of any specific issue were open or settled, what kinds of demands would be seriously considered, and how the various demands and conflicts would be processed. Such ministerial definitions exerted all-important top-down control on the day-to-day process.

Such ministerial structure-defining decisions primarily reflected the ministry's own view of correct policy. The minister often seemed to be responding to group pressures when in fact his earlier messages had partially defined the pressures that would come forward. He encouraged and acted on those group demands that supported his policy preferences; he resisted demands he thought wrong. It was widely assumed that the truckers were a powerful lobby, that, in some mysterious, undefined fashion, they could exert great, decisive pressure on the minister. But the simple fact is that the truckers won only when they and the minister held similar policy preferences; when the two parties disagreed, the truckers always lost. The minister seemed to be playing a predominantly political game, and often said he was, when in fact cognitive-instrumental factors, the minister's own policy convictions, dominated this political game.

I focus first on the bottom-up forces, mainly by examining the relationship between interests groups and the ministry. I then consider in detail the minister's great top-down, structure-defining power.

INTEREST GROUPS AND STRUCTURAL POWER

An interest group has relatively little influence with a minister if it must rely on overt communication and visible pressure, especially in a parliamentary system where policy proposals are often formulated behind closed doors and where announced policies often are approved by the House without change. Each group in this trucking system much preferred to have its views understood by the minister and taken into account during the very early, intragovernmental drafting of proposals. Ideally, a group wanted the minister to keep off the agenda, to refrain from even considering, any proposal he knew would offend that group. In fact, the group wanted all the key players to know what would offend the group and consequently to avoid offence. Similarly, the more clearly other players understood what a group favoured, the more easily they could figure out how to placate or bargain with this group.

In other words, each group sought structural power, the power that results when other people base their actions on invisible calculations about a group's likely reactions. Structure-level power is difficult to see because it often works through non-events, through actions people might have taken but, on the basis of anticipated reactions, decided not to. Although the semi-popular political culture attributed great influence to the noisy, desk-pounding groups, in fact a group's reliance on such visible, process-level moves revealed its lack of structural power and thus its basic weakness. Openly exerting pressure was a second-best strategy, a sign that the group had failed in its primary goal.

The players valued 'systemness' because it gave them greater access to structure-level power. It also generated clarity and predictability. All players wanted to base their relationships more on internalized images and anticipated reactions than on overt interaction and events. It usually is resource consuming, structurally confining, and politically dangerous to learn about other people's viewpoints by acting first and then observing their responses to this action. By contrast, if each player internalized a cognitive map of the various group viewpoints and could thus anticipate likely group reactions, the actions of each player could be more rational and efficient. Systemness enhanced the ability of the players to understand and influence each other. The more systemic this field became, the more mutual power was generated.

If I know what you would find rewarding, I better understand how to evoke your support or co-operation and better understand the extent of my bargaining power over you. If a group can better estimate the array of support and opposition on a given issue, and thus better predict the outcome of deliberations on this issue, the group can more easily avoid wasting resources on lost causes. By anticipating reactions, we can avoid confrontations with other players and avoid an embarrassing retreat from a publicly stated position – or at the very least we can safely predict that a confrontation will occur.

THE INSIDERS' SYSTEM

In some respects, the structure of this policy system exhibited a vertically disconnected, 'two cultures' gap. Some of the system's ground rules were emphasized in public performances and made a key part of the system's legitimating self-image. Another set of less publicly articulated, insiders' rules seemed designed to help the ministry and the interest groups build more clarity, predictability, and structure-level power into their relationship. These rules also reflected broader liberal-democratic, cultural perspectives on how the political game should be played; and they sometimes reflected the political game's own macro-level requirements, which were imposed on players in top-down fashion.

Politics, it was assumed, is basically about conflict between self-interested groups, which means that each group must generate a clearly defined set of interests and demands. Sublimation and ritual combat are thrust on groups in top-down fashion. Even if the group has nothing to say, it still must take a stand. And groups are supposed to disagree even if doing so means staging a fight over trivial, inconsequential issues. This system, perhaps most policy systems, demonstrated a limited capacity to deal with subtle, sophisticated ideas; it could consider issues only by first greatly simplifying them, often by fitting them into a bipolar, unilinear model. Given such a model, specific policy moves could be seen in terms of more or less regulation, tighter or looser restraints, favouring or opposing truckers, and other simple distinctions of this kind.

According to these insider rules, each interest group had a responsibility to decide exactly what it wanted and to convey these demands, in clear terms, to other players. Over a period of years, there should be continuity in the statements that a group issues. If the group was reconsidering some part of its previous program, it should give everyone early, advance warning. Within a short period of time, the group should make only marginal not sudden, wholesale changes in its demands. Similarly, the minister, rather than unleash surprises, should give early notice of any pending policy shift. A group should not demand some proposal unless it actually can mobilize its membership in support of this proposal. If an interest group gave first priority to item X, and if the minister later accepted the group's demand on item X, the group should treat this as an important rather than minor concession, in line with its own initial allocation of priorities.

At the same time, the ground rules allowed for inevitable, politically inspired misstatements. It was the role of the interest-group leader to demand more than the group expected to receive and to legitimate the group's demands by portraying them as the correct embodiment of more general, widely accepted values. No one thought a group ever would say that it was content or that its program had been realized. It was bad politics to boast about one's recent victories, far smarter to magnify one's discontents and minimize one's recent policy gains. Because the minister wished to be seen as a tough negotiator or even-handed mediator rather than the captive of any one group, no group would praise the minister for being extraordinarily sympathetic to its concerns. Everyone assumed that the group's public statements would be couched in dramatic, overblown rhetoric, which portrayed a growing crisis, predicted imminent disaster for the group's constituents, demanded emergency action, etc. Behind the scenes, however, a group was expected to be reasonable, to accept compromise, to signal to others what was more and less important in its demands, and to accept defeats without smashing the larger structure.

Because one wanted better information on where people stood and what their future reactions might be, silence could be unnerving, conflict often informative and functional. An interest group should speak out early on an issue bearing on that group's interests. How vehemently one spoke would indicate the priority one assigned to this issue. Silence was often taken to mean assent, but it was better to have explicit assent. A group was criticized if it kept silent during the initial consideration of a proposal and later, after others had invested much time and energy in this issue, launched major objections. To avoid this possibility, the minister sometimes prodded silent groups into showing their hand early.

Compared to the interest-group leader's relatively uncomplicated role, the minister performed many subroles and addressed many constituencies. Often a minister's specific act would be difficult to interpret because it could be fit into several possible contexts, each of which gave the act a different meaning. An indication from the minister that item X was being reviewed might be notice of a pending policy shift and thus a concession to the early-warning norm; or it might be a symbolic gesture, an attempt to placate certain groups by reassuring them that their concerns were 'under study.' If the minister formally consulted with various groups on proposal Y, he sometimes was serious about proceeding with Y but sometimes wanted to show how disagreed the key groups were and thus how inappropriate it would be to proceed.

Everyone disliked such ambiguities, and, consequently, certain clarifying rituals were developed, as the following examples show. (1) Following a truck-related accident, it was assumed that the minister would respond with a strongly worded anti-trucking statement in the House, deploring the industry's record on highway accidents, threatening to crack down on the giant trucks, reassuring everyone he was not going to be pushed around by the 'trucking lobby.' But OTA understood that this was a self-contained, expressive performance, which, at most, might be followed by a two-week intensification of roadside inspections. (2) The minister was expected to attend OTA's annual meeting and make sweeping, pro-industry statements, but OTA members knew that such expressions of support did not imply any new, specific pro-trucking measures. At the same time, if his comments were more restrained or, worse yet, if he sent the deputy minister in his place, this was a bad omen, perhaps indicating a pending increase in the gas tax. (3) When shipping groups denounced recent 'unreasonable' increases in trucking rates, the minister would order a study of PCV Act amendments giving government the power to disallow rate increases; but everyone knew this was a token move, designed to appease shippers until the furore over recent rate increases died down. (4) During periods of federal imperialism, when the Ontario cabinet was eager to keep key groups loyal to continued provincial jurisdiction, the minister's claims to be reviewing possible changes in the regulatory system were meant to be taken literally.

THE OFFICIAL VERSION

The more publicly emphasized, official ground rules were largely a product of the transportation culture. These rules produced the kind of greatly simplified imagery that large-scale systems apparently require. According to this official version, the trucking sphere was dominated by conflicts between competing economic interests, primarily carriers vs shippers and trucking vs other modes. In the presence of such conflicts, the minister's policy, and much of the system, should be founded on even-handedness. By formally consulting with all contestants and acting as an honest broker rather than as advocate of any one camp, the minister would guarantee political fair play. Even-handedness also was sound economics. Because these conflicts were best resolved through undistorted market forces, government should avoid a policy that conferred market advantages on any one camp, that created artificial, politically subsidized winners. The minister portrayed himself, inaccurately, as nothing more than a passive responder to interest-group demands, eager to solve trucking problems but often stymied by conflicting interests, unable to proceed unless he could find some solution on which the key interests agreed.

In line with this self-image and the resulting norms, the minister often conceived of trucking issues within a tripartite trucker/shipper/railway structure. This meant fitting diverse interests and players into one or another of these blocs, reducing a complex field into a simplified three-team structure. And each of the three blocs was expected to articulate, or have attributed to it, a clear set of demands, a precise viewpoint. Such a structure was built on useful fictions, on inaccurate over-generalizations. The structure required such fictions. How could the minister mediate between truckers and shippers unless each bloc produced a precise viewpoint, clearly at odds with the other? How could the system deal with issues central to the interests of the trucking industry unless it knew exactly 'what the truckers wanted'? In reality, while CN and CP often could agree on a railway viewpoint, there was no 'trucking viewpoint' or 'shipping viewpoint' on any of the issues under consideration. 'Shippers,' of course, included most businesses in Ontario. Moreover, it was assumed that shippers spoke not only for themselves but for the recipients of goods, the consignees, and for the ultimate consumers, an assumption that simplified the consultational framework and that gave shipping groups additional legitimacy, but one that put even more of a representational burden on shipping associations. Because the system required a 'truckers' viewpoint,' it stubbornly ignored the great diversity and conflicting viewpoints within that industry, happily accepted OTA as the authoritative voice of Ontario trucking, and in effect equated those segments best represented by OTA with the entire industry. To simplify things even further, OTA was urged to reduce its demands to a set of short, trigger-like phrases, as if it were engaged in collective bargaining and presenting its list of demands to the mediator.

Interest groups in this system rarely sent the crisp, consistent messages urged by the insiders' ground rules. When the minister referred to the truckers and other key groups as difficult, volatile, or unreliable, he was acknowledging the gap between rules and practice. This unreliability emerged in part from the ambivalent attitude of trucking and shipping groups toward key regulatory issues, for reasons explored in previous chapters. Either the demand was vague – 'board reform,' 'rate regulation' – or the group held a yes/no, approach-avoidance attitude toward the demand (e.g., for rigorous enforcement). The group would criticize the minister for ignoring its demand, but might also criticize him for adopting it; witness the truckers' rebellion against his 1963 decision to proceed with OTA's twenty-five-year-old demand for rate filing.

But some of this volatility and unpredictability in interest-group behaviour was the product of top-down, system-induced forces. Demands were often vague, empty labels because the system pushed each group to send static, highly simplified accounts of its viewpoint, accounts that became subject to loss of meaning, ritualization, and related pathologies. Moreover, the system imposed too simple a structure on a diverse, fragmented field. Only if one began with the assumption that such a diverse bloc like 'truckers' or 'shippers' were capable of producing a single viewpoint, did their resulting positions seem vague, unstable, unreliable. This gap between stability-seeking norms and volatile interest-group behaviour widened after 1975, when new trucking groups challenged OTA's right to speak for the entire industry, and when the two major shippers' groups, the Canadian Manufacturers' Association and the Canadian Industrial Traffic League, adopted divergent views on the central deregulatory issues.

ISSUE SUBSYSTEMS: SHIPPERS VS CARRIERS

The minister played the key role in defining and altering this system's structure. In the ministerial view, the trucking field naturally divided into separate issues, each of which had a different character or texture, each of which should be processed in a distinctive manner. Based on this ministerial viewpoint, the system divided into differently structured issue subsystems, each with its own policy premises, ground rules, and distinctive patterns of ministry/group interaction. The system's public, self-legitimating statements, then, inaccurately suggested that one structure, even-handed ministerial mediation among conflicting economic interests, characterized all trucking issues, when in fact it characterized some but not others.

The official version best described issues perceived by the minister as shipper-vs-trucker questions. On matters like shipper liability for illegal trucking transactions or 'intercorporate trucking,' the extent to which a trucking transaction between two corporations with some degree of common ownership should be viewed as an internal, private-trucking transaction, the minister behaved very much like a labour mediator, shuttling between both sides to find some middle-ground settlement. But on the great majority of basic, day-to-day shipper/trucker conflicts – e.g., over lost or damaged goods, the truckers' alleged failure to fulfil promises, or mislabelled or poorly crated goods – the minister would simply urge the two sides to hammer out their differences through renewed private discussions. Most shipper/trucker conflicts, in other words, were matters to be resolved through intergroup negotiations not public policy. Here, even-handedness meant non-intervention.

Although OTA wanted the minister to treat the private-vs-commercial-trucking battle as an internal industry question and to assume a sponsor-like responsibility for protecting the regulated core from this private threat, the minister instead insisted on seeing this as a shipper-vs-trucker issue. Seen in this light, he was unwilling to impose restraints on private trucking because that meant curbing the business firm's basic right to ship its own goods. The minister conceded that he had some responsibility for protecting the regulated core and that, if this core were being decimated by some unchecked, epidemic-like expansion of private trucking, he might intervene; but in the meantime he did not see private trucking as a serious threat to the core's survival. To OTA, even-handedness meant that the minister at least should impose the same burdens, the same licence fees and performance standards, on both private and commercial trucking. In reply, the minister, invoking a different but traditional version of even-handedness, said that shifts in a status quo to which all sides had become adjusted would unfairly give one side unanticipated, unearned advantages over another.

HIGHWAY SAFETY

Except for the movers of household effects, trucking is a business that serves other businesses rather than the public at large. The perception that most Ontario residents had of trucking was based not on their experience as customers of that industry but on their view of the truck on the road. Consequently, while regulatory issues attracted little mass attention, the 'truck in traffic' was a high-visibility issue. The popular attitude toward trucks as vehicles was a strongly negative one, and this attitude became part of a pervasive, vague hostility to the industry. Trucks were a nuisance, a source of noise and smells, a menace to the pedestrian, and a threat to the peace and quiet of residential neighbourhoods. Trucks punished the roads, creating dangerous cracks and potholes. While augmenting the highway repair bill in this way, the industry allegedly escaped paying for its fair share of construction and repair costs. Private motorists, who, in effect, competed with trucks for road space, criticized trucks for hogging the road and slowing down traffic or, conversely, for moving at dangerously high speeds. And it was widely believed that trucks caused a disproportionately large number of traffic accidents. Even many truck-free accidents presumably were caused by road damage attributable to trucks. Supporting these anti-truck complaints was a broad, formidable coalition, which included automobile and motorist associations, most municipal councils in the province, most newspapers, and most ratepayer and neighbourhood-improvement associations.

Eventually this list of grievances underwent successive simplifications. Diverse complaints against the truck were condensed and focused on the simple assumption that 'trucks cause accidents.' The OTA response was probably correct: these groups had decided to emphasize highway safety because it was a serious issue with mass appeal; but 'safety' remained a surrogate or façade for various anti-truck grievances, both serious and trivial. When it came to identifying exactly how trucks caused accidents and what the appropriate policy response would be, further simplification occurred. Some groups in the anti-truck coalition thought speeding trucks were the problem and lower speed limits for trucks the solution; but other groups said that accidents often resulted when frustrated motorists tried to pass slow-moving trucks. Eventually the coalition decided to focus on one aspect of the safety issue, the size of trucks, and to focus on one solution, newer, tougher provincial limits on truck size and weight. Convinced this coalition spoke for mass public opinion in Ontario, most members of the legislature, from all political parties, endorsed the idea of reducing highway accidents through tougher limits on truck size.

That the minister sided with the truckers on this issue was seen by the anti-truck bloc as evidence of the 'trucking lobby's' great, backstairs influence. The deregulators' subsequent 'capture and cartel' argument confirmed these earlier suspicions. But had the minister viewed this issue in political terms, he surely would have sided with this formidable, incensed anti-truck coalition, backed by a near-unanimous legislature. On this and the highway-finance issue, OTA was less a 'lobby,' wielding threats or promises, than a grateful client, whom the minister protected from a very popular anti-truck crusade. On both the safety and finance issues, the minister sided with the industry because he thought the truckers' viewpoint was correct and the opposing viewpoint an expression of some vague, emotional hostility to trucks. The minister's response, in other words, was mainly cognitive-instrumental, a product of his own policy convictions. As the minister told the House and apparently believed, the widely advocated weight and size limits would impose inefficient, smaller loads on truckers, with shippers and consumers eventually paying the price. But more important, all the serious studies, all the solid evidence, on the safety issue consistently supported OTA's arguments.

Four major Ontario inquiries into problems of highway safety, in 1937, 1956, 1976, and 1983, found that trucks were involved in fewer accidents than their numbers on the road would lead one to predict. And large trucks were no more likely to cause accidents than small trucks. Given the high structural quality of post-1945 roads and highways, road damage had ceased to be a serious cause of accidents. In proposing policies designed to reduce accidents, none of these commissions gave priority to truck-related issues. Highways should be designed in a manner that created fewer steep grades and fewer sharp curves and that gave motorists longer, less-obstructed views of the road ahead. The law should require *all* drivers to be periodically retested, and all vehicles to be periodically inspected. Speeding limits should be reduced. If any one issue deserved primary attention, it was drinking drivers rather than trucking.

Moreover, the safest truck was not necessarily the smaller one but rather the one with road-gripping tires, improved brakes, better rear vision for drivers, wider axles, a larger number of axles, greater distance between the axles, and other structural features of this kind. If the provinces allowed higher weight and size limits for vehicles containing these newer safety features, truckers would be given an incentive to acquire such vehicles, and these features would spread more quickly through the industry. OTA argued, and these provincial inquiries generally agreed, that using higher limits as an incentive to spur the adoption of new safety features would do more to improve highway safety than would a rigid adherence to size limits. However, since these safety features were less visible and dramatic than truck size, it would be difficult to convince the public of this view.

The minister opposed lowering the weight and size limits. Along with OTA, he believed that, as new safety features became a part of truck design, the limits should be raised. But he could not totally ignore political considerations or so formidable an opposition bloc. In pursuing higher limits, he told OTA, one had to move slowly, select the right moment, 'educate' people, avoid getting too far ahead of public opinion. Perhaps to counter the popular 'trucking lobby' or 'capture and cartel' fears, OTA and the minister publicly exaggerated their differences on this issue and occasionally engaged in ritual combat. The minister often denounced 'monster trucks' and the 'trucking lobby'; none the less he gradually but steadily edged the weight and size limits upward. Although publicly complaining about the inefficiencies caused by needlessly low limits, and sometimes irritated by the minister's gradualist, start-and-stop strategy, OTA knew that the minister protected truckers from even lower limits.

As early as 1930, the minister had accepted the notion, urged by truckers, truck manufacturers, and engineers, that allowable, 'safe' truck size could be defined only in relation to the kind of truck (single frame, tractor and single trailer, etc.) and in relation to the kind of safety features (size and distribution of axles, type of brakes) contained in a given truck. The resulting regulations on truck size and weight comprised a long, complex schedule of varying limits for various kinds of truck, comprehensible only to readers with some understanding of truck design. The anti-truck coalition, however, could deal with this schedule only by fitting it into a much simpler framework, for example, by assuming that any amendment either 'raised' or 'lowered' the limits. One obviously must fight rule changes involving big, visible jumps, like a change in the number of trailers that could be linked to one tractor. But most amendments raised some limits, lowered others, and reshuffled the categories; and here the coalition found it difficult to formulate a reponse. The coalition usually solved this problem, and simplified things further, by attending only to the top end or ceiling of the entire schedule, the maximum allowable size for any truck. This meant that a minister could raise many of the other limits in this schedule without attracting attention. All the drama and mass appeal lay in the issue of curbing the 'giants,' not in debating the safety problems of smaller trucks or quibbling about what weight concessions one should give to a truck with a certain array of axles.

This coalition could not understand why it failed to get more support from within the trucking industry. Tough limits on truck size presumably defended small trucking companies operating smaller trucks from being outcompeted by large firms operating monster trucks. Not only did this view incorrectly assume a neat correlation between size of truck and size of trucking company, and incorrectly assume that large and small firms competed against each other in the same micro-markets, it also made sense only if the regulations consisted of a one-sentence limit on the largest vehicles. Because the schedule set limits on size in many categories, for the small as well as the large truck, almost every trucking firm found these limits an irritating restraint.

These regulations were altered annually to take account of changes in truck design. Exactly how the size and weight rules should be adjusted in the light of these design changes was defined by the minister as a 'technical' question, best resolved by the 'experts,' that is, truck manufacturers, engineers, and trucking executives. Because of this ministerial definition, OTA officials acquired a major role in drafting annual revisions. The major threat to this close working relationship was the truckers' own characteristic ambivalence and aggressive individualism. OTA officially said that a schedule linking size limits to design features was a sign of sophisticated thinking; but many truckers said the schedule was too sophisticated for any human being, even a trucking lawyer, to comprehend. In talking to the minister, OTA would urge the minister to raise limits for trucks containing some new feature; but some truckers, attached to the older models, would say that this new feature really was a change for the worse. And if the minister did raise the limits for trucks containing some new feature, as OTA had urged, many OTA member firms would criticize the minister for pushing them into premature acquisition of new vehicles. On weight and size limit issues generally, OTA members tended to over-react to specific events, concentrate too much on short-run skirmishes, endanger OTA's rapport with the minister by launching all-out attacks on the minister over some specific changes in this year's schedule.

PAYING FOR THE ROADS AND HIGHWAYS

A central element in Canada's twentieth-century transportation policy was the decision to construct an elaborate highway network. At the beginning of the century, the question of whether to build highways was debated, but only briefly. Once it became clear that the automobile would occupy a central role in the lives of most Canadian families, once most voters became motorists, the outcome was no longer in doubt. Roads had always been a provincial responsibility, delegated by the provinces to the municipal governments. To respond to the demands of the automobile, however, the provinces gradually assumed responsibility for the construction of major, intermunicipal roads. The central question after 1920 was how these heretofore non-interventionist provincial governments would finance such a large-scale undertaking. The answers that Ontario worked out between 1920 and 1927 were treated by subsequent ministers as a basic settlement. This settlement structured and dominated all further highway-finance considerations.

The settlement can be summarized as follows. Roads of lesser importance, the 'local' roads, would be financed by municipal governments out of real-property taxes. Despite the warnings of pay-as-you-go conservatives, the Ontario government decided to finance much of its highway construction through the issuance of long-term bonds, to be retired when most of the highway network was completed. A special sales tax on gasoline would compel highway users to shoulder much of the highway-finance burden and presumably would tax motorists in proportion to their use. Although much smaller in amount, the fees motorists paid for securing motor vehicle permits (the 'driver's licence') and motor vehicle registrations and the PCV licence fees paid by regulated truckers also would be applied to highway construction. Because highways benefited not just motorists but all provincial residents – improving access to and from many communities, strengthening tourism and other aspects of the provincial economy – it was thought appropriate that a significant portion of highway costs be met from general revenues, by the taxpayers at large.

From the outset, in the 1920s, the same broad coalition that fought the trucking industry on highway safety issues strongly urged the cabinet to approve an additional, special tax on trucking. 'Making the truckers pay' had broad, enormous appeal. It was only fair that truckers pay more because they allegedly inflicted extraordinary damage on the roads and, unlike private motorists, benefited commercially from their road use. A trucking tax would relieve the financial burden on private motorists and general taxpayers, and it would act as a financial deterrent on the growth of trucking. For the railways and their many municipal council allies, a special tax would mean that truckers finally were being compelled to pay their fair share of highway costs. Moreover, because the amount of additional gasoline consumed does not increase in direct proportion to increase in vehicle size, and because long-trip vehicles use less gas per mile than short-trip, stop-and-start vehicles, it was widely believed that the gas tax inadvertently subsidized truckers at the expense of cars, and subsidized large trucks at the expense of small ones. To correct this invalid cross-subsidization and to check the use of very large trucks, the special-tax advocates wanted to base this tax on the weight of each truck and the distance it travelled. The cabinet had included a weight-distance tax in the original, 1926 PCVA, in fact had initiated regulation partly to identify the trucking firms to be taxed. The act required each trucking firm to keep a log for each of its trucks and to periodically submit these records so that provincial officials could make the necessary tax calculations. But it quickly became apparent that the vast majority of trucking firms did not keep such records and that the provincial government had no interest in creating a record-examining inspectorate. Because this tax was 'impossible to enforce,' and because gas-tax revenue far exceeded the most optimistic earlier estimates, the cabinet decided to abandon the weight-distance tax in 1927, despite an intense, broadly based campaign for its retention. At this point, with the weight-distance tax abandoned, the minister thought the major financial issues settled.

The finance and highway-safety subsystems had very similar structures. For more than fifty years, the anti-truck coalition, commanding great support within the legislature and apparently among the public at large, argued that the settlement was too generous to truckers and that some version of the weight-distance tax should be revived. Swimming against this strong political tide, the minister kept insisting that the truckers paid their 'fair share,' although he would not elaborate. Ministers repeatedly told the House that an irrational antipathy to trucks had created this demand for punitive levies on one of Ontario's most important industries and that punishing the truckers ultimately would hurt all shippers and consumers.

The campaign for a weight-distance tax reached its peak during the 1955–65 period, when there was growing concern about how to pay for the massive post-war highway construction program; but even at this high point in the campaign, the minister gave far more serious consideration to the creation of toll roads than to a special tax on truckers. The campaign receded in the 1970s, when highway construction declined and there seemed no urgent need for a new user charge.

On finance issues, the OTA/minister relationship was highly structured and ritualized. The truckers were content with the 1927 settlement, willing to see user charges periodically increased in line with inflation, and concerned mainly to resist any revival of the special trucking tax. But if OTA said that current tax rates were reasonable, people might assume that the industry thrived and could well afford an additional tax. Instead, OTA portrayed the typical trucking firm as caught in a cost/price squeeze, barely breaking even, teetering on the edge of viability, and thus likely to be pushed over the edge by even a small increase in the gas tax or licence fees. Both before and after the announcement of an increase in user charges, the minister would adopt a tough line, would remind truckers that they were being subsidized by a 'taxpayer-financed highway system,' and would tell the House that he was not going to be intimidated by the trucking lobby; less publicly he would reassure truckers that this was just a routine, inflationary increase, not a departure from the basic settlement. In the period between such tax increases, when the minister was mainly interested in repelling demands for a special trucking tax, he would insist that the industry paid more than its fair share of highway costs and probably subsidized private motorists.

There was one key difference between the safety and finance subsystems. To maximize his discretion and maintain his advantage over various revenue-providing groups, the minister deliberately kept many aspects of the financial settlement vague. He carefully avoided making the kind of precise commitment that interest groups could turn into an entitlement and use as an argument for lessening their financial burden. On the question of user charges vs general revenue, all he would say was that user charges should pay for 'most but not all' of highway costs. On how user charges should be allocated between truckers and private motorists, he would only insist that the existing arrangements were roughly fair – exactly how or why, he refused to say – and that one could never secure more precise equity on such matters. Moreover, the amounts spent on highways and the amounts collected from user charges would vary independently of each other; so the people paying such charges could not argue for a reduction or a freeze because highway expenditures had been reduced in recent years or because user-charge revenue, calculated as a percentage of total highway costs, had exceeded some crucial threshold, like 66 per cent. It was to prevent such precise calculations and a resulting sense of entitlement that the minister initially had opposed the creation of a separate Highway Fund and opposed any statutory earmarking of these charges for highway purposes. The users' share of highway costs might rise to 90 per cent, as it did during the 1930s, or fall below 50 per cent, as it did in the 1950s. All such fluctuations, the minister said, were within the bounds of the settlement.

No issue better demonstrates the minister's ability to structure and restructure these issue subsystems as he saw fit, without paying great mind to what the various groups wanted. While making this 1927 settlement the major structuring element in all highway-finance debates, refusing to depart from it, insisting that he consistently adhered to it, the minister and his cabinet colleagues really were redefining it substantially. After 1960, the cabinet increasingly viewed the gas tax not as a user charge related to highway construction but as one among many sources of general revenue. If more aggregate revenue were needed, the cabinet would announce small increases in all provincial taxes, the gas tax included. Thus, while highway expenditures levelled off after 1975, the gas tax continued to rise. By the mid 1980s, annual gas-tax revenue significantly exceeded annual road-and-highway expenditures. To trucking and private-motorist associations, this seemed a major departure from the settlement. Hadn't the minister consistently said that user charges should pay for most but not all highway costs. In defending the newer practices and insisting they were consistent with the original settlement, the minister produced two very novel interpretations of what that settlement had included. First, he said, highway users were being treated fairly and in line with the settlement as long as they received benefits commensurate with what they paid. Second, the old settlement had been intended to preclude the introduction of some new, qualitatively different, user charge, not to put some ceiling on the gas tax.

STRUCTURING REGULATORY ISSUES

On regulatory questions the minister again structured the process; and he did so in line with his own preference for a minimal regulatory system. He insisted that the initial 1926–33 versions of the PCV Act had settled the key regulatory issues, a settlement he saw no need to elaborate on or re-open. In this subsystem, he saw his role as that of the paternal non-interventionist: resisting group demands for a more restrictive, suffocating system, saving these groups from their own folly rather than simply meeting their demands. To keep truckers loyal to continued provincial jurisdiction, he approved a few system extensions, but they were relatively innocuous ones, like a trucking-only licensing board, unlikely to trigger a cumulative, tar-baby effect.

According to the ministry view, business groups usually over-reacted to every small bleep in the market, always saw their rivals engaging in 'destructive competition,' too quickly demanded government protection from new technology or new market practices, as the early railway campaign for legal restraints on trucking and the later trucking campaign against combined trips amply demonstrated. Time and market forces, rather than public policy, were the best solutions to such problems. Truckers and shippers might think they wanted a 'more effective regulatory system,' but they would never stomach the accompanying increases in government surveillance and intrusiveness. Because these groups explicitly rejected increased intrusions, one could not take their demands for 'better protection' at face value and one should feel no urgent need to act on them. The group most loudly demanding rigorous enforcement would be the first to criticize the minister for proceeding with it. If he were wrong whatever his response, the minister would rather stick to his non-interventionist guns and be damned for inaction. Nor did one have to respond, except rhetorically, to those demands that waxed and waned in predictable, cyclical fashion, usually in response to recent events. For example, the shippers demanded 'rate regulation,' i.e., a legal ceiling, only when trucking prices were rising; and truckers more vehemently demanded a crack-down on grey and black marketeers during economic recessions. The minister also recognized that the consensus on vague labels was more apparent than real. Shippers and truckers urged rate regulation, but the former meant a legally enforced ceiling, the latter a legal floor. Both blocs urged more extensive regulation, at least before 1975, but truckers meant tighter entry control, shippers meant more elaborate performance standards. The truckers wanted 'rigorous enforcement' aimed at black-market truckers; shippers wanted it aimed at truckers who failed to process claims on lost or damaged cargo. Many ministers said and apparently believed that this weak, frail regulatory system represented a reasonably acceptable middle-ground compromise, a stable equilibrium. More pervasive regulation simply would produce more private trucking and larger grey and black markets and would provoke a political reaction from all those people inconvenienced by the additional restraints.

OTHER SUBSYSTEMS

From the minister's viewpoint, issues internal to the trucking industry, issues that set trucker against trucker, had their own distinctive structure and were to be treated differently from the broader regulatory issues. The truckers' demand for an increasingly elaborate letter-category licensing system, which would give recognition to the various segments and would minimize cross-overs between them, was thought to be such an internal issue, and the minister largely complied with trucking demands. He also accepted the notion that, once this letter-category system was created, it required a certain amount of elaboration and sharpening of language, so that firms did not sneak across boundaries by exploiting legal ambiguities. OTA also convinced the minister that the general-goods, LTL, or A-category trucker was the most essential part of the industry and that letter-category rules should restrain other categories more than this one. But once the other categories began to organize and voice their concerns more effectively, in the later 1970s, the minister switched to a more mediating, even-handed role on conflicts between categories.

To a great extent, the minister accepted the view that the regulated trucking was the essential but vulnerable nucleus of the industry, which had to be protected from the peripheral sector. Because the regulatory system presumably heaped burdens and imposed constraints on this nucleus, and because this system was the creation, in a sense the property, of the minister, both OTA and the minister agreed that he had an obligation to protect regulated truckers and the system from grey- and black-market threats. The minister saw regulated-vs-private-trucking issues not as an internal industry question but as a trucker-vs-shipper question, on which he must remain an even-handed mediator. On regulated-vs-peripheral-trucking issues, however, the minister was clearly a protector of the regulated sphere. In pursuit of this protector role, the minister was prepared to bend his minimalist preferences and concede some modest extensions in the system: for example, drawing freight forwarders into the system, restricting the behaviour of leasing companies, expanding the shippers' liability for illegal transactions. Throughout the 1960–75 period, the minister worked closely with OTA and the trucking lawyers to find more elaborate, more precise language that would stamp out pseudo-leasing, phony buy-and-sell arrangements, and other grey-market practices. But because neither the minister nor OTA was willing to accept the preconditions of a serious enforcement effort, little could be done about the black-market truckers, who openly flaunted the regulatory system. Moreover, both OTA and the minister knew that the system extensions noted above would not be enforced. The minister genuinely wanted to protect regulated truckers from the peripheral sector, but, given insignificant enforcement, all he could offer were symbolic-expressive rewards rather than better protection.

For decades, OTA criticized the minister's tendency to break up the various trucking issues and allocate them to different subsystems, so that 'one hand did not know what the other was doing.' The minister was urged to adopt a holistic approach toward the industry, to recognize how intimately interconnected these issues were. But what OTA really wanted was a more consistent ministerial performance of the sponsor/protector role. Before increasing the gas tax, imposing higher performance standards, or rejecting some increase in weight-and-size limits, the minister should recognize what a damaging effect his actions would have on trucking profits and operating efficiency. Here and elsewhere, the minister consistently refused to extend the sponsorship role. The OTA argued that, because the federal government was biased in favour of rail, Ontario and other provinces should seek inter-modal, nation-wide evenhandedness by becoming champions of trucking. But the minister said he was responsible for pursuing balance and equity only within the Ontario political system. The minister occasionally intervened to defend the truckers from over-zealous municipal councils imposing allegedly excessive restraints on the movement of trucks within municipal boundaries. The OTA wanted him to go further, assume jurisdiction over intramunicipal trucking and eliminate the list of exempt goods, and thus choke off the peripheral firms' major sources of income. But the minister did not feel strongly enough about his sponsorship role to do battle with hundreds of municipal councils or to provoke a fight with Ontario's farm groups over the abolition of exempt goods. Nor did the minister think it was Ontario's role to protect Canadian trucking firms from the American threat. The regulatory system ignored the nationality of firms making applications. In the later 1970s, the minister said that continued regulation, at the provincial level, was an essential safeguard against wholesale Americanization of the Canadian trucking industry; but this was a purely rhetorical-expressive invocation, an attempt to ground the system in legitimate, Canadian themes.

THE SYSTEM DISRUPTED

During 1975–80, this fifty-year-old system was jolted out of its normal orbit. The system's stability had been based in good part on its low visibility; but the deregulation movement helped draw trucking questions into a much larger public arena. Trucking now acquired importance because it was a battleground in a larger war, an essential link in a larger move to deregulate transportation and other parts of the economy. By 1975, regulated truckers wanted the minister to stamp out grey-market practices by extending the regulatory system and closing legal loopholes; deregulators, federal officials, and the increasingly vocal non-regulated truckers urged the minister to move in the opposite direction; and both sides intensified their pressures for a definitive trucking policy that would clarify the minister's future direction. For the first time, trucking became a cabinet-wide issue; and it managed to split the cabinet. The minister responsible for trucking defended regulation by attributing to it a long list of sweeping achievements and objectives. But some cabinet members wanted the cabinet and the Conservative party to embrace trucking deregulation as part of a more general shift to the right, and these members were able to insert a reference to trucking deregulation in the 1975 Speech from the Throne.

To divert attention from these internal splits and buy some time, the minister created a select legislative committee on trucking regulation, the first full-scale inquiry into the program since 1936. Proceeding largely through public, formal hearings, at which participants reinvoked the standard cultural themes, the committee not surprisingly emerged with a restatement of the classic, initial rationale for trucking regulation. Given evidence of the existing program's very limited achievements, the committee urged the minister to move toward a strengthened, expanded, more pervasive system, precisely the kind of interventionist advice that ministers had long resisted. Having provided a clear, stable policy for so many decades and having managed the system's structure with a firm hand, the minister now seemed uncertain and on the defensive. He said he favoured neither more pervasive regulation nor deregulation but rather 'regulatory reform,' which he refused to define. Pressed for some kind of response to the select committee report, the minister introduced some very minor changes in the PCV Act, heralded them as major 'reforms,' but then either withdrew them or let them die on the agenda. For the central players, accustomed to much more structure and clarity, all this was, to use OTA's term, 'a farce.'

In 1980, the minister decided to start the review process again, this time delegating the task to a PCV Act review committee located inside the ministry and representing all the relevant interest groups, as well as a wide sampling of policy professionals. If the various interests on the committee could agree on a specific reform package, the minister said he would endorse it and bring it to the legislature. Everyone welcomed this initiative because it dispelled much of the previous confusion, gave the debate a clear locus, and provided the kind of prior consulation that all groups liked. The intergroup, behind-the-scenes horse-trading that dominated this committee's sessions encouraged a more pragmatic, realistic rather than expressive-rhetorical approach to the issues. Because the committee worked to produce not a report but a specific piece of legislation, there was less expressive posturing, far less invocation of standard cultural themes, far more tough-minded negotiation on specifics. (The select committee, by clearly revealing the minimalist, inadequate nature of the existing system, had made it difficult for any group to urge a continuation of the status quo.) Given this dash of realism and pragmatism, some of the traditional worries seemed less formidable. For example, as soon as one recognized that the existing system allowed American truckers to do whatever they liked, it was more difficult to see deregulation as some opening of the international floodgates on a heretofore protected trucking industry.

It was this realist insight into the inadequacies of the old system that led reformers to see enforcement as the Gordian knot that first had to be untangled. Unless one could figure out how to produce a better-enforced system, for example, how to draw in the unassimilated periphery, subsequent discussions about substantive changes would become the kind of expressive ritual that earlier discussions of PCV Act amendments had been. The committee's solution to the enforcement problem, and perhaps its single most-important contribution, was to separate entry control and identification. Under the new plan, all truckers, including private truckers, carriers of exempt goods, intramunicipal truckers, owner operators, and leasing companies, would have to register in a Commercial Vehicle Operators Registration (CVOR) program. A CVOR would be granted to any applicant who passed a non-rigorous written test dealing mainly with road safety, vehicle maintenance, and truck-related legislation. CVOR's purpose was all-inclusive identification, not entry control. Because virtually no one would be denied a CVOR, presumably no firm would want to operate illegally, outside this system. Firms found to be violating either the traffic laws or trucking regulations would be subjected to penalties based on a demerit system, similar to the 'loss of points' system used in the case of motor vehicle permits ('drivers' licences'). A firm that lost all its points in a given year would have its CVOR suspended. All truckers would pay a CVOR registration fee, a modest move toward spreading the financial burden more evenly between regulated and unregulated truckers; and the operator's licence fee, paid only by regulated truckers, would be reduced, on the assumption that revenue from this fee should pay only for administration of the regulatory system, not for the highways as well. By and large, OTA liked CVOR, while shippers and peripheral-sector truckers were suspicious. None the less, the minister and legislature approved the CVOR system in 1987. To improve future enforcement, the minister also promised he would initiate regular reporting practices, would rely much less on roadside inspections, and would initiate on-site inspections of business premises; but, because ministers had often promised or threatened these things, one cannot be certain how seriously this commitment was intended.

The committee's goal was to create a more modest but more effective system, to discard some regulations but secure tough enforcement of the ones that remained. Commercial truckers would still have to apply to OHTB for operators' licences, but they would be judged primarily on their 'fitness,' that is, on their having passed the CVOR written test and having demonstrated some familiarity with efficient management practices in the trucking business. Existing carriers could still force a hearing on an application by arguing that the proposed new service would be contrary to the public interest or would have economically disastrous effects on current service providers, but in such cases the burden of proof would lie with the existing carrier, not the applicant. After a five-year transition period, this ability to force a hearing would disappear, and only a fitness test would remain. Truckers would be required to issue rate schedules but not to file them with the province. The terms of shipper/trucker contracts could remain confidential. Owner operators would be eligible to apply for operators' licences and thus would be unambiguously defined as employers or managers rather than employees. Most of the restraints on the behaviour of freight forwarders, brokers, and lessors, which OTA and the minister had written into PCVA during the 1960–75 period, would be swept away. However, the letter-category aspects of licensing would remain. And in one area, mainly as an enforcement device, the committee favoured more restrictive licences. It urged the minister to use limits on fleet size, written into specific licences, as a penalty for non-compliance.

On the assumption that the very detailed terms of PCV licences often imposed inefficient operations on firms and made such licences almost impossible to enforce, the future licences would be simpler, would grant much wider authority, and would be assembled in building-block fashion. Rather than have each licence name specific goods or towns, each licensee would be authorized to operate freely within one or more stipulated regions and would be authorized to carry all goods within one or more broad categories. Regulated truckers were ambivalent on the subject of licence simplification because broadened authority benefited both the licence holder and his rivals. Moreover, licences that provided less protection against one's rivals would lose some of their current capital value.

Mainly because of the horse-trading that produced it, this reform package, as embodied in the proposed Truck Transportation Act, commanded broad interest-group support. All the key groups, including OTA, felt uncomfortable about some parts of the package but keen about others. OTA eventually decided to oppose the new bill; but even the association recognized that, if the provinces failed to pursue measures of this sort, the federal government might intrude and implement its own, more sweeping version of deregulation. In the end, OTA's opposition was restrained rather than all-out. Although these reforms were endorsed by both the outgoing Conservative and new Liberal governments during the 1984–5 period, both governments preferred to move slowly, while waiting for some clarification of how far the federal government would demand the provinces move. However, this act, based largely on the review committee's report, was reintroduced in November 1987 and appeared headed for final approval.

8

Pathological Processes in Policy Systems

Why do governmental attempts to solve public problems so often produce disappointing results? One may think of cognitive-instrumental (or CI) rationality as a necessary but not sufficient cause of policy success; and one may conceive of CI irrationality – that is, confused, misinformed, aimless, often self-defeating action – as an important source of policy failure. Although this irrational conduct may sometimes spring from ad hoc, personal decision making, there also are systemic or structural factors that regularly produce such conduct and that explain why disappointing policy results are common or endemic rather than random or occasional. One way to describe the systemic sources of CI irrationality is to see them as a set of recurring, patterned, identifiable system malfunctions or 'pathologies.'

In the transportation case described in preceding chapters, behaviour often was irrational because the ideas on which it rested were inaccurate, over-simplified caricatures, shielded from evidence or experience; or the ideas were based on apparently meaningful but in fact vague, condensed, or empty concepts. Such ideas were intellectual traps, which protected people from reality and blocked the formulation of constructive solutions. The pathologies helped explain why this maladaptive culture emerged and lasted. But why did these pathologies occur in the first place, and why did they reappear so often?

One could answer this question by citing factors unique to the preceding case; for example, the unusual problems associated with describing, representing, and regulating a complex industry like trucking, the common Canadian tendency to project American arguments onto local problems in lieu of studying those problems. Or, perhaps, the pathologies described in preceding chapters are common, even inevitable, features of any policy system. If so, understanding the reasons why these pathologies so often occur, understanding the structural factors that produce them, may yield some additional insights into the policy-failure problem. In this chapter, I assume that the pathologies described in the preceding case study are common occurrences in all policy systems, and I derive from this case some suggestions as to why these pathologies so often appear.

POLICY-MAKING RATIONALITY

Using policy to solve public problems, formulating accurate, useful CI ideas in a policy-making setting, is an intrinsically difficult and often frustrating process. Policy systems deal with large-scale, complex, often poorly understood problems, some of which will stubbornly resist any attempted public solution, and many of which can be transformed or alleviated but not 'solved.' Often the problem is changing while we attempt to grapple with it. In many cases, no one has any useful insights or even modestly promising solutions. We must show great patience, freely experiment, commit large amounts of effort, and often be content with very limited, dubious successes. It probably is wise to treat most ideas sceptically, as tentative hypotheses that might prove useful or true in certain limited ways, as hypotheses one would want to keep reassessing and changing on the basis of their performance.

Just as any truth is a partial, limited truth, any policy objective is a partial, limited good. It may or may not achieve anything worthwhile. If it does, it will achieve certain valued results and not others – in fact, will achieve certain results at the expense of others. It is never a pure good because never cost-free. The costs of pursuing any objective include not only the resources required to implement it, but the value of other activities not pursued because denied these same resources. Moreover, any objective, if pursued and achieved, clashes with other objectives – e.g., increased regulation with autonomous business decision making, a freer transportation market with regional equity or export development. A naïvely absolutist approach presents goal A as an unqualified good thing, ignores the costs, ignores the way in which it clashes with other good things, and implies that 'the more of A, the better.' Given this approach, the government's achievement of A always seems to be shockingly inadequate.

But the key question really is: How much of A do we want? What is the optimum amount of A achievement, given its costs, recognizing that, in supporting A, we are robbing values B, C, and D of resources, and also recognizing how A directly clashes with values J, K, or L? The central questions, then, are trade-off questions. Given limited resources, how do we want to allocate them among valued objectives? If more of policy A means less of policy B, how much of each do we want?

In place of tentative commitments, testing through experience and trade-offs, we may instead develop rigid, excessive commitments to greatly simplified ideas, to absolute truths and unqualified objectives. This naïve-absolutist approach not only obscures a more calm, measured assessment of various solutions, it inflates expectations, promises too much, makes excessive commitments, and consequently makes the very limited results seem that much more disappointing. The pathologies discussed in this study help produce this naïve-absolutist approach. Exactly how and why is what the rest of this chapter considers.

THE SEARCH FOR SHORT CUTS

For its players, the policy-oriented CI game is intrinsically uncertain, frustrating, disappointing, perhaps tedious. As players, we pursue short-run action that *might* move us somewhat closer to certain long-term policy objectives, which in turn, often many years from now, *might* successfully address some features of a problem; but even then a debate will likely occur over whether there has been true success or not. Often the amount of energy and commitment we expend is far in excess of the satisfying results or solutions achieved. A central problem in this game – in the political game as well – is how one sustains player motivation despite these disappointments, especially how one sustains short-term commitment to a long, means-end chain, which might or might not produce eventual results.

To fill the short-run gratificational gap, players often seek out short cuts, some quick fix or cure-all that will produce sudden, sweeping results. We want very much to believe that a sure-fire, no-fail panacea exists, just waiting to be discovered. Wish fulfilment produces fundamentalism, fixation, projection, vertical disconnection, self-closure. We seize upon some recent proposal, attributing to it excessive importance and extraordinary curative powers. A proposal may acquire this status through fortuitous, irrational circumstances, just by being available when we were eagerly searching for something to fix on. Often we unquestioningly apply to the relevant problem some model that allegedly worked wonders in another setting, filtering the evidence so that only its benefits are perceived. In fact, we busily scan other settings to find such solutions, and intersystem, policy hucksters aggressively hawk the latest sure-cure. As a result, we become excessively committed to the proposal, insufficiently critical, locked into an idealized rather than balanced or measured view of the proposal, unable to assess its costs and benefits, unable to trade it off against other valued objectives.

The search for short cuts often produces faddism. Because the recently adopted proposal cannot possibly fulfil all the goals attributed to it, we angrily reject it, as if we had been duped or betrayed. Initially the proposal's limitations are ignored; later its merits, although perhaps modest, also are ignored. In place of a patient search for small but cumulative gains, the system lurches from one cure-all to another.

TEMPORAL DISCONNECTION

Many theorists have argued that all systems exhibit a natural tendency to wear down, to drift from order to disorder, unless there is an investment of effort to maintain order. The process is often called entropy. One might also think of it as temporal disconnection, a process whereby the connections and meanings defined at a given time tend to fall apart or dissolve. For example, ideas become removed from their original context and acquire a different, unrelated meaning. An interest group, having identified its interests and linked them to some demand, subsequently loses sight of the original objective and settles for something else unrelated to, or much less satisfactory than, the original demand.

Inertia is a form of temporal disconnection. An idea or practice acquires a life of its own and persists despite the disappearance of the original, justifying context. The familiar, the here-and-now, acquires undue importance at the expense of the possible, even when the latter may constitute an improvement. Generalizations outlive their supportive evidence; a group persists with certain demands even though they no longer serve the group's interests; certain policy solutions or programs survive even though the initial problem has vanished; values or practices may command support but for reasons no one can remember.

CULTURAL ENTROPY

Idea systems, for example the case law surrounding Canadian railway regulation, sometimes undergo a natural process of growing sophistication and elaboration. But perhaps all cultures also undergo a natural entropic drift toward less meaning, clarity, and order. Cultural systems evolve in this direction because specific ideas tend to become detached from their initial rationale, supportive evidence, or meaning. As policy cultures undergo entropy, they become less adaptive, more trap-like.

When a concept is subjected to frequent use, there may be a tendency for the label and its referents to become disconnected, for the referents and the concept's meaning to erode. Through use, the idea loses subtleties and complexities; it becomes a simplified, vulgarized cartoon of its initial meaning. Perhaps the longer an idea is in circulation, the greater the loss of meaning, which would explain why Canada's transportation culture is both one of the oldest and one of the less adaptive. Eventually the idea may become an empty cliché (e.g., even-handedness), a very familiar label that everyone uses, assumes to have meaning, but cannot define. Labels largely devoid of meaning, especially the overly familiar cliché, give system members an illusion that they are meaningfully discussing policy issues or that they agree on certain issues.

There probably is a correlation between the extent of meaning lost and the size of the social system within which ideas circulate. Ideas developed by and for a journal-reading community of policy professionals must be greatly simplified when made part of a mass political system or when transmitted by the mass media to large audiences with diverse interests and backgrounds. In such cases, the complexities and subtleties are either squeezed out at the beginning, to make these ideas palatable for a mass audience, or the complexities gradually fall away as these ideas are transmitted in chain-like fashion across many connecting links. Not only the size of the system but the circulating medium is relevant. Groups that negotiate face to face daily can sustain more complicated ideas than a system in which ideas must be broadcast to mass audiences in large-scale public performances. The underground culture described in preceding chapters circulated among a very large audience but through the medium of many small, two-party transactions. It retained much of its clarity, complexity, and realism because it did not have to be acted out in public performances, where it would have been not only simplified but entrapped in much of the official culture's symbolism and mythology.

As an idea becomes more simple, many of the qualifications, conditions, and limitations fall away. An idea valid only in a given context breaks loose of that context and is assigned increasingly wide applicability. The tentatively formulated hypothesis becomes a sweeping assertion. A goal initially seen in measured, cost-benefit terms begins to acquire panacea-like status, as the cost side of the equation falls away. Naïve absolutism often results from simplification, fundamentalism, and fixation: the conversion of a limited, tentatively asserted, complex idea into a much simpler, unqualified great truth or cure-all.

While meaning tends to erode, new meanings are glued to a concept through the process of symbolic accretion. As each concept acquires more and more referents, the cultural system drifts toward fuzziness and disorder. A sharply defined idea converted into a vague, multivalent, emotionally charged symbol becomes a blunt intellectual instrument and an obstacle to clear thinking. One cannot invoke the concept without activating a vast assortment of unintegrated referents. Through this accretion process, limited solutions are irrationally invested with vast remedial importance and converted into panaceas.

THEATRE

Ideas stated in dramatic terms are intrinsically enjoyable. They provide some of the short-run gratifications needed to sustain the political and CI games, and so acquire great importance in these games. But we badly distort reality by imposing a dramatic structure on it. Dramatization can be a dangerously seductive device, helping to produce simplistic, vulgarized cultures. Because the cost-benefit, trade-off realities of rational policy formulation are basically uninspiring and non-heroic, these realities receive short shrift in most dramatic portrayal of policy problems.

Ideas are captivating and appealing if conveyed in striking, visual, often emotionally charged images (e.g., fragmentation, balkanization). Bold overstatement, strong contrasts, unqualified generalizations, are more dramatic than gradations, subtle shadings, or highly qualified, tentative assertions. We are attracted to a larger argument (e.g., differentiated, non-competing transportation niches, principles vs politics) if it contains some symmetry, underlying logic, and conflict. We often want the argument cast in the form of a story, preferably a familiar, patterned narrative involving growing tension and then resolution – for example, the problem that became a crisis until this great policy breakthrough occurred, the regulatory program that was designed to police an industry but then was captured by it. We like unilinear, bipolar constructs, in which pro-regulators fight deregulators, or recent proposals move to either the left or the right, because such constructs are simple and symmetrical and because they always involve a dramatic tension between this and that. But such constructs encourage a two-sides-only, yes/no view of policy problems; and they portray all proposals as a straight-line move toward either one pole or another. Heroic accounts begin with ringing statements of general principle and then urge us to ride fearlessly toward the problem, ready to fight the vested interests armed only with the correct principles. Such accounts foster fundamentalism and inhibit a mundane, undramatic assessment of trade-offs. As much of this study tries to show, a pre-occupation with dramatic events, the clash between leaders, or the emergence of a new policy paper often distracts attention from less interesting but far more important events, like the policy implications of a regulatory board's many small decisions.

THE RITUALIZATION OF POLICY SYSTEMS

Drama is one way in which expressive games intrude on either political or cognitive-instrumental ones; attending more to the underlying, symbolic meaning of actions than to their apparent, manifest meaning is another such expressive intrusion. This latter intrusion, like the first, is inevitable; but like the first it inhibits our ability to pursue CI policy-related rationality. Expressive games always intrude, because we are inevitably and legitimately interested in deriving from other people's actions some clues to their motives, character, or future direction. But it is difficult to use ideas as sophisticated, policy-related instruments when people attend more to the deeper, indicative meaning than the manifest content of these ideas. One way to make this point is to describe a policy system that has been subjected to very extensive expressive intrusion, a system that has been pervasively 'ritualized.' Although my account is overstated (for dramatic effect), much of it applies to the previous case study.

In such a system, the allocation of symbolic pay-offs through public performances acquires undue importance. The players in a policy system are pushed toward 'posturing,' the enactment of a position or stance as an end in itself. It is in such a setting that officials and interest-group leaders feel compelled to 'take a stand,' even when they have nothing to say. Saying the right thing often becomes more important than, becomes a substitute for, pursuing actions that would solve problems. And the interest group seems more interested in symbolic pay-offs – for example, an official report that adopts some of the group's distinctive language – than in tangible policy solutions. Politicians give priority to the strategic manipulation of symbols, and groups are too easily diverted from their original intent with token reassurances. If the government says it is moving toward objective X, it merely is reasserting the value of X and reassuring the advocates of X that the government takes them and their demand seriously. When a leader says that a given program achieves X, she only means that it would be nice if the program did, or she is legitimating the program by linking it to the correct values. Rather than resolve differences or make choices, policy statements provide a balanced allocation of verbal rewards to a variety of concerned groups, so that each part of the report says the 'right things' for a different constituency.

Not only is talk often a substitute for action, but, when action is pursued, resources are focused on showy, ineffective solutions rather than on invisible but more effective ones. Or emphasis may be given to token, ineffective efforts, designed only to show that something is being done. The ritualization of policy systems contributes to impatience, dramatization, and the fundamentalist search for panaceas. An official cannot tell concerned groups how difficult it will be for government to alleviate their suffering, how unpromising most proposed solutions appear, how unlikely it is that there will be any significant amelioration for at least ten years. Such remarks, although true, would suggest to the concerned group that the official assigns low priority to the problem and to the group concerned or that the official is afflicted by self-doubts, vacillation, or just plain incompetence. To send the right symbolic messages, officials inevitably over-dramatize and over-promise, even though doing do can create dashed expectations and more anger later on.

It is obviously rational but, for similar reasons, often difficult to monitor the effectiveness of an existing program. Officials frequently will avoid a program review because of the symbolic message it conveys, because the groups supporting the program will interpret the review as an assault on the program.

TEAMS

Affiliative perspectives inevitably intrude on CI and political games and inevitably inhibit the pursuit of CI or political rationality. As much of the social-psychological literature demonstrates, we cannot treat our own beliefs as merely cold, possibly useful intellectual instruments. I am strongly committed to my beliefs because they help identify who I am and how I differ from others and because they are an important source of my self-esteem. For social systems as well, beliefs have an identifying, boundary-maintaining, and legitimizing function. Such affiliative considerations help convert tentative, complex hypotheses, which are supposed to be used as instruments and assessed on the basis of the results they produce, into sweeping, simplistic, semi-sacred values, to be expressively reaffirmed. A group cannot coldly assess ideas that help define, and thus symbolize, the group. Nor will this group look kindly on outsiders who coldly assess such ideas. By embracing a given belief or proposal, a group envelops that idea with its systemic mantle and demands that others see such ideas in partly affiliative terms. Therefore, the more affiliative considerations intrude into political and CI games, the more extensively will these games be ritualized.

When certain ideas represent a sponsoring group, insiders display solidarity through ritualistic reaffirmation of these ideas. Similarly, how outsiders handle our ideas reveals what they think of us, and this response becomes far more important to us than the substantive merits of what they said. Affiliative intrusions also strengthen the reliance on simplistic, dramatic constructs, such as a unilinear, bipolar distinction between insiders and outsiders, this team and that team. One's response to messages depends less on their content than on their sponsor. Thus, the ideas that belong to each group can be simplified and partially shielded from evidence because the group need not take too seriously what outsiders, especially 'the other side,' say.

MORE ON POLITICS AND DRAMA

Political intrusions contribute further to the vulgarization and dramatization of policy-relevant ideas. Ideas are simplified because each group screens out whatever is contrary to its demands and self-interests.

To secure and maintain the enthusiastic support of one's constituency, and at least to secure the attention of outsiders, one must overpower other stimuli bombarding those same audiences. It is difficult to mobilize mass support for ideas that are subtle, qualified, based on a long chain of argument, stated in a hypothetical or tentative fashion, based on facts and language that some people will understand but others will not. Political mobilization requires a shrill, emotionally charged defence of sweeping solutions, conveyed through simple, visual images, and clearly marked, black/white distinctions, perhaps summarized in a few short, attention-grabbing phrases. If we want other players to internalize an image of our group's demands, we must give them a greatly simplified, stark version of those demands. Political mobilization thrives on the condensed, vague symbol (new leadership, bold departures), which evokes a strong response but conveys little precise meaning and thus binds its sponsor to little precise action. One cannot rally the troops, and keep them rallied, on behalf of possibily successful, marginal improvements or of proposals that contain a slight net advantage of benefits over costs. The political process requires fundamentalism, absolutism, over-commitment. One must urge a heroic, unqualified commitment to certain sure-fire panaceas. This process rarely rewards the sponsor of accurate, cautious, qualified statements.

POLITICS AND AFFILIATION

In liberal democratic societies, the political game is officially portrayed as a passive arena or market in which contending sides pursue previously defined, perhaps economically based 'interests.' But, as well, the political game generates its own structure, which it then imposes on players. Liberal-democractic politics is supposed to be about conflict or disagreements between players who are aggregated into groups, blocs, or teams. This kind of political game requires a pronounced affiliative framework. The game would be difficult to play if it consisted of a great many unaffiliated individuals, if there were amorphous teams, lacking identity or stability, or if there were too many teams contesting at once. Each group must have interests or demands; the interests must differ, otherwise how could one tell one team from another; and we must assume that each side is pursuing clever, politically rational strategies designed to advance those interests. To give each team a viewpoint and identity, we minimize the importance of intrateam differences and of overlaps in team memberships. Conflict among interests is presumably the whole point of the game. Each team needs conflict with an enemy in order to mobilize internal resources and explain external failures. If conflict with other teams does not naturally arise, one must find some grounds on which to stage conflict, hence a search for ritual combat.

If a group has no viewpoint, if it doesn't know what to say, on a certain issue, it must none the less say something, even if that something is not central to the problem at hand (sublimation). Having issued a commitment on a public stage, the group has acquired affiliative, proprietary responsibility for this idea, and the group's reputation for sagacity is at stake. Having approved a certain policy move, the government becomes its sponsor and is judged by how well it works. A group must gain approval of its demands in order to sustain its reputation for political effectiveness. If we withdraw or reassess publicly made commitments, others might interpret this to mean we previously made a mistake, and presumaby will make more, or that we are afflicted with Hamlet-like vacillation and self-doubt. Instead, one shores up the commitment by investing it with increasing, although often inaccurate, importance, validity, and remedial powers (reverse mobilization). We often engage in similar overattributions to justify our commitment of energies to some controversy (ritual combat). In these ways, the requirements of the political game push players toward over-commitment, fixation, and absolutism.

A combined affiliative-political game, politics conceived of as a battle between teams, thrives on simple, bipolar constructs, such as left vs right, shippers vs carriers, road vs rail, federal vs provincial. We think of political debate in terms of a pro and a con on any given issue. Parliamentary systems naturally produce bipolar choices; the government is either wrong or right. Any policy proposal is seen as a move in one direction, either toward or away from a given objective, either toward one team's preferences or toward the other team's. Thus, policy choices are conceived of in binary, this-or-that, yes/no terms, rather than as trade-offs or 'how much' decisions. And decisions of the latter sort are discouraged by the way in which each team digs in behind an unquestioning defence of its own position. Groups (e.g., the trucking associations) may cling to simple, binary ideas (road vs rail) because these identify the teams and create clearly marked boundaries between them; more sophisticated ideas are resisted because they would blur such boundaries.

The underground culture described in the preceding case study remained a gritty, realistic account of market practices because it was not acted out in public performances before large audiences, did not become anyone's affiliative property, did not have to be sold to potential supporters, and did not have to be legitimated by being enmeshed in official cultural symbolism.

POLITICS AND EXPRESSIVE PERFORMANCE

Political intrusions into policy-oriented, CI games add to the ritualization of such games by augmenting the symbolic significance of events and behaviour. Because they lack sufficient information on issues of great concern to them, interest groups will carefully scrutinize the moves of other key groups and the minister for underlying indications of future intent, often incorrectly attributing vast symbolic significance to what are, in fact, trivial moves. Sometimes this overattribution is a deliberate, rational political move. By over-reacting, the group shows that it is unified, militant, ever-vigilant, over-sensitive, and not to be trifled with. But often excessive interest in the symbolic meaning of actions arises because the group has limited information on an issue of great importance to it, and therefore desperately grasps at symbolic straws. Overattribution emerges in the same way that rumours and other irrational responses occur: the group tries to fill an information void on an important issue by resorting to very speculative interpretations of recent actions. Overattribution is a major vehicle through which symbolic accretion occurs.

In other ways as well, politics encourages the ritualization of policy-related processes. There must be some short-term, intrinsic gratification to sustain a group marching toward long-term, ultimate objectives. To mobilize a group on behalf of some specific move, one must overstate the importance of that move, treating it more as an end in itself than merely as one link in a very long chain. (To show that the game is important and worthy of one's commitments, all the players may join in attributing excessive importance to recent proposals and events.) For that group, winning out on that specific demand becomes an important, intrinsically gratifying reward because it is seen as a symbolic indication of major progress toward those ultimate objectives. But there is always the danger that these short-run victories will obscure, or replace, the eventual destination. When this displacement occurs, a group accepts symbolic pay-offs in place of any substantive moves to adopt its demands or to solve public policies. Through similar ritualizing processes, a demand, once formulated, becomes disconnected from its original rationale, and its substantive merits cease to be important. To provide short-term gratification and to preserve the team's reputation, winning on behalf of this demand becomes all-important, and how others respond to this demand becomes a key test of which side they are on. The group may play to win even though this demand no longer serves the group's or anyone else's interests.

Although leaders may try to maintain motivation at a constantly high pitch, there is a natural ebb and flow in the players' enthusiasm and involvement. Having achieved a certain short-run goal, supporters will relax their efforts, savour the victory, and neglect to proceed with the necessary implementing steps. Again, means become converted into ends; the tactical gain becomes confused with an end to the war.

ABSOLUTISM AND AMBIVALENCE

Rather than try to make trade-off decisions among competing objectives, policy systems often make excessive, rigid commitments to sweeping, unqualified objectives. To suggest that any one of these values is a limited good or to pose the 'how much' question would be read as a symbolic indication of too little commitment to these good things. Given an absolutist position, trade-offs will alway seem to be an illegitimate sell-out of the correct values. To descend from the level of absolutes is undramatic, unappealing, not gratifying. Policy systems, either a one-policy system or the larger, all-policy system, are better at identifying grand objectives than at making detailed comparative decisions about how these various objectives are to be implemented.

One can evade the trade-off confrontation through temporal segregation, so that this week a study will urge more spending on the arts, next week's study will recommend a doubling of spending on scientific research, the week after a study will urge more support for the fishing industry, and so on. Where the objectives not only compete for funds but clash directly, 'ambivalence' is the major process through which one avoids having to make comparative, how-much choices. We favour X, but when X is implemented and it clashes with other good things, we draw back. And we keep repeating this approach-avoidance cycle. Rather than try to make some specific trade-offs between X and Y, for example, between transportation as a business and as a policy instrument, we sometimes urge X and sometimes Y, or we issue muddy statements that embrace both but fail to clarify how they are to be reconciled.

If one does little more than identify the general objectives to be pursued, one is then left with the problem of explaining why all these good things are not implemented. In the real world, at more specific levels of the hierarchy, the specific how-much decisions are somehow made; but an absolutist policy culture will always find these real practices illegitimate, distasteful, disappointing. Working within such a culture, the Canadian transportation policy system had difficulty bringing its official ideas down to the level of specific policies and difficulty in legitimizing the specific how-much decisions being made by firms in the marketplace and by regulators hearing detailed cases. The result was two coexisting, unconnected cultures, one outlining the correct values, the other describing real practices. And one can always invoke a dramatic 'principles vs selfish interests' story to explain why the system doesn't behave the way it should.

Perhaps there also is an unfortunately absolutist streak in one part of the liberal-democratic culture. According to this culture, policy solutions must result from a purely cognitive-instrumental game, from an objective, seminar-like search for the right solutions. Other games inevitably intrude. Yet, in some settings, like the family or the work-place, we can simultaneously pursue several games without becoming terribly confused or easily deceived. Confusion occurs in policy systems partly because the intrusions are considered illegitimate. Thus the various players must attempt to deny or disguise these intrusions. A culture that deplores political, affiliative, or expressive intrusions into policy-making systems inhibits the development of a more sophisticated cognitive perception of those systems. By contrast, our culture could help produce a less confused, more clear-headed approach to the simultaneous performance of multiple games in policy systems if it began by legitimizing this phenomenon.

Sources

CHAPTERS I AND 8

A good summary of the micro-economists' approach to regulatory failure can be found in Barry Mitnick, *The Political Economy of Regulation* (New York: Columbia University Press 1981). 'Political realism' dominates U.S. studies on policy making: a good recent illustration is J. Anderson, *Public Policy-Making*, Third Edition (New York: Holt, Rinehart 1984) or T. Dye, *Understanding Public Policy*, Fifth Edition (Englewood Cliffs, NJ: Prentice-Hall 1984). For political realism plus the concept of policy system or 'subgovernment': R. Ripley and G. Franklin, *Bureaucracy and Policy Implementation* (Homewood, IL: Dorsey 1982) and Ripley and Franklin, *Congress, the Bureaucracy and Public Policy* (same publisher 1980). A. Wildavsky's *Speaking Truth to Power* (New York: Wiley 1979) is an example of recent attempts to examine the relationship of political to cognitive-instrumental rationality.

The systems theory outlined in chapter I is my own free reworking of the central ideas in Talcott Parsons, 'Pattern Variables Revisited,' in *Sociological Theory and Modern Society* (New York: Free Press 1967); Parsons, 'On the Concept of Value Commitments,' in *Politics and Social Structure* (New York: Free Press 1969); Parsons, 'Social Structures and the Symbolic Media of Interchange,' in P. Blau, ed., *Approaches to the Study of Social Structure* (New York: Wiley 1975). See also Parsons et al., *Toward a General Theory of Action* (New York, Free Press 1951), chs I, II; Niklaus Luhmann, *The Differentiation of Society* (New York: Columbia University Press 1982); Luhman, *Power and Trust* (New York: Wiley 1979); J. Alexander, *The Modern Reconstruction of Classical Thought: Talcott Parsons* (Berkeley and Los Angeles: University of California Press

1982); G. Cooke, 'Sanction Situations and Sanction Interaction – Concepts for Action Theory,' *Sociological Inquiry* 52 (1982): 37–46; V. Lidz, 'Transformational Theory and the Internal Environment of Action Systems,' in K. Knorr-Cetina and A. Cicourel, eds, *Advances in Social Theory and Methodology* (London: Routledge and Kegan 1981); D. Rueschmeyer, 'Structural Differentiation, Efficiency and Power,' *American Journal of Sociology* 83 (1977): 1–25. I try here to extend my own earlier attempt to apply this kind of systems theory to policy phenomena in Kaplan, *Reform, Planning, and City Politics* (Toronto: University of Toronto Press 1982). My notion of systems pathologies owes much to Neil Smelser's *Theory of Collective Behavior* (New York: Free Press 1962); and to the 'garbage can' view of decision making, for example, J. March and J. Olson, 'Organizing Political Life,' *American Political Science Review* 77 (1983): 281–96. For policy culture: J. Gusfield, *The Culture of Public Problems* (Chicago: University of Chicago Press 1981). On 'structure and event,' see A. Giddens, *Central Problems in Social Theory* (Berkeley and Los Angeles: University of California Press 1979). For multiple games and rationalities: K. Boulding, *Ecodynamics* (Beverly Hills, CA: Sage 1981) and J. Habermas, *Reason and the Rationalization of Society* (Boston: Beacon 1981). For systems as an outcome of aggregative, bottom-up processes: M. Crozier and E. Friedberg, *Actors and Systems: The Politics of Collective Action* (Chicago: University of Chicago 1980).

The notion that policy making should involve 'how much' decisions, trading off competing values, a notion I develop further in chapter 8, is central to the way in which economists approach such questions. See, for example, R. Poole, ed., *Instead of Regulation* (Lexington, MA: Heath 1982) or R. Amacher et al., eds, *The Economic Approach to Public Policy* (Ithaca, NY: Cornell University Press 1976).

ON PRIMARY SOURCES GENERALLY (CHAPTERS 2 TO 7)

My conclusions rely heavily on the following sources, which could be cited in almost every subsection of each chapter. First, the major inquiries: Royal Commission on Rail Transportation, 1917; Royal Commission to Inquire into Railways and Transportation in Canada (Canada), 1931–2, hereafter referred to as the Duff Commission; Royal Commission on Transportation (Ontario), 1936–7, hereafter the Chevrier Commission; Royal Commission on Transportation (Canada), 1950–1, the first Turgeon commission; Royal Commission on Transportation (Canada), 1955, the second Turgeon commission; the Royal Commission on Transportation

(Canada), 1962, the MacPherson commission; Select Committee of the Legislature on the Highway Transportation of Goods (Ontario), 1976–7, hereafter the Ontario select committee; and the very extensive files, hearings, correspondence, research reports of the Public Commercial Vehicles Act Review Committee (Ontario), 1981–5, hereafter the PCVA Review Committee. The typical major inquiry on transportation produces some very useful background research papers, receives about 300 submissions, holds public hearings extending over roughly 75 sittings and filling perhaps 25 volumes, and thus generates a 40-foot-high column of documents. For the MacPherson commission, one would have to quadruple all such estimates. There also are a number of lesser inquiries cited below, most of which received extensive submissions and some of which held public hearings.

Transportation issues also played a part in the submissions and hearings of committees dealing with more general issues: the Commission on Dominion-Provincial Relations, 1939–40 (Rowell-Sirois); the Special Committee of the House of Commons on Post-war Reconstruction and Reestablishment, 1944–5 (hereafter the Post-war Reconstruction Committee); and the Royal Commission on Canada's Economic Prospects, 1955–6 (the Gordon commission).

Among the 'trade journals' so often referred to below, the two most important are *Bus and Truck Transport* and *Canadian Transportation and Distribution Management*, every issue of which was read from January 1925 to July 1987. Others used are *Canadian Driver Owner*, 1974–87, and *Truck Canada*, 1953–83.

Although many of these journals have experienced several name changes over the course of their history, I consistently use the more recent name. The importance of these sources cannot be overstated. Each issue reviews all the current policy issues, describes the specific operations problems of transportation companies, closely scrutinizes the latest moves of the relevant minister, and often reports extensively on trade association viewpoints and internal differences.

Also systematically examined were the trucking and transportation stories contained in the Public Archives of Ontario's (PAO) vast collection of newspaper stories from province-wide newspapers (examined for the period 1920–70), the trucking files of the *Globe and Mail* (1945–87), and similar files for the *Financial Post* (1950–80).

This study would not have been possible without my securing access to a vast amount of miscellaneous, unpublished material contained in the Ontario Trucking Association library. In particular, I should note the

Charles LaFerle Collection, a sixty-one-volume collection of basic documents on all Canadian transportation matters covering the 1930–70 period.

In the period since 1970, the hearings of the House of Commons Standing Committee on Transportation have become rich sources of information on transportation issues.

All the primary sources cited can be found in the following Toronto collections: the Public Archives of Ontario, the J.P. Robarts Research Library, the library of the Ontario Trucking Association, the Ontario Ministry of Transportation and Communication, the Metropolitan Toronto Public Library, the Legislative Reference Library of the Ontario Legislature, the York University Library, and the library of the Ontario Highway Transport Board. Many people, at all these places, provided me with great assistance, for which I am grateful.

CHAPTER 2: THE CANADIAN TRANSPORTATION CULTURE

For suggestions that there are pathological elements in this culture, see H. Darling, *The Politics of Freight Rates* (Toronto: McClelland and Stewart 1980) and F.W. Anderson, 'The Philosophy of the MacPherson Royal Commission and the National Transportation Act: A Retrospective Essay,' in K. Studnicki-Gizbert, ed., *Issues in Canadian Transportation Policy* (Toronto: Macmillan of Canada 1974). That such pathologies can be found in U.S. transportation culture is developed in H. Levine, *National Transportation Policy: A Study of Studies* (Lexington, MA: Heath 1978).

Interventionist, Canadian, and Other Themes These themes, although based on my reading of many sources, are best summarized in the final reports of major royal commissions, the 1917, Duff, both Turgeon, and MacPherson commissions. See also W.T. Jackman, *Economic Principles of Transportation* (Toronto: University of Toronto Press 1935), chs 1–4; A.W. Currie, *Canadian Transportation Economics* (Toronto: University of Toronto Press 1967), ch. 1 and passim; H. Purdy, *Transportation, Competition and Public Policy in Canada* (Vancouver: University of British Columbia Press 1972), ch. 1 and passim; and Norman Bonsor, *Transportation Economics: Theory and Canadian Practice* (Toronto: Butterworths 1984). Because these themes, the railways, and regional protest are central to Canadian history, one finds them treated extensively in any standard account of the post-Confederation period.

Early Railway Policy The single best source is W. Glazebrook, *A History of Transportation in Canada* (Toronto: McClelland and Stewart 1964; republication of the 1936 edition). Jackman and the reports of the 1917 and the Duff commissions also give good summaries of early policy. Because Harold Innis was a member of the first Turgeon commission, this commission's records contain a large collection of Innis's reflections on early rail policy, written in 1950–1. See as well R. Schmidt, 'Transportation Expansion and Development in Canada to 1927: A Political Economy Approach' (MA thesis, Queen's University 1976).

Regional Protest See Currie, chs 5, 9; Darling *The Politics of Freight Rates*; J. Baldwin, 'The Evolution of Transportation policy in Canada' (Ottawa: Canadian Transport Commission [hereafter the CTC] 1979); submissions by various regionally based interest groups and by provincial governments to all the standard royal commissions on transportation; 'Transportation Paper,' submitted by the premiers of four Western provinces to the Conference on Western Economic Opportunities, Calgary, 1973. The Ontario government's submissions to the two Turgeon and to the MacPherson commissions attempted to rebut these Western and Maritime claims. The (Ontario) Department of Highways Historical Collection (boxes 53–4) in the Ontario archives contains a good deal of material on how Ontario prepared its submission to the first Turgeon commission. On the Crow and the Maritime subsidy more specifically: Purdy, chs 9, 10; Currie, chs 4, 5; R. Lyons and F. Tyrchniewicz, *Freight Rates and the Marketing of Canadian Agricultural Products* (Winnipeg: University of Manitoba 1977); H. Darling, *An Historical Review of Direct Transport Subsidies in Canada* (Ottawa: CTC 1975); C. Edsforth, 'Statutory Rates and Their Effect on the Freight Rate Structure,' 1952 (OTA library); the LaFerle Collection, vols 9, 10, 21, 40. On branch lines and branch-line subsidies, see Purdy, ch. 15.

Integrated Network See road vs rail below.

Planning vs Politics This theme is spelled out in the post-war non-interventionist literature described below.

Left vs Right See various submissions of the Canadian Manufacturers' Association and other business groups to the Duff, the first Turgeon, and the MacPherson commissions. The CCF/NDP position is derived from House debates: for example, the debates on the National Transportation

Act in September 1966. For the public-vs-private enterprise issues in rail policy and CNR recapitalization, see Senate, Special Committee on Railways, hearings, February–May 1938; Currie, ch. 17.

Road vs Rail, Integrated Network, Distinctive Market Niches This was a central issue in the submissions, hearings, and final reports of the various commissions: Duff, Post-war Reconstruction, Turgeon (first), Gordon, and MacPherson. See also J. McDougall, 'Motor Competition and Railway Labour Costs,' *Canadian Journal of Economics and Political Science* 5 (1939): 52–6; J. Rollitt, 'Competitive Aspects of Road and Rail Freight and Passenger Rates,' *Canadian Journal of Economics and Political Science* 5 (1939): 40–52; T. Kuhn, 'The Economics of Road Transport' (PhD thesis, McGill University 1957); J. MacDougall, 'The Report of the Duff Commission,' *Canadian Journal of Economics and Political Science* I (1935): 77–98; D.W. Carr, 'Truck-Rail Competition in Canada,' report prepared for the MacPherson commission, 1961; J.-C. Lessard, *Transportation in Canada* (published by the Government of Canada 1956); Currie, ch. 19; Purdy, ch. 17; *Bus and Truck Transport* editors, 'A Political History of Canadian Highway Transportation,' *BTT*, May–November 1950; R. Wolff and C. Kuczer, *The Future of the Truck and Rail Modes as Carriers of Freight in Canada* (Toronto: University of Toronto/York University Joint Programme in Transportation [hereafter the Joint Programme] 1979); S. Mozes, 'The Canadian Trucking Industry ...' (MA thesis, Dalhousie University 1972); Maritime Transportation Commission, *The Atlantic Provinces Transportation Study* (1967); *Mid-Canada Transportation Scene* (Winnipeg: Centre for Transportation Studies, University of Manitoba 1973); and T. Oum, 'A Cross-Sectional Study of Freight Transportation Demand and Rail-Truck Competition in Canada,' *Bell Journal of Economics* 110 (1979): 463–82. Inter-modal issues were a major focus of stories in *Canadian Transportation and Distribution Management* from 1925 on and in the *Financial Post* stories I examined for the post-war period.

Trucking: Federal or Provincial See sources for chapter 4.

The Need to Regulate Trucking; Consensus and Dissensus This issue figured prominently in the submissions and hearings for the Duff commission and the Chevrier commission in Ontario and also was extensively discussed in the trade journals during 1925–35. See also railway and trucking association submissions and testimony in relation to the first Turgeon and the Gordon commission; Royal Commission on Transportation (Nova Scotia), *Final Report*, 1936; C. Archambault, 'Road Transport in Canada,' 1958 (OTA library); Dominion-Provincial Conference, 'Statement on Trucking,' 1932 (Robarts Library); J. Munro, 'The History of Motor Carrier Transportation and Its Regulation in Canada' (MBA thesis, Indiana University 1963). For a good account of classic, pervasive railway regulation: I. Feltham, 'Transport Regulation in Canada,' *Transportation Law Journal* 6 (1974): 43–70.

The Culture of Rates The rates issue figured prominently in all royal commission submissions and hearings. The second Turgeon commission dealt exclusively with rates. Roughly nineteen volumes of the LaFerle Collection focus on rates. The issue also has been a central concern of the trade journals. Aside from these sources, I have used Darling, *The Politics of Freight Rates*; Currie, chs 2–11; Purdy, chs 6–8; Bonsor, *Transportation Economics*, chs 2, 3, and 6; T. Heavor and J. Nelson, *Railway Pricing under Commercial Freedom: The Canadian Experience* (Vancouver: University of British Columbia 1977); Henry and Associates, 'Rail Freight Rates in Canada,' 1939; D. Bell, *Freight Rates and Transport Policy* (Toronto: Joint Programme 1978); C. Edsforth, 'The Canadian Freight Rate Structure,' 1952 (OTA library); M. Prabhu, 'Freight Rate Regulation in Canada,' *McGill Law Journal* 17 (1971): 292–359; D. Maister, *Regulation and the Structure of Trucking Rates in Canada* (Ottawa: Anti-Inflation Board 1977); Maister, *Regulation and the Level of Trucking Rates in Canada* (Washington: National Academy of Sciences 1978); Maister, 'Regulation and the Level of Trucking Rates in Canada: Additional Evidence,' *Transportation Journal* 18 (1978): 49–62; D. LaPrade, 'Rate Regulation and Price Discrimination in the For-Hire Trucking Industry' (MA thesis, Lakehead University 1979).

Post-war Non-interventionism For the non-interventionist and deregulationist case: House of Commons Special Committee on Regulatory Reform, *Report*, 1981; G. Reschenthaler, ed., *Perspectives on Canadian Airline Regulation* (Toronto: Butterworths 1979); W. Stanbury, *Studies on Regulation in Canada* (Montreal: Institute for Research on Public Policy 1978), chs 4–7; M. Westmacott, *The Canadian Transport Commission and the Public Interest* (Ottawa: Canadian Consumer Council 1977); L. Courville, *Responsible Regulation: Rules versus Incentives?* (Ottawa: C.D. Howe Research Institute 1980); G. Reschenthaler and B. Roberts, 'A Reexamination of Canadian Airline Regulation,' *Logistics and Transpor-*

tation Review 11 (1978): 3–28; ECC, *Responsible Regulation: An Interim Report* (Ottawa 1979); ECC, *Reforming Regulation* (Ottawa 1981); K. Ruppenthal and W. Stanbury, eds, *Transportation Policy: Regulation, Competition, and the Public Interest* (Vancouver: University of British Columbia 1976), especially the chapters by Water and Germane; papers for National Conference on Regulatory Reform, 1981; Parliamentary Task Force on Regulatory Reform (Canada), *Discussion Paper* (1980); J. McManus, *Federal Regulation of Transport in Canada* (Ottawa: Consumer Council of Canada 1972); K. Ruppenthal, ed., *Transportation Subsidies: Nature and Extent* (Vancouver: University of British Columbia 1974). For an application of the micro-economic approach to regulatory failure in Canada, see R. Cairns and C. Green, *Political Economic Theories of Regulation* (Montreal: Centre for the Study of Regulated Industries, McGill University 1979).

Non-interventionism: Rhetoric and Reality For descriptions and assessments of federal transportation mainly in the 1955 to 1975 period, see E. Chambers et al., 'Bill C-20: An Evaluation from the Perspective of Current Transportation Policy and Regulatory Performance,' *Canadian Public Policy* 6 (1980): 121–30; papers for the symposium on 'Canadian Transportation Research – The Future,' Ottawa 1967; Conference on Canadian National Transport Policy, papers, Joint Programme (Toronto), 1972; M. Kliman, 'The Setting of Domestic Air Fares: A Review of the 1975 Hearings,' *Canadian Public Policy* 3 (1977): 186–96; J. McManus, 'On the "New" Transportation Policy after 10 Years,' in K. Ruppenthal, ed., *Studies in Regulation* (Vancouver: University of British Columbia 1979), pp. 209–25. The key primary documents are Transport Canada, *Transportation Policy: A Framework for Transportation in Canada* (Ottawa 1975) and *Interim Report on Freight Transportation in Canada* (Ottawa 1975); House of Commons Standing Committee on Transportation and Communication, hearings on the Nat. Transportation Act, September–October 1966; House debates on NTA, September 1966. For the board/minister relationship, see H. Janisch, *The Regulatory Process of the Canadian Transport Commission* (Ottawa: Law Reform Commission of Canada 1978); J. Langford, *Transport in Transition* (Montreal: McGill-Queen's University Press 1976); W. McMaster, *The Canadian Transport Commission: Independence vs. Accountability* (Toronto: Joint Programme 1980); M. Kircher, *A Study of Public Affairs and Policy Processing in Transport Canada* (Toronto: Joint Programme 1978); A.R.

Wright, 'An Examination of the Role of the Board of Transport Commissioners ...' (MA thesis, Carleton University 1962); and J. Hazard, 'The Institutionalization of Transportation Policy – Two Decades of DOT,' *Logistics and Transportation Review* 23 (1987): 33–56.

Deregulation Minister of Transport, *Freedom to Move* (Ottawa 1985); hearings of the House Standing Committee on Transportation on the document *Freedom to Move*, November–December 1985; hearings of the Committee on Bills C18, C19, March–April 1987; Canadian Transportation Research Forum, *Proceedings* (Toronto: 1980); S. Barone et al., 'Deregulation in the Canadian Airline Industry,' *Logistics and Transportation Review* 22 (1986): 421–48; A. Ellison, *U.S. Airline Deregulation: Implications for Canada* (Ottawa: ECC 1981).

Reforming Grain Transportation Submissions to and hearings by the House of Commons Standing Committee on Transportation, January–April 1983; House of Commons *Debates* for most of May and June 1983; *Globe and Mail* stories and trade journal accounts for the 1977–84 period; A. Abouchar, *An Economic Analysis of the Hall Commission Report* (Toronto: Ontario Economic Council 1977); Commission on the Costs of Transporting Grain by Rail, *Report* (Ottawa 1976); Grain Handling and Transportation Commission, *Grain and Rail in Western Canada* (Ottawa 1977); J. Gilson, *Western Grain Transportation: Report on Consultation and Recommendations* (Ottawa: Transport Canada 1982); D. Harvey, *Christmas Turkey or Prairie Vulture? An Economic Analysis of the Crow's Nest Pass Grain Rates* (Montreal: Institute for Research on Public Policy 1980).

Trucking Deregulation The pros and cons, mostly the cons, are summarized in N. Bonsor, *The Costs of the Regulatory Process in the Canadian For-Hire Trucking Industry* (Ottawa: ECC 1980); J. Berry, *The Impact of Regulation: The Case of Trucking* (Ottawa: Anti-Inflation Board 1977); Blyth, Eastman, Dillon, and Co. 'Trucking Regulation Reform,' prepared for CTC, 1973; M. Boucher, *Economic Analysis of Regulations Governing the Quebec Trucking Industry* (Ottawa: CTC 1979); M. Cairns and B. Kirk, *Canadian For-Hire Trucking and the Effects of Regulation* (Ottawa: CTC 1980); R. Hirschorn, *Trucking Regulation in Canada: A Review of the Issues* (Ottawa: ECC 1981); R. Lord and J. Shaw, 'A Comparative Examination of Regulation and the Operation of Intraprovincial Firms in

Alberta and Ontario,' in *Studies in Trucking Regulation* II (Ottawa: ECC 1980); R. House and Associates, *Economic Regulation of the For-Hire Trucking Industry* (Ottawa: Anti-Inflation Board 1977); D. MacLachlan, 'Canadian Trucking Regulations,' *Logistics and Transportation Review* 8 (1972): 59–81; MacLachlan, 'Canadian Trucking Regulations, *Bell Journal of Economics and Management Science* 3 (1972): 98–129; J. MacRae and D. Prestcott, *Regulation and Performance in the Canadian Trucking Industry* (Ottawa: ECC 1981); MacRae and Prestcott, *Additional Evidence on the Effects of Regulation on Rate Levels in the Canadian For-Hire Trucking Industry* (Guelph: University of Guelph 1979); J. Palmer, 'A Further Analysis of Provincial Trucking Regulation,' *Bell Journal of Economics and Management Science* 4 (1973): 49–71; Palmer, 'Taxation by Regulation? The Experience of Ontario Trucking Regulation,' *Logistics and Transportation Review* 10 (1974): 207–12; D. Maister, *Regulation and Performance in the Canadian Trucking Industry* (Ottawa: ECC 1980); J. Sloss, 'Regulation of Motor Freight Transportation,' *Bell Journal of Economics and Management Science* 1 (1970): 327–66; Sloss, 'The Regulation of Motor Freight Transportation in Canada: A Reappraisal of Policy,' (Cornell University 1975, mimeo; PAO); G. Wilson, *The Economics of Trucking Regulation* (Toronto: Joint Programme 1977); M. LeBlanc, 'Economic Regulations and the Motor Carrier Industry in Canada,' (University of New Brunswick, 1973, mimeo; PAO).

CHAPTER 3: THE CANADIAN TRUCKING INDUSTRY

The standard account of the industry can be found in most of the submissions and in the final reports of the various royal commissions: Duff, Turgeon, MacPherson, Chevrier, Gordon, the Ontario Select Committee, etc. My own account of the industry is based in good part on the discussions of specific operating firm-level problems contained in the trade journals. I also rely on the detailed testimony that individual trucking and shipping firms provided about their specific problems, relying on Turgeon, Mac-Pherson, the Ontario select committee, and Ontario PCV Act Review Committee. This testimony and most of the studies cited below deal with a range of problems and do not neatly fall into one or another section of this chapter. From time to time, the *Financial Post* and the *Canadian Banker* publish excellent summaries of recent trends in the trucking industry.

Many of the studies cited under trucking deregulation in chapter 2 also describe the industry. In addition, I drew on the following: Department of

Consumer and Corporate Affairs (Canada), *Trucking Industry: Analysis of Performance* (1976); G. Chow, *An Analysis of Selected Aspects of Performance of For-Hire Motor Carriers in Canada* (Ottawa: Consumer and Corporate Affairs Canada 1980); CTC, *The Canadian Trucking Industry: Issues Arising out of a Review of the Current Information* (1975); Interdepartmental Committee for the Study of Competition and Regulation in Transportation (Canada), *Competition and Regulation in the Inter-City Trucking Industry in Canada* (1981); idem, *Definition and Characteristics of the Trucking Markets* (1980); M. Kim, *Regulation and the Production Structure of the Trucking Industry in Canada* (Toronto: University of Toronto Press 1979); J. Diamond, *Cost and Capital Characteristics of the Canadian Trucking Industry* (Ottawa: CTC 1980); G. McKechnie, *The Trucking Industry* (Ottawa: Privy Council Office 1968); Roads and Transportation Association of Canada, *Proceedings*, 1975 conference on trucking; Commission of Inquiry Concerning Employment in the Undertaking of Transporting Goods Interprovincially and Internationally by Means of Motor Vehicle (the Murchison commission), *Report*, (1967); Kates, Peat, Marwick, and Co., *Trans-Newfoundland Corridor Transportation Study, Volume B: the Trucking Industry* (Ottawa: CTC 1974); CTC, 'Size and Market Share of Canadian-Domiciled For-Hire Carriers Engaged in Freight Transportation' (1975); Harries and Associates, *The Alberta Trucking Industry* (Ottawa: CTC 1979); M and B Transportation Consulting Associates, *The For-Hire Trucking Industry in the Atlantic Provinces* (Ottawa: CTC 1982); Commission of Inquiry into Newfoundland Transportation (Government of Canada), *Report*, 1978–9; A. Dartnell, 'The Transportation of Freight by Road in Canada' (PhD thesis, McGill University 1967); House and Associates, *The Economics of Urban Goods Movement* (Ottawa: Transport Canada 1979); idem, *Manitoba For-Hire Trucking Industry* (Manitoba Trucking Association 1974) and *The Institutional Framework of the Canadian Trucking Industry* (Ottawa: Transport Canada 1980); M. Nelymuk, 'A History of the For-Hire Trucking Industry in Ontario' (Faculty of Administrative Studies, York University, undated); F. Nix and A. Clayton, 'Notes on the Canadian Trucking Industry' (1979; OTA library); Transport Canada, *Freight Transportation in Canada* (1975); idem, *Competition in Trucking: Industry Conduct*, and *Competition in Trucking: Institutional Framework* (1979); idem, *Ownership Patterns and Foreign Influence in the Canadian Trucking Industry* (1980); Trimac Consulting Co., *Operating Costs of Trucks in Canada* (Ottawa: Transport Canada 1976); R. Westin, *Research and Education Needs of the Canadian Trucking Industry* (Toronto: Joint Programme 1977); Acres Research and

Planning Ltd, 'Atlantic Provinces Transportation Study,' prepared for the Maritime Transportation Commission, 1967, esp. vol. 3; Royal Commission on Truck Transportation in Newfoundland, *Report* (1962); A. Craig, *Trucking: British Columbia's Trucking History* (Saanichton, BC: Hancock House 1971).

Studies on more specialized issues include Transport Canada, *Ownership Patterns and Foreign Influence in the Canadian Trucking Industry* (1980); idem, *Freight Forwarders* (1984); G. McLaughlin, *The Bulk Freight Shippers' Point of View* (Ottawa: CTC 1978); K. Englehart and J. Palmer, 'Entry Regulation and the Urban Cartage Industry' (1978; available at OTA, PAO, Robarts Library); D. Wyckoff and D. Maister, *The Owner-Operator: Independent Trucker* (Lexington, MA: D.C. Heath 1975); Maister, 'Motor Carrier Use of Owner Operators: Efficiency or Exploitation?' *Transportation Research Forum Proceedings* 20 (1979): 447–55; R. Mayes, *A Second Look at Energy and Trucking* (Vancouver: University of British Columbia 1976); idem, *Energy, Labour, Regulation, Government Policy: Some of the Truckers' Problems* (Fredericton: University of New Brunswick 1978); G. Baillie, 'Trucking Bankruptcies in Canada, 1950–72,' prepared for Transport Canada, 1974; CTC, *Isolated Communities* (1978); J. Diamond, *The Dominance of the Large Carrier in Canadian Trucking* (Toronto: Joint Programme 1982); idem, 'The Large Carrier in Canadian Trucking,' prepared for Transport Canada, 1982; Department of Labour (Canada), Commission of Inquiry Concerning Employment in the Undertaking of Transportating Goods Interprovincially and Internationally by means of Motor Vehicles, *Report* (1967).

The Ontario studies used in this chapter are Ministry of Transportation and Communications (MTC), *Industrial Transportation Requirements Study* (1978); Ministerial Inquiry into the Dump Truck Industry (MTC), *Report* (1978); Ministry of Agriculture (Ontario), *Transportation of Farm Products and Livestock* (1948); MTC, *Owner-Operators of Trucks and Truck Transportation Brokers in Ontario* (1980); MTC, *Report on Private Trucking, Leasing and Common Carrier Industry Concentration*, 3 vols (1982); PCVA Review Committee, *Intermediate Transportation Services* (1981). Ontario Highway Transport Board, Class R (Dump Trucks) Licences Field Investigation, *Report*, (1982); MTC, *Truck Transportation in the Province of Ontario* (1975); Stevenson and Kellogg, Ltd, *A Study of Cartage and Intercity Trucking* (1975), prepared for MTC; MTC, *Study of Cartage* (1976); Ministry of Energy (Canada), *Energy Conservation in the Ontario Trucking Industry* (1976); E. Biggs, *Report to the Ontario Government on Farm-Related Trucking* (1980). Hearings and submissions relating to the Ontario Highway Transport Board's 1966 'Inquiry into PCV Act Operation ...' provided a very thorough view of segmentation in the Ontario industry.

The views of shippers are best summarized in the submissions made to the usual commissions by the Canadian Industrial Traffic League and in the published proceedings of this organization's annual meetings. About fifteen volumes of the LaFerle Collection in the OTA library contain papers, newspaper stories, OTA-CITL correspondence on the daily issues (broken promises, lost goods, late deliveries, mislabelled goods) involved in shipper/trucker transactions.

CHAPTER 4: INTEREST-GROUP RATIONALITY: TRUCKING IN CANADIAN POLITICS

My account of CTA is based on CTA's annual submissions to the federal minister responsible for transportation, 1938–87; CTA submissions to, and appearances before, all the various royal commissions and inquiries: Turgeon, MacPherson, Gordon, Rowell-Sirois, the Postwar Reconstruction Committee; speeches and proceedings of the annual CTA meetings (especially speeches by the CTA's executive director and the president); the extensive trade-journal accounts of CTA moves, especially the more sympathetic accounts to be found in *Bus and Truck Transport*. In addition to it normal submissions, the following statements or reports by CTA are especially important: *Statement on Agreed Charges and Other Railway Rate-Making Practices* (1955); *A Report on National Rail Subsidization* (1959); *Control and Regulation of Extra-Provincial Highway Transport* (1966); *Trucking in Canada*, a report prepared for CTA by E. Steeves (1967); *Regulation of Freight Forwarders* (1971); *Statement on Transportation Policy* (1976); *Federal Role in Motor Carrier Regulation* (1976); *Interprovincial Sales Tax Arrangements for Canadian Transportation Companies* (1977); *A Perspective on Collective Rate-Making* (1981); *Western Grain Transportation* (1982). See also CTA submissions in 1971 and 1974 to the Murchison commission dealing with working conditions in trucking. The CTA appeared before the House Standing Committee on Transportation on 28 June 1955 (on combined trips, take-overs, various railway practices); 3 November 1959 (same subject); 9 November 1966 (on the National Transportation Act); 7 March 1968, 2 April 1969 (on extension of Maritime subsidy to trucking); 21 February 1983 (on the Crow); 21 November 1986 and 9 March 1987 (on deregulation).

I have also drawn on the annual reports of various provincial trucking associations (contained in the OTA library) and the trade-journal reports of annual provincial trucking-association meetings.

The following items provide useful information on federal/provincial relations in the trucking field but also deal in part with the trucking associations: R. Logan, 'Public Policy and Extra-Provincial Trucking in Canada' (MA thesis, University of New Brunswick 1970); J. Munro, 'The History of Motor Carrier Transportation and Its Regulation in Canada' (MBA thesis, Indiana University 1963); idem, 'Regulation of Motor Freight Transportation: A Comment' (1971; OTA library); Alexander Peel, 'A Regulatory Structure for Canadian Motor Carriers' (MBA thesis, University of California, Berkeley 1957); Tillo Kuhn, 'The Economics of Road Transport' (PhD thesis, McGill University 1957).

Political Culture For the Howe-inspired effort to federalize, see the above-cited works by Logan, Munro, and Peel; the trade journals for this 1935–9 period; House of Commons *Debates*, 17, 18 March 1937, 5 April 1939; Senate *Debates*, 11–15 November 1938. For the 1949–53 constitutional reinterpretation, see Attorney General for Ontario et al. v. Winner et al. v. S.M.T. (Eastern) Ltd. et al. (1954) DLR 657; Privy Council, Appeal no. 23, 1952.

Market Changes Most of the post-1950 works cited under road vs rail in chapter 2 deal with combined trips and railway take-overs. Such intermodal issues were the major focus of *Financial Post* stories from 1950 to 1970 and of stories in *Canadian Transportation and Distribution Management*. Vols 13–15 of the LaFerle Collection (OTA library) contain speeches and other material on the piggyback and railway take-over issues, 1950–70. Railway incursions into trucking are discussed in I. Feltham, 'Common Ownership in Canada with Particular Reference to Regulation and Acquisition of Motor Carriers,' *Transportation Law Journal* 6 (1974): 43–70; H. Romoff, 'Multi-Modal Transportation: Some Comments Based on the Canadian Experience,' *Proceedings*, Transportation Research Forum, 1970.

Ten Economies or One? In addition to some of the works on trucking deregulation cited under chapter 2 and some of the industry descriptions cited under chapter 3, the following studies describe the various provincial regulatory systems and indicate how similar they are: Centre for Public Sector Studies, University of Victoria, *Motor Carrier Regulation in British Columbia* (1978); Alberta, Select Committee on Intraprovincial

Trucking Regulations, *Report* (1977); H. Janisch and K. Ward, *Compilation and Analysis of Selected Provincial Regulatory Statutes* (Federal-Provincial Consultative Committee on Regulation, 1979); F. Nix et al., *Motor Carrier Regulation: Institutions and Practices* (Ottawa: ECC 1980).

My account of the interprovincial issues rests in good part on the CTA's annual, post-1954 submissions to the Canadian Conference of Motor Vehicle Transport Administrators (CCMVTA), on the submissions made by various other groups to CCMVTA, and on the official, statements issued by this body following its roughly annual meetings. The Joint Federal-Provincial Advisory Conference of Ministers of Transport (1973–87) meets less often and issues very brief statements, but again the submissions are important summaries of the problems. Interprovincial questions receive extensive coverage in the trade journals; and they were thoroughly aired in the MacPherson hearings. I based my conclusions about differences of viewpoint within the trucking community on the trade-journal reports on annual meetings of the various provincial trucking associations and on the submissions made by these associations to CCMVTA. The LaFerle Collection in the OTA library contains three volumes (30–2) of speeches on interprovincial questions in 1950–70; the Leslie Frost papers (Ontario archives) contain extensive, scattered correspondence with other provinces on trucking issues; and boxes 17–18 of the Ontario Select Committee records contain extensive correspondence on interprovincial issues.

I also draw on the following overviews: G. Belanger, *Ontario-Quebec Reciprocity on Licensing* (Toronto: Joint Programme 1971); H. Parenteau and G. Belanger, 'A Report on Reciprocity' (1976), prepared for Ontario Select Committee on the Highway Transportation of Goods; R. House and Associates, *Extra-Provincial Motor Carrier Licensing Reciprocity Study*, 3 vols (Ottawa: CCMVTA 1977); J. Day, 'Proposed Uniform Regulations Relating to Truck Contracts of Carriage and Truck Bills in Canada' (1971), prepared for CCMVTA.

Section III For CTA/Ministry relations in 1967–73, I rely mainly on the trade journals and the proceedings of CTA's annual meetings. See also A. Clayton, 'Truck Transport Regulation,' Roads and Transportation Association of Canada, 1975; R. House, 'Regulation under the National Transportation Act and Conflict of Jurisdictional Authority,' York University, 1972 (available at Joint Programme); Federal-Provincial Advisory Council on Motor Carrier Regulation, *Report*, 3 vols (1972); Menzies Group Limited, *Section III ...*, 3 vols (MTC 1972); R. Schultz, *Federalism, Bureaucracy, and Public Policy: The Politics of Highway Transport*

Regulation (Montreal: McGill-Queen's University Press 1980). I also had access to transcripts of Schultz's 1978–9 interviews with the major participants in these 1967–73 events. On the extension of the Maritime rate subsidy to trucking, see Federal-Provincial Committee on Atlantic Region Transportation, *Report* (1968); hearings of the House Standing Committee on Transportation, March 1968, March–June 1969.

CHAPTER 5: REGULATING THE INDUSTRY

My account of Ontario's program in trucking regulation is based in good part on the submissions, hearings, and background papers relating to the four major reviews: the Chevrier commission (1936–7), the OHTB 'Study and Review of PCV Act Operations in Ontario' (1965–6), the Ontario Select Committee on the Highway Transportation of Goods (1976–7), and the work of the Public Commercial Vehicles Act Review Committee, 1980–5. Each of these reviews produced a mountain of evidence. Submissions by many trade associations, for example by OTA and the Canadian Manufacturers' Association, provide what I have called the standard, exaggerated account of what Ontario regulation has achieved; but when one gets beyond the usual cultural themes and rhetoric, a detailed, realistic description of the program (and the underground culture) emerges. In this connection, submissions by specific firms are often more revealing than trade-association statements, and the give-and-take of hearings is more useful than the original submissions. The work of the PCV Act Review Committee is especially informative because it proceeded through informal discussions, without the usual public posturing, and proceeded over a five-year period through a series of committee proposals and private responses. (More on review committee sources is provided below under chapter 7.)

As usual, the trade journals were rich, indispensable sources on specific, monthly concerns. I also relied heavily on OTA's internal statements to its members, described in the section on chapter 6. Although there were relatively few 'events' in this program's history, the trade journals and the newspapers (the *Globe and Mail* and the newspaper archives of the Ontario archives) devoted elaborate, special attention to the adoption of a 'public necessity' criterion in 1932, the creation of OHTB in 1955, the adoption of rate filing in 1963, the 1975–80 confusion, and, of course, the work of the various review commissions.

The 'Department of Highways Historical Collection' in the Ontario archives contains a large body of internal departmental memoranda on trucking and of correspondence between the minister and various interest groups for the 1920–55 period. While this material unfortunately is scattered through fifty-seven boxes, especially important are boxes 9, 11, 12 (origins of PCV Act); boxes 16, 17 (the 1932 amendments, the 1932 Dominion–Provincial Conference); boxes 20–3, 29, 31, 44, 51 (demands for extensions in the program); box 53 (on the creation of OHTB). There is more correspondence between the relevant interest groups and either the premier and the trucking minister, and, as well, correspondence between the minister and premier, in the premier's papers, which brings one down to roughly 1961. Again the trucking material tends to be scattered. Because the federal government controlled trucking during much of the 1940s, the Hepburn (1930s) and Frost (1950s) papers are especially important. Trucking issues appear in perhaps seventeen of the Hepburn boxes, twenty-six of the Frost boxes.

The Canadian Industrial Traffic League's (Ontario Division) various submissions, appearances before hearings, and correspondence with the minister provide the best summary of shipper viewpoints on the Ontario program. Similarly, the Railway Association of Canada best represents the CN and CP viewpoints.

The single best source of the minister's views on regulation is contained in his annual speeches to the OTA meetings. The summaries of the discussions following such speeches (appearing both in trade journals and in OTA's archives) tell us much about OTA/minister relationships. The OTA library also has an extensive collection of all the minister's speeches to various interest groups on trucking issues. Almost annually the minister provides a detailed interview with one of the key trucking journals, usually *Bus and Truck Transport*. The more official, culturally legitimate view of things is presented in the minister's statements to the legislature or in official pronouncements. There are few full-dress legislative debates on trucking policy but one can find some discussion on the initial PCVA (31 January 1926) creation of entry control (24 February 1932), the creation of OHTB (8, 9 March 1955), and the institution of rate filing (12 February, 5 March 1963). (For the period before 1946 one must rely on detailed, quasi-official newspaper accounts, called 'the newspaper Hansard.') The post-1975 debates and ministerial statements are noted below and in the sources for chapter 7. There is a great deal of information, unfortunately scattered, in the minister's answers to opposition questions, about sixty per year, on trucking issues.

Only for the recent period has one been able to secure information on the policy-making process within the ministry and on the relationship between the minister and the senior civil servants. The key documents here are MTC, *Towards a Transportation Policy Analysis and Evaluation Process* (1978) and *Essays on Policy Development: 1979–80* (1981).

The annual reports of the OHTB provide a good running account of changes in legislation and regulations, but reveal little about how the board makes its decisions.

For a brief but insightful summary of Ontario's program, see D. Maister 'Remarks on the Economic Regulation of Trucking,' prepared for the Review Committee, 1982. Other informative general accounts and assessments are M. Patton, *Report to the Hon. T.B. McQuestor, Minister of Highways on Trucking Regulation* (1934); L. Thomson, 'The Report of the Chevrier Commission,' *Canadian Journal of Economics and Political Science* 5 (1939): 220–9; P.D. Grenfell, 'Road Transport in Ontario' (1958; MTC library); D. Gillen, 'The Economic Issues of Trucking Regulation in Ontario,' a report prepared for the Select Committee, 1976; M. Rappoport, *History of the PCV Act and Related Laws and Regulations* (MTC 1981); N. Bonsor, 'The Regulation of Ontario Trucking,' in *Government Regulation* (Toronto: Ontario Economic Council 1978); MTC, *Trucking Services to Small Communities* (1982) and *Small Community Study* (1984). See also the following background papers summarizing various aspects of the program for the PCV Act Review Committee and all appearing in 1981–2: 'Trucking Industry Structure,' 'Costs of Regulatory Administration,' 'Small Communities,' 'Intermediate Transportation Services' (on brokers, leasing, freight forwarders, etc.).

Regulation to What End Hearings for the Chevrier commission and for the 1966 OHTB PCV Inquiry summarize the program's early history, including interest-group complaints about the program's minimal or aimless character.

Minimalist Regulation This is based largely on the minister's speeches to OTA and on his interviews with trade journals.

Regulation Pursued for Too Many Ends For the minister's inflated statements about what the program achieves, see Ontario Legislature, *Debates*, 29 October 1975; 10 June 1976, 7 November 1978, 15 May 1979.

Northern Development This issue was thoroughly reviewed by the Select

Committee. See also submissions to the minister, to the Select Committee, and to earlier bodies by various northern groups and municipal councils. In addition, see N. Bonsor, *Transportation and Economic Development in Northern Ontario* (Toronto: Ontario Economic Council 1976); MTC, *An Investigation of Freight Rates and Related Problems in Northern Ontario* (1976) and *Freight Reduction in Northeastern Ontario* (1977); R. Summerly, *Freight Rates and Regional Development* (MTC 1974); Submission of the Ontario Lumber Manufacturers' Association of Ontario to the Minister, 1974; and OTA's reply to this submission. Boxes 14 and 16 of the Select Committee records deal with northern issues.

Licensing as Politics; Micro-market Planning; Impact of Entry Control
The 'political' factors are often discussed in OTA's internal news bulletins to its members; but they also surfaced when the Ontario legislature's Standing Committee on Resource Development investigated this issue in March–April 1977. See the committee hearings and the committee's 'Report on the Ontario Highway Transport Board,' 1977, briefly discussed in the legislature on 27 May 1977. My account of how the OHTB makes its decisions is based largely on an extensive sampling of the OTA's internal newsletters, which describes board proceedings. I also sampled the transcript of hearings on cases that OHTB began to provide in 1978. A few frank assessments of the board's quirky nature appeared in the Select Committee hearings, but there was far more evidence on this issue presented in the less public proceedings of the PCV Act Review Committee. My numerical descriptions of how the board deals with cases is based on OHTB annual reports, checked against my own tabulation of cases for four widely separated years. My conclusions about how OHTB makes decisions, based on primary evidence, are consistent with other accounts: J. Willis, ed., *Canadian Boards at Work* (Toronto: Macmillan of Canada 1963), pp. 93–112; R. Rohmer and D. Saul, *Practice and Procedures before the Ontario Highway Transport Board* (no date or publisher); S. Cole, *The Highway Transport Board*, special lecture of the Law Society of Upper Canada (Toronto: Law Society of Upper Canada 1971); S. Flott, 'The Ontario Highway Transport Board and the Development of Road Transportation Policy in Ontario' (Osgoode Hall Law Faculty 1973); Flott, 'Reflections on Trucking Regulation in Ontario,' paper delivered at the University of Toronto, 1984; A. Manouchehri, J. MacRae, and D. Prestcott, *A Logit Analysis of Ontario Highway Transport Board Decision Making* (Guelph: University of Guelph 1981–2). For more official views:

'The Ontario Highway Transport Board, 1958–1965,' paper prepared for the 1966 PCV Act Inquiry; OHTB, *The Meaning of Truck Rate Filing* (1963) and *Report on Procedures and Policies* (1979).

Enforcement My own account relies on the general sources listed at the outset. Partly informative, partly 'official' accounts include MTC, *Summary of Commercial Vehicle Inspection Program* (1975), *Operational Efficiencies of Truck Inspection Stations* (1981), and *Truck Compliance Rates* (1981).

CHAPTER 6: INTEREST-GROUP RATIONALITY:
THE ONTARIO TRUCKING ASSOCIATION

This chapter rests mainly on the OTA's own statements: its annual submissions to the minister, which began in the early 1930s; its submissions to the Chevrier commission and to the 1976–7 select committee; and its several appearances at the select committee hearings. Since Chevrier allowed OTA counsel to cross-examine all witnesses, these extended hearings provide a rich account of the association's viewpoints and its relationship to all other players in the later 1930s. Because an OTA representative was a member of the PCV Act Review Committee, the records of this committee are similarly informative for the 1980–5 period. I have examined the speeches given by the OTA executive director and the association president at every annual OTA meeting since 1933, although there are a few gaps in the OTA records; and I've sampled the speeches given by trucking executives and the summaries of discussions held at these meetings. As previously indicated, the premier's papers contain all the correspondence between the OTA and either the premier or the minister responsible for trucking matters down to 1961; and the Department of Highways Historical Collection contains all minister/OTA correspondence down to 1955. For the more recent period, the OTA library has a full record of its letters to the minister, but only a partial record of his replies. See also OTA's submissions to the OHTB study on use of bills of lading, 1958; the OHTB review of the PCV Act (also OTA's appearance at hearings and its formal response to the final report), 1965–6; the Rappoport commission on the dump-truck industry, 1975; the Biggs commission on farm-related trucking, 1979; the OHTB review of the dump-truck industry, 1979, the OHTB inquiry into international trans-border trucking (and OTA's written submission in response to the final report), 1981–2. OTA also periodically makes submissions to the Ontario minister of labour on labour-related issues in trucking. For OTA's own history of trucking regulation in Ontario, see OTA, *The Golden Age of Trucking, 1925–85* (1986). The association's roughly monthly report to its members, called, at various points since 1930, OTA *Bulletin*, OTA *Round-Up*, *News Round-Up*, is candid and very informative. In 1983, OTA also began a new monthly, *Ontario Trucking Today*. As well, the trade journals give very extensive coverage to OTA's viewpoints, meetings, and sometimes to its internal debates.

Finding a Constituency OTA's constituency-defining problems can be studied through the above sources and as well through the annual reports of its various specialized divisions, for contract carriers, tank trucks, dump trucks, etc. In the 1980s, some of the various segments also created their own journals: for example, CAM-DO, the journal of household movers.

Cartel and Guild An article that greatly influenced how Canadian business groups perceived both OTA and trucking regulation is J.E. Annable, 'The ICC, the IBT and the Cartelization of the American Trucking Industry,' *Quarterly Review of Economics and Business* 13 (1973): 33–47. For OTA viewpoints on grey-market practices, intermediate roles, etc., see OTA *Freight Forwarders* (1969); *Memorandum on 'Lease' Operations* (1977); and *Owner-Operators* (1980); see also its correspondence with the minister on the 1981 report on owner operators; the Biggs report on exempting farm goods from the PCV Act, 1980–1; on the 1982 MTC report relating to leasing. Volumes 24–5 of the LaFerle Collection contain miscellaneous material on brokers and freight forwarders.

Rationalizing the Industry; Two Cultures; Rationalization and Regulation The trucking journals, as major advocates of rationalization, deal exhaustively with this issue. For example, these journals are the key source of information on real rate-making practices. See also submissions of the Niagara Frontier Tariff Bureau and the Canadian Transport Tariff Bureau to the select committee, to the PCV Act Review Committee; the annual addresses by bureau representatives to OTA meetings; R. House and Associates, *Tariff Bureaux in Canada* (Ottawa: Ministry of Transport 1960). Boxes 4 and 5 of the Select Committee records deals with tariff bureaux. A summary of industry culture and practice on bills of lading can be found in the submissions and hearings relating to the OHTB inquiry and in the final report, *Report on the Requirement of Use of Bills of Lading by*

Highway Carriers in Ontario (1958). My account of what the larger firms think is based on trade-journal and OTA summaries of discussions at annual OTA meetings.

What Kind of Regulatory System My description of OTA's role in board proceedings is based on the association's internal monthly newsletter summarizing board proceedings.

'Rate Regulation' Aside from the usual sources noted above, the trade-journal accounts of how truckers responded to the adoption and subsequent results of rate filing, 1962–71, provide a good summary of this issue.

The Threat of Private Trucking For a good summary of this issue see MTC, *Report on Private Trucking, Leasing and Common Carrier Industry Concentration*, 3 vols (1982); also the submissions and later responses to this study. (This material also summarizes the 'concentration of ownership in trucking' issue.) I also relied on the annual reports of the Ontario Private Truckers' Association; as well, this association began issuing proceedings of its annual meetings in 1983. On intercorporate trucking, see E.M. Walker, 'Corporate Linkages in the Trucking Industry' (MTC 1977); OTA's submission to the MTC Committee on Intercorporate Trucking, 1982; and the *Final Report* of this committee in 1983.

Licence Categories The single best source of this topic is the submissions and hearings involved in the 1966 OHTB inquiry into the PCV act, an inquiry that focused almost entirely on the letter-category and related segmentation issues.

New Departures See OTA's 'Submission to the PCV Act Review Committee' (1980), 'Response to the *Interim Report* of the PCV Act Review Committee' (1981), 'Response to *Responsible Trucking*' (1982), 'Response to the Public Trucking Act' (1984).

CHAPTER 7: THE STRUCTURE OF A POLICY SYSTEM

Much of this chapter is based on the same sources described at the outset of the section on chapter 5 and to an extent the material described at the outset of the chapter 6 section.

Interest Groups, Structural Power, Insiders' System I rely mainly on the trade journals, which very closely scrutinize the minister's every move; the minister's speeches to various interest groups; the ensuing discussion at these meetings; the minister's interviews with trade journals; and ministerial responses to questions in the legislature. The rules of the game often are most clearly revealed when someone is being criticized for violating them.

The Official Version This version is the one the minister most often presents to the House, for example, Ontario legislature *Debates*, 3, 8 April 1952, 15 March 1957, 1, 16 March 1964, 8 April 1965, and on other dates too numerous to list. It also regularly appears in his speeches to OTA.

Issue Subsystems; Shippers vs Carriers The minister's position here is illustrated by his statements in debates over intercorporate trucking and shipper liability, Ontario *Debates*, 17 February, 19, 21 March 1977; 1 March 1978; 3–5 April 1979, etc., and again in his speeches to OTA.

Highway Safety I rely heavily on the submissions, hearings, and final reports relating to the Chevrier commissions, 1936–7; Commission of Inquiry into Problems of Highway Safety, 1956; Select Committee of the Legislature on Highway Safety, 1976–7; Ontario Commission on Truck Safety, 1982–3. See as well submissions and final report of an Ontario Department of Transport Committee inquiry into motor vehicle noise, 1963–4; OTA, *Twin Trailer Operations in Ontario* (1973), *Guide to Safety on Load Security* (1976), and *Safety Is Good Business* (1982). The views of the anti-trucking bloc are covered extensively and sympathetically by the newspapers: see the *Globe and Mail* and the newspaper collections of the Ontario archives. The trucking journals closely follow detailed issues relating to weight-and-size rules and other highway traffic regulations. The legislature has never had a great debate on safety issues. It approves small changes in traffic legislation every year, and there also are many questions to the minister on safety issues.

For accounts of the earlier period that deal with both the highway safety and finance issue, see A. Rowan, 'History of the Motor Vehicle Branch' (no date; Ontario archives); MTC, 'History of the Motor Vehicle Branch, Department of Highways, 1903–32' (1934); Royal Commission on Public Roads and Highways (Ontario), *Report* (1914); Select Legislative Re Laws Respecting Motor Vehicles and Highway Travel, *Report* (1923) and hearings preceding this report.

Who Pays for the Roads and Highways? The key sources are documents, hearings, etc. relating to the Chevrier commission in 1936–7 and to the Select Committee on Toll Roads and Highway Finance, 1956–7; the trade journals; the minister's appearances at annual OTA meetings, minister appearances at other groups like the Ontario Good Roads Association, the Ontario Motor League. Again the legislative debate is fragmented into a large number of opposition questions, but there was a full-dress debate on the toll roads report on 19 February, 15, 18, 19, 21 March, 1 April 1957. For more information on Ontario: 'Financial History of Ontario Highways, 1919 to 1934' (undated, Ontario archives); M. Gross, 'Some Aspects of Road Financing and Administration, 1791 to 1958' (undated, Ontario archives); C. Archambault, *Theories, Objectives and Practical Problems of Road Finance*, prepared for OTA (1956); OTA, *Equity in Motor Vehicle Taxation* (1962); *Highway Financing and Related Problems* (1964), and *PCV License Fees* (1973). More general sources containing material on Ontario are Roads and Transportation Association of Canada, *For-Hire Truck Fuel Taxes in Canada* (Ottawa 1977) and *Report of Vehicle Fuel Tax Committee* (Toronto 1983); Canadian Tax Foundation, *Taxes and Traffic: A Study of Highway Finance* (1955); N. Bryan, *More Taxes and More Traffic* (Toronto: Canadian Tax Foundation 1972); G. Campbell, 'An Analysis of Highway Finance and Road User Taxes in Canada' (PhD thesis, Purdue University 1956); E. Guillet, *The Story of Canadian Roads* (Toronto: University of Toronto Press 1966); Z. Haritos, 'Rational Road Pricing Policies in Canada,' 1971, prepared for Transport Canada.

Structuring Regulatory Issues; Other Subsystems I rely on the usual sources: ministerial appearances before interest groups, his interviews with trade journals, minister's correspondence with these groups (available in the archives for the pre-1960 period), and the OTA's more recent correspondence with the minister (available in the OTA library). On the Americanization issue, see OTA, *International Transportation of Goods* (1959); submissions and hearings of MTC inquiry resulting in *Ontario-USA Reciprocity Study*, 3 vols (1977–80); submissions to a similar OHTB inquiry and the final report entitled *Report to the Minister on the Balance of Trade in International Trucking Services between Canada and the United States* (1983); Cubukgil and Associates, *Recent Trends in Transborder Trucking between Ontario and the United States* (MTC 1987); and for the official view, Minister of Transportation and Communications (Ontario) 'Statement to Transborder Trucking' (1984).

The System Disrupted Because this confusion consisted of visible events, it was extensively reported in the *Globe and Mail*, in the trade journals, and was the source of constant questions from opposition members. The confusion was played out in the Ontario *Debates* throughout the 1975–80 period, although some important ministerial statements appeared on 11 December 1975, 8, 10 June 1976, 7 November 1978, 15 May 1979, 8 May 1980. Several of these statements contained useful background papers, summarizing recent events. See also K. Bailey, 'The 1976 Select Committee on the Highway Transportation of Goods: How Can We Understand It?' (York University 1984).

The System Reformed? In addition to the usual sources, this section rests heavily on the extensive files, reports, hearings of the PCV Act Review Committee: *Interim Report* (1981); *Responsible Trucking* (1982); minutes of meetings of committee; collection of material entitled 'Responses to *Responsible Trucking*' (1983); 'Discussion Paper on *Responsible Trucking*' (1983); 'Proposal for a Public Trucking Act' (1984); collection of material entitled 'Responses to the Public Trucking Act' (1985); License Rewrite Subcommittee, minutes of meetings and *Report*, 1984; Transportation Regulatory Reform Implementation Project, miscellaneous papers, and correspondence, 1984–6.

Index